Richard Savage

Prince Schamyl's wooing : a story of the Caucasus-Russo-Turkish War

Richard Savage

Prince Schamyl's wooing : a story of the Caucasus-Russo-Turkish War

ISBN/EAN: 9783743338807

Manufactured in Europe, USA, Canada, Australia, Japa

Cover: Foto ©ninafisch / pixelio.de

Manufactured and distributed by brebook publishing software (www.brebook.com)

Richard Savage

Prince Schamyl's wooing : a story of the Caucasus-Russo-Turkish War

PRINCE SCHAMYL'S WOOING

A STORY OF THE CAUCASUS—
RUSSO-TURKISH WAR

BY

RICHARD HENRY SAVAGE

AUTHOR OF

"MY OFFICIAL WIFE"
"THE LITTLE LADY OF LAGUNITAS"
Etc., Etc.

NEW YORK
THE TRADE SUPPLIED BY
THE AMERICAN NEWS COMPANY
1892

COPYRIGHT, 1892, BY
RICHARD HENRY SAVAGE.

(All rights reserved.)

Press of J. J. Little & Co.
Astor Place, New York

CONTENTS.

BOOK I.

PRINCE CHARMING AND THE ROSE OF TIFLIS.

		PAGE
CHAPTER	I.—The Mess-Room of the Guard Uhlans.—Children of the Flag.—Coming War Clouds.—A Princely Judas, - - -	7
"	II.—Brothers no more.—At the Turkish Ambassador's Ball.—A Royal Deserter.—Diplomatic Spider-Webs, - - - -	25
"	III.—In the Cavalry School.—Called by Gortschakoff.—Dimitri's Doom.—In the Golden Horn, -	42
"	IV.—The White Countess's Boudoir.—With General Ignatief in Constantinople.—Where is your Brother?—On the Bridge of Karakein, - - - -	62

BOOK II.

THE DESERTER.—CROSS AGAINST CRESCENT.

CHAPTER	V.—A Stormy Interview.—The Rose of Tiflis.—Schamyl's Quest.—The White Cross of the Grand Duke, - - - - -	91

CONTENTS.

		PAGE
Chapter	VI.—Missing.—Under the Shadows of Ararat.—A Mother's Memory,	117
"	VII.—Tcherkess against Kurd.—An Old Friend with a New Name,	136
"	VIII.—Abdallah's Ruse.—Schamyl's Spy in Kars,	158
"	IX.—In the Wolf's Den.—Kars.—The Message of the Rose.—Ahmed, my Lover!	177

BOOK III.

WINNING THE ROSE.

Chapter	X.—The Cannons Speak.—Hassan Bey's Message.—Moussa's Battle in the Night.—Face to Face.—Turns of the Tide.—The Medjidieh Redoubt,	203
"	XI.—The Storming of Kars.—At the Armenian Convent.—Old Hassan's Faith.—Ghazee's Flight.—Safe at Last!	230
"	XII.—Beyond the Danube.—Victory.—Constantinople.— G r o n o w ' s Warning.—The English Fleet.—On the Verge.—Peace at Last.—Schamyl's Vision,	258
"	XIII.—By the Neva.—Ghazee's Revenge!—At the Opera.—The Lost Handkerchief.—Dr. Abdallah,	283
"	XIV.—Home Again.—In the Orbelian Palace.—Finding a Sister.—The Opening of the Neva,	301
"	XV.—An Emperor's Gift.—The Brides of Dargo.—Tidings of Ghazee.—A Last Shot.—Under the White Tower.— T r e a s u r e - Trove.—Kismet,	324

PRINCE SCHAMYL'S WOOING.

A STORY OF THE RUSSO-TURKISH WAR.

BOOK I.

PRINCE CHARMING AND THE ROSE OF TIFLIS.

CHAPTER I.

THE MESS-ROOM OF THE GUARD UHLANS.—CHILDREN OF THE FLAG.—COMING WAR CLOUDS.—A PRINCELY JUDAS.

"HURRAH for Suleiman Effendi!"

Glasses crash. The walls ring again to the guardsmen's cheers. Foaming wine flows in rivers of gladness!

First in bonhomie, the dare-devil Uhlans of the Imperial Guard are the gayest mess in all mad St. Petersburg. Just a "good-by" breakfast to "Captain Suleiman," who has won all hearts while serving as Military Attaché of the Turkish Embassy! A dozen of the daredevil Russian Uhlans surround the jolliest little Turk who ever smoked a chibouque.

It is a fateful time. December snows whirl down in great cottony flakes without. Merry-jingling bells tinkle as the troikas fly by. The city by the Neva is in the high tide of its winter social splendor.

A general restlessness of the conquest-craving Muscovites gives "élan" to a season of feverish gayety. This is 1876; the Conference of Constantinople wearies along at the never-ending task of patching up the elastic map of Turkey!

Peter's Town is filled with the "cream of the army." There is a flavor of "war" everywhere. Mobilization is the pivot of all gossip. When these falling snows shall pass away, the tramp of the legions of the White Czar will shake the land. But, in the mess-room of the Uhlans, only hospitality reigns. Beside the rich board (through clouds of smoke) and over the vari-colored wine glasses, gallant faces beam kindly on that gay Moslem, "Suleiman."

His embassy will soon be gravely wending its way toward the Bosporus—ushered forth with hollow Slavic official courtesy. Captain Suleiman has his summons to report at once in Constantinople. He will be a cyclopædia of valuable information at the Turkish War Office.

In his diplomatic séjour of three years, Suleiman gathered hosts of friends. A bright-eyed, merry man, a capital rider, a game "bon vivant," and a charming host!

His red fez has added a point of flaming color to many a dazzling fête. Calmly he engulfs the wine of Shiraz, and eke that of Roederer.

He can twist a papyrus, tell a story, and criticise

the ankles of the unsurpassed ballet with any of the "jeunesse dorée" of the Guards.

Though Suleiman dances not, he has an extensive acquaintance with the voluptuous priestesses of the "opera coulisses."

In short, a Turk à la mode—whatever slips from the orthodox Islamism his easy nature has brought about, he piously regards a diplomatic sacrifice to his country's "interests."

Sighing to think of his last passage over the hair-like bridge of Al Sirat, he drowns these gloomy presages of conscience in the soul-entrancing wine. Reverently he murmurs, "Mashallah! Bismillah!"

He is beloved of the Uhlan circle. He has taught many a gay Muscovite rider a trick or two picked up on the Armenian plains. He is "a soldier every inch of him." . . . Yet a Turk! a Turk!

Suleiman raises his glass, and (in the easy French of his adopted calling) invokes the blessing of Allah upon the friendly circle of swordsmen.

The train is making up now at the Moscow station, which will bear him flying homeward via Odessa.

Thence the steamer will waft him over the Euxine to the romantic shores of the Golden Horn.

This Moslem is affected in his heart of hearts. Will he meet the brave Uhlans next in the swamps of the Danube or on the plains of Armenia?

It is the "fortune of war" with his friends. To Suleiman Effendi it is Kismet.

There is a suspicious sparkle in his eye as he grasps each outstretched hand. All the morning there has been an exchange of tokens. A cigarette case here, a dagger there—all the little trifles of cameraderie at parting. . . .

When the grave mess-steward announces Suleiman's sleigh, he rises. Now he fights his way to the door with a last warm cry:

"Au revoir, mes frères!" "Bonnes chances aux braves! Vivent les Uhlans!"

Pausing in the arched entrance of the great mess-hall, he throws his arms around a young giant, and whispers in Turkish a few words.

The three black orloffs dash away with a wild clash of their bells. Suleiman is "en route."

Gathered around the smoking-table, the knot of officers indulge in those incomparable cigarettes—the delight of the Russian.

In this glittering circle no one is peer to the stately *Mohammed Ahmed Schamyl*, who seats himself in silence as he enters with Suleiman's last words ringing in his ears.

Prince Schamyl's dark eyes gleam with strange tenderness as he takes a cigarette from his old chum in the Corps des Pages, Paul Platoff, a dashing captain of horse artillery of the Guard.

Schamyl is the only member of the Uhlan mess who is at once a Russian officer and a Moslem born.

Indescribably haughty and graceful in his bearing, *Ahmed Schamyl* retains the charm of the wild Circassian mountains in whose snow-crested gorges he was nurtured.

The youngest son of the great warrior Sultan Schamyl of Daghestan, his twenty-seven years of life in camp and court have been busy. Tall, dark, with flashing, brilliant eyes—as lissome as a panther, the young major bravely bears his splendid Circassian uniform of the Imperial Personal Body Guard.

It needs not the silver cartridge cases, heavy jewelled belt dagger, and the Damascus "chaska" in its rich sheath, with the natty astrakhan turban, to indicate the caged "Prince of the Caucasus."

While Platoff and his friends pledge the success of the coming war, Ahmed Schamyl's mind wanders away to a stirring future hidden yet by the smoke wreaths of battlefields nearing every day.

The "good-by" of little Suleiman, whose embassy is practically closed, grieves this alien soldier of the Czar.

Back from the past, with all its record of early life in Page Corps and cadet school (long before he had learned to whisper burning words to the spirited maids of honor in the Winter Palace), comes the memory of the day, when, as a lad of nine, he clung to his mighty father as he proudly descended from the eagle-nest of "Aul Gunib."

Thirty years of bitterest war against Russia ended when the Prophet-Chief of the Caucasus surrendered to the chivalric Prince Baryatinsky.

Ahmed Schamyl remembers well his august father, now lying dead at Medina, among the holy shrines of the great Mohammed.

His mother . . . Ah! Perhaps, in the war cloud which is drifting toward him, some flash of strange light will tell him of that sweet-faced woman who is only a hallowed fairy of his childhood days, "la dame blanche."

In his regimental mess-room, surrounded by the

gay comrades of his later days, strange fancies haunt the mind of the noble Circassian soldier.

He has dearly loved the man who left him but a few moments past. In a short military apprenticeship in the Caucasus years gone by, at Tiflis, he met Suleiman, whose father was a Pacha at Erzeroum. Many a lively day of chase by the rolling Kura, many happy hours listening to the old legends of Georgia, Armenia, and Anatolia, cemented a friendship, renewed, when, as captain of the Etat-Major, "Suleiman" came to St. Petersburg "en diplomate." His Turkish comrade is gone.

Ahmed Schamyl quaffs the regimental loving cup, but his heart is sad. Suleiman's last whisper thrills him yet.

"We will be brothers, Ahmed! even if we meet on the field, sword in hand!"

Thus old friends meet as new foes under warring flags!

Suleiman's blade will flash under the crescent! Ahmed (a royal-born warrior-prince), of a prophet-sire, who was a Moslem of the Moslems, will head his undaunted Circassians under the Greek cross, and fight for the Czar!

Paul Platoff's laughing challenge rouses him.

"Dine with me, Ahmed! We will go and hear the gypsies sing to-night. They have some new beauties."

Schamyl agrees. Anything is better than this rattling round of wild "shop" talk.

Fast and furious grows the fun. On all sides would-be generals are settling the diplomatic mysteries of the exciting hour.

"Constantinople Conference," "Allied Powers," "Bismarck," "English Fleet," "Balkan Passes," "Ignatief's policy," "Gortschakoff's demands"—all these stock phrases mingle with the rattle of dice and the chat of the social hour.

Young Schamyl sees the faces of his brother officers gravely peering through smoke wreaths, as they grapple with the unsolved Eastern question. Blood may solve it, but not talk. Making his way through the friendly throng—for he is not on duty—Schamyl grasps cloak, sabre, and turban. Platoff's sleigh bears them both to the artillery caserne.

Throwing himself idly down on a fur couch, the moody prince gazes on his Russian "brother of the heart."

Paul's rifle battery will probably join the heavy invading columns of the Danube army. The general plans are divined by the initiated.

Himself—he is only "a leaf in the storm"—whither will he drift? No one knows.

"Ahmed," begins Platoff, "I wanted to have a serious talk with you. I heard a rumor to-day at the Galitzins, which I did not like at all."

"Well?" slowly speaks the Circassian, as he draws mighty puffs from his chibouque.

"It relates to your brother, Prince Ghazee," continues the artilleryman.

Schamyl's brow instantly darkens. He knows, in the lonely bitterness of his secret heart, he has no *real* brother. For "Jamal-Eddin," the oldest of great Schamyl's sons, lies dead under the drifted sands far away in Armenia. He clung a devotee to the Turkish service; dying a Moslem as true as ever listened to the muezzin's call from airy height. Him the young guardsman remembers but dimly.

For when his warrior father came down from his inaccessible eyrie at Gunib, in "fifty-nine," and sheathed his sword forever, Jamal-Eddin did not join the train accompanying the defeated warrior to his refuge at Kaluga in the land of the White Czar. Golden captivity had no charms for Jamal-Eddin.

Ahmed recalls the splendid state in which the old king of the Caucasus spent his exile, far from the romantic land of the "Thirty-five Years' War."

It is now six long years since the fiery captive hero asked the Czar the last boon of going forth in his old age to Arabia, to die beside the tomb of the great Prophet at the Holy Cities.

His brother! Then it is surely "Ghazee Mohammed" the Guardsman—brother only in name.

"What of my brother?" coldly queries the princely youth.

"Several general officers were there—all growling over the coming campaign. They hate so suddenly to leave these lovely witches of society and of—the ballet," said Platoff with a sneer. "Your brother was named. I caught a few words. Old Lazareff said he would not be trusted with any command."

"Why?" demands Schamyl, fiercely, half starting up.

"Because his relations with Countess Nadya Vronsky are too well known."

"And?"—Schamyl's eyes are very eager.

"I don't know where Vronsky picked her up. He's dead and gone, poor fellow! But she was from the Balkans somewhere. I am told she is the mainstay of the Turkish *chargé d'affaires* in all his intrigues—a dangerous bit of dimity."

Schamyl paces the long room like a tiger. Platoff quietly resumes.

"I wanted you to know what is going around. It may hurt you in your chances for separate command."

"How can it hurt me, Paul?" demands Ahmed.

"They say," replies Platoff, "that a great uprising in the Caucasus will be the Turkish stroke in our rear; that the great Schamyl's son will lead the Moslems. He is to be made Chief Pacha of Armenia as a reward!"

Ahmed's eyes are blazing like a lion at bay. "They claim he will desert and betray the Czar," he hisses. "Is that the lie?"

"Exactly so, Ahmed," kindly rejoins Platoff. "I knew you ought to hear this at once. You can trust me, Prince, can you not?"

"To the death, Paul!" Schamyl answers, as he measures the room with the light stride of a wolf of the Ukraine.

There is silence. The deep boom of the giant bells of St. Isaac's breaks the stillness. It is a feast day. Fifty-two Sundays and the same number of feast days make an agreeable change in the Muscovite year. This is a masterly stroke of Russian "tyranny."

Ahmed places his hands on Paul's shoulders. "Look here, Platoff, I will trust you. I am going to see this man. Before I do, I will give you my heart. I want your advice."

"Sit down, Ahmed! Tell me what you wish," answers Paul. He pities the young prince's outraged honor. Ahmed's eyes are hopeless.

Both sons of Schamyl wear the Czar's uniform. "Noblesse oblige." Schamyl a warrior—yes! But a traitor and deserter—never! . . .

Ahmed raises his head from his hands after a moment's thought. He speaks partly to himself.

"I am not like the others. My father was a great soldier, priest, king, and open rebel. He was born on the glittering crests of the peaks of unconquered Daghestan. He fought for his own land.

"Forty long years the cannon's roar and the crash of volleys echoed through the lovely valleys of Circassia.

"Four times he drove great Russian invading armies back in defeat and gloom. When he came down from Gunib and took a soldier's oath to Baryatinsky, the honor of the family was then engaged. The Czar Nicholas kept faith. The Emperor Alexander has done the same. My father lived like a king; the great Czar allowed him to go and die like a prophet on holy ground."

Platoff nods assent.

"You know, Paul, this gloomy, middle-aged, red bearded conspirator has nothing in common with me. The Czar has educated us as reigning princes, attached us to his court, and preserved our personal wealth. There will be one Schamyl to draw a sword loyally under our flag! I must save the family honor!" Schamyl's eyes blaze in rage.

"Thank God, Ahmed! you speak like a man," cries Paul, with joy at his heart.

"I never knew my mother," softly says Ahmed. "Schamyl's three sons had each a different mother. I sometimes think there is a mystery held back, Paul! I am dark, like a Georgian. My father was light of hair and eyes.

"Ghazee has held himself aloof from me for years. In fact, we have been strangers since our father died. He does know of my birth, but hates me cordially, I fear. He is silent. He has no heart to give any one. My father had his mystic dreams, his wild exaltations, and all his dark secrets died with him. Of course, you know, Paul, he had several living wives, à la Turque."

Platoff bows.

"I think my blood may bring my loyalty from the weaker side, perhaps from a Russian mother. Who knows?"

Ahmed's eyes are dreamy. His thoughts fly away to the grand old Pontic realm, where the giant peaks of Ararat and Kasbek buttress the blue skies with their silvery, massy crests.

"Have you ever thoroughly questioned old Sergeant Hassan?" interpolates Paul.

Ahmed starts.

"Useless! He is a gloomy old man, half pagan, half Moslem.

"When he came back from Medina, after my father's death, he attached himself to my person. He must know all, for he fought twenty years at my father's side. I think he knew my mother. He carried me in his arms on some of our retreats.

"On my hunting trip to the Caucasus (after I

left the cadet school), he showed me all the scenes of my father's campaigns.

"When I would question him, the sergeant always growled:

"'I have sworn on the Sultan's amulet.' He would go no further."

"But he is in your power now," eagerly cries Paul.

"True," rejoins Ahmed, "yet he loves me. He would not serve Ghazee, though he gave him the sacred amulet my father carried in the fifty pitched battles as a holy charm.

"My sire was a mystic seer.

"You know his gloomy ascendency over his warriors, devotees, or dupes as you might call them. He deposited some Arabic scrolls for Ghazee, with his last wishes. He sent him this sacred amulet, on which his followers swore that awful oath of the old fire-worshippers, and with it the message,

'REMEMBER!'

"Ghazee, my stony-hearted brother, is twenty years older than I am. When I spoke on these matters to him, he turned on his heel, ejaculating, 'I have nothing to tell you.' His eyes are fixed on a shadowy crown. The old sergeant has been a faithful henchman to me. It is strange, Paul, he clings to me yet. I am not a Mohammedan in faith, as you know."

Paul crosses himself piously.

"Old Hassan is a stern Moslem. He is true to Prophet Schamyl's dying command, yet serves his Christian son, and will not obey the head of our once royal house, Ghazee, the Russian-bred Moslem.

"I wonder, dear Paul," Ahmed sadly concluded, "whether my stray bullet will come along before I pierce this mystery. The war will be on us as soon as spring grass peeps out on the southern plains."

"Prince," replies Paul Platoff, "I am touched with your loneliness, yet we talk now of our duty.

"You must begin to unravel this knot. See Ghazee—at least prevent him disgracing the name of Schamyl. Do not let him be a deserter and a fugitive. Think of your prospects, your own future command, the succession to the Caucasus, as its chieftain of the sword.

"You have spoken nobly here, Ahmed. You alone can save the honor of the name of Sultan Schamyl. It has given you as royal a heritage as that of the Hapsburgs, Hohenzollerns, or even the Romanoffs—a heritage of glory."

"I thank you, Paul," cries Ahmed. "I will seek Ghazee to-night. . . . Where are his haunts now?"

"Ah! that is the most compromising thing. The Turkish Chargé, Countess Nadya Vronsky, and Prince Ghazee Mohammed Schamyl are a plotting triumvirate. Don't go in there. We had Captain Suleiman to-day at déjeuner. Remember how you might be suspected. Not too much Turkish friendship!"

"True," gloomily replies Ahmed. "This is the icy land of Doubt and Distrust. I will drive up with my sleigh after dinner, and see him. You shall know all."

Paul Platoff's maître d'hotel announces dinner.

It is a masterpiece, "en petite comité," for Platoff, of an old Boyar family, is a "rara avis," noble yet not a prince, Russian and yet no prodigal.

Ahmed's face brightens as the two friends run over the chances of the campaign. Bulgaria, Servia, Bosnia, Herzegovina, the Danube advance—all are canvassed. Black Sea complications and the great Asiatic struggle in the Caucasus, Anatolia, Georgia, and Armenia, conned with eager eyes.

"This time we will take and keep Kars, Batoum, and Erzeroum," Ahmed prophesies.

Platoff merrily drains his glass. "True, cher ami, the Emperor needs a road to Baku and—— "

"Turkistan," finishes Schamyl, with a grim forethought of that great future struggle for the heart of Asia, Persia and India, which will swing England and Russia yet into a war "à l'outrance."

"You ought to serve in your own land, Ahmed," says Platoff, thoughtfully. "You know the frontier well."

"I know every gorge and valley from the great pass of the Elburz, from sea to sea, and as far as our eagles will soar—for we must stop now at Trebizond."

"Why so?" interjects Platoff.

"England," sententiously rejoins the Circassian.

"Try this Chambertin," hospitably commands the gunner. "I pledge you one toast."

Ahmed's eyes are inquiring vaguely. There is a roguish smile on Paul's face as he answers:

"Maritza, the Rose of Tiflis."

"With hearty good-will," is Ahmed's response.

They both know the Princess Maritza. Among

the noble beauties of the Catherine Institute, none has ever surpassed the budding Georgian heiress of the great house of Deshkalin.

With two lovely patrician girls of her own age, this beauty of the Trans-Caucasus was sent to St. Petersburg in charge of the wife of the governor of the great domain.

Happy Ahmed! On guard at the palace, during her brief stay in the suite of the Empress, as maid of honor, the young soldier has listened to the glorious beauty while their voices mingled in the almost forgotten tongue of her native land. To the envy of the other curled Guardsmen, Schamyl has the rare ability of using her own Georgian dialect.

While he sips the velvety Chambertin, Ahmed sees again Maritza's flashing dark eyes, liquid with the light of unchallenged beauty's dower.

"Ah! The star-eyed lady is far away now, Paul! There are many gallants around the vice-regal court of Tiflis."

It is indeed true that the peerless Georgian has returned, with new Russian graces, to charm the pleasure-loving circle at the great headquarters, on the border where Russia, Persia, and Turkey join.

"She owns some of your old family domains, Ahmed?" questions Paul.

"En vérité!" laughs Ahmed. "My dear boy! The Deshkalins control the greater part of our heritage, from the black pass of Dariel to the rose-gardens of sunny Tiflis. My royal father held the land with forty thousand mailed horsemen—a strong title. We have now money, thanks to the magnanimity of the Emperor. But the house of Schamyl has nothing left in lands but one old eyrie of Gunib and the romantic hunting parks of Dargo!" . . .

Slowly sipping their coffee over cigars and liquors, the two friends commune as to the possibility of a Turkish uprising in the Caucasus.

"If Ghazee plays the Emperor false, Ahmed, you may not be sent to your native mountains, but over to the swamps of the Dobrudsha.

"How could they count one brother as a renegade, and give the other full sway? The Emperor cannot know all."

"Ah! Paul, it is sad!" cries Ahmed, with clenched hands. "I cannot denounce even such a brother in advance!

"Can I plead a loyalty for myself which I have not yet proved? But!"—his eyes flash—"the field will tell the story." . . .

"I counsel you to do nothing to prevent your Moslem half-brother from slipping out now, Ahmed," wisely remarks Paul, studying the noble face of the young Uhlan.

"Why?" wearily queries Ahmed.

"Bring it to a head to-night. You are not able to keep him faithful. Let him go. War will not be declared for three months. If he goes *now*, you can prove your innocence.

"If he deserts at the last moment, you are ruined for this campaign."

"Paul, I thank you." Ahmed springs up, promising to return and report.

There is an ugly look in the glittering dark eyes of the Uhlan. It bodes no good to Ghazee. Tossing his cloak over him, lightly swinging his heavy "chaska" to its belt, with the stride of a mountaineer Ahmed descends the stairway. . . .

A clatter of bells, a flash past the window, Schamyl whirls by like the drifted leaf in the storm toward his bitter tryst.

"Gallant fellow," ruminates Paul, as he tries a few pages of a naughty French novel. "I think there will be a stormy scene. Ah, well! this is a case of Kismet."

The Battery captain's eyes wander over the seemingly trite pages. He hurls the volume at his dog.

"Basta!" he cries. "I wish I could dance the mazurka just once more with lovely Maritza, the Rose of Tiflis. Great God! what eyes!" Platoff has recourse to the papyrus—he half closes his eyes. This scheming Ghazee! . . .

"By St. Vladimir!—I have it! I see that devil Ghazee's scheme. He pursued Princess Maritza here with desperate attentions. He hopes to see the Crescent pushed as far as the line of the Caucasus. If he aids the movement, he may be Pacha of Georgia. Will he reign supreme over this fairy domain, and wear the Rose of Tiflis on his heart?"

Paul excitedly takes a draught of vodki. "I must warn Ahmed about this. He will—he must protect her! Yes! it would be strange to see Sultan Schamyl's two sons cross swords, in their own land, over this lovely Rose of Georgia."

Platoff is heart whole and a philosopher. "I must go and tell my brother Ivan. He can inform Prince Gortschakoff how true Ahmed is. Our foxy old premier can guess the rest.

"Ahmed must serve in his own land. Great

George! what a country for battery practice!" Platoff wanders in the smoke of yet unfought fields. Dreams! . . .

As Platoff dreams and smokes, Ahmed, raging at heart, drives to his brother's splendid town-house.

Ghazee Mohammed does not disdain a luxury which impresses even the lavish Russ.

The obsequious dvornik informs him that his Highness sups with the Ottoman Charge d' Affaires. The young prince dashes thither. The palatial halls are all lit up.

"Ah! Cards, conspiracy, women, and low plotting." Ahmed gnashes his teeth. "Old Ben Schamyl ruled like a Sultan, not thus debasing himself before his inferiors."

Drawing up before the Legation, the major scrawls a few words in the patois of his boyhood on a card. The dragoman bows, he knows too well the fiery Circassian would not brook a moment's hesitation. He returns with timid eagerness, hat in hand.

"The Prince will be there. Salaam—Highness."

For twenty minutes Ahmed drives up and down before the great Catherine statue on the Nevsky. As he sees a well-known troika approach, he springs from the sleigh, and his high Circassian boots crunch the crisp snow of the square, where, placed above her many sculptured lovers, the Great Catherine (a bronze goddess) is enthroned in the crystalline winter starlight.

Yes, his brother is coming! His brother and his enemy—now! Perhaps!

CHAPTER II.

BROTHERS NO MORE.—AT THE TURKISH AMBASSADOR'S BALL.—A ROYAL DESERTER.—DIPLOMATIC SPIDER-WEBS.

"You want me! For what?" Ghazee's heavy foot strides along by the side of the agile Ahmed.

A lumbering, sullen, red-bearded man of middle age is the head of the house of Schamyl. His voice bears neither tenderness nor passing interest. He would be back with Mustapha Pacha.

"Ghazee, I have a few words to say to you. You can answer or not, as you wish. You have never been a kind brother to me, yet we bear the same name. You *still* wear a Russian uniform."

"Proceed," growls Ghazee. "Be brief."

Ahmed's eyes blaze like black diamonds. His voice rings like a bell. They are far beyond the driveway, where sleighs laden with lovers dash along (meteors of the night), swift and spectral as the black coursers of Fate.

"Are you going to desert your flag in this war?"

"Who says so?" snarls Ghazee.

"A man I am going to shoot to-morrow for lying, if you say it is not true," is the cutting response.

"Where is this talk?" demands Ghazee, fiercely.

"In the salons, the clubs, the casernes," hisses Ahmed, facing his brother, like a duellist, à la barrière.

"I have no answer. Go to the devil!" is the not over-judicious remark of the senior.

Ahmed lightly springs upon his companion. He grasps his wrists and eyes him steadily.

"Are you mad?" he queries.

"No! I am going to keep out of this war. I will not be questioned." Ghazee has cut the bond at last.

Ahmed drops his wrists.

"I will give you till noon to-morrow to resign unconditionally from the Russian service, or I will denounce you myself. I shall report at the Ministry of War." The young man is wild with shame.

"You may throw away your *own* honor. You shall not ruin me. If you go, go as a man, not as a renegade and traitor. You shall not stay and play the spy."

The silent stars shine down on two princely brothers facing each other, under the shadows of Catherine's lofty monument.

"Now, by the grave of my father, dog, fool, and lickspittle of the Giaour, I curse you by this! To Eblis, the home of the damned! I swear it!"

The amulet of Ben Schamyl glitters in the pale starlight. Ahmed's hand seeks his dagger. He drops it in wonder. Is his brother mad?

"We meet again, as deadly foes," is the last snarl of Ghazee, who turns his back.

Ahmed, motionless, sees the retreating form of the man who is brother no more. Surprise paralyzes him. It is over.

The troika dashes away. Standing, drawing lines in the flake snow with his sabre sheath, Ahmed Schamyl knows he is now alone in the world. It is then true. Ah! disgrace!

Leisurely walking to his sleigh, he drives to Platoff's house. His being is stagnated.

At least, his brother's blood is not on his hands yet. Yes! Paul is waiting still.

The two friends meet without a word. Ahmed throws himself down.

Platoff can hear his own heart beat.

After a few moments, Schamyl wrings his hand.

"I'll tell you all to-morrow, Paul. Come to my quarters at four."

Mechanically draining a stirrup cup, he smiles faintly and clanks down stairs.

His face looked green and stony in the lamp-light as he passed the door.

"Just the way Bolski looked when he fell with Orenburg's sword in his heart," thinks Platoff. He sleeps, for another day's revelations wait him.

Paul Platoff's dreams were not pleasant.

While he tossed and turned, there was yet high revel at the Turkish Embassy. There is music, flowers, feasting, dancing.

Groups of men and women "à la mode," and everywhere "vive la bagatelle." The Russian life of the salons. Prince Ghazee Schamyl pushes his way through the gay crowd. Unheeding laughing salutations, and merry challenges of rosy lips, he seeks one well-known figure.

Ah, yes! There enthroned, with her amber hair, and steady, cold blue eyes, Nadya Vronsky queens it in her place of honor.

Brushing aside the smaller fry of her adorers, the burly prince whispers a word.

Offering his arm with the aplomb of a veteran of

many Petersburg seasons, Ghazee leads the lady to an alcove.

A few whispered syllables throw an ashy pallor over the beauty of her haughty Austrian-like face.

"To-night, Prince?" she murmurs. Her bosom heaves. It is a lightning stroke.

He bows sullenly. "Tell him he must give me fifteen minutes at once, in his own room."

"And what of me?" There is a quiver in the voice of the cold countess.

"That you will learn when you join us. Be careful. Do not be observed."

He bows low, and saunters carelessly into the buffet supper-room, nodding to a friend here and there. A club rendezvous for a roulette duel? Yes. Passing through a portière, the prince pushes his way into the privacy of the sanctum of Mustapha Pacha. He drops on a divan.

Ghazee Mohammed Schamyl lifts his head calmly as the dark-bearded Chargé glides in, closing the door. There is an eager question in the diplomat's eyes—"What stroke has fallen?"

"It is all over, Mustapha!" Ghazee growls. "I leave to-night or never! But how? I may be arrested any moment. That mad fool Ahmed has heard it in the clubs."

"Do you speak Persian?" Mustapha quickly queries. His lightning mind suggests a way out.

Ghazee nods.

"You are saved!" cries the host. Mustapha then claps his hands. The valets pour in. In ten minutes Ghazee is no more the Guardsman, *en demi-tenue.*

He is a shawled, turbaned Persian merchant.

"Is the stain on my hair dark enough?" Ghazee queries.

"The rest at the Bazaar," replies the diplomat. A dozen nimble hands have aided in the task of disguise. Countess Nadya Vronsky enters the secret room. She aids in the last drapery touches.

"I have full passports viséd for these travelling merchants who go to Hamburg. Iskander, my Armenian secretary, will attend to all. He will pass you on the steamer. Give him any cipher letter for me."

There are tears in Nadya Vronsky's eyes. "You go alone?" she falters.

"Yes, if I can," growls Ghazee. "Now, get down with the other fools, and leave the ball as soon as you can. No nonsense! Go openly, with an air of fatigue.

"Don't whimper when I am gone. You'll get to Constantinople soon enough."

The Vronsky's head drops in her hands. Bitter tears steal through her jewelled fingers. He sneers his parting advice:

"Now end this. Mustapha will look out for you. Wait for his wishes. I must leave. They would not dare to search this Legation; but the Russian dogs will watch every one leaving, and play their clumsy part as spies."

If ever Nadya Vronsky's heart clung to an idol, Ghazee was that divinity of her strange affections—a paradox of love.

Throwing her arms around him, she whispers: "At Constantinople, soon?"

"Yes, yes!" rapidly speaks Ghazee, pushing her to the door. He roughly embraces her.

She is gone. The door is locked.

"Now, Mustapha, have your people destroy my entire uniform and cloaks here. Let my driver be told I have gone to the club with a friend. Give me a good dagger! Yes, that's right. Now, send this ring to Dimitri, my Greek maître d'hotel, to-morrow—after we pass Cronstadt. He knows the sign.

"I must not linger here now. Send that devil of a woman down to Constantinople, by Vienna—not too quick." Ghazee leers to himself. "You can trust her with anything for me."

"Do you wish anything more?" anxiously queries the Sultan's representative. He craves the safety of solitude.

"Yes, your flask—some of that old cognac. Cigars? No. Cigarettes? Yes.

"There! Now you will soon be with us. How do I go out?" Ghazee is ready for flight. "More safely by the servants' entrances?"

"Here! Osman will conduct you. Now, depend on Iskander. Allah be your guide. Money?"

"No."

"Well, Iskander will furnish you any amount at Hamburg!"

Before the last words are finished Prince Ghazee Mohammed Schamyl has disappeared. The Imperial Guard has lost an officer.

Drowsy porters, scullions, and the "valetaille" cast but a contemptuous eye on the passing Asiatic who disappears in the night. Some peddling jewel merchant—trash and turquoises!

As his attendant guides him, Ghazee hears above, the ceaseless clatter of the wassail rout.

His path of treason begins in darkness. A few paces and a passing sleigh is caught. In an hour Ghazee slumbers in the midst of the Persian travellers. His guardian Osman lurks on watch over the traitor.

Mustapha Pacha mingles once more with his guests. A dozen cavaliers throng around, eager to escort Countess Vronsky to her carriage. As she takes leave of her host, he suavely remarks:

"Ah! madame, your faithless prince has gone to the club, I see—a little roulette."

The circle of cavaliers hear of the departure of Ghazee Schamyl with joy. The path is now open to lesser luminaries. They struggle for the escort of the fair goddess.

Before the tired beauties who graced the diplomat's fête have taken their morning chocolate Ghazee Schamyl is tossing on the high rolling waves of the Gulf of Finland. Cross-legged and seated with a crowd of Persians, he fingers his heavy dagger, as man after man, who might know him, passes along the deck.

Yes! Death before capture. His brow is dark. It is an hour of fate!

There is fair example in the half-frozen Persian merchants to warrant Ghazee muffling up his face. Wrapped to the eyes, shivering and fearful of the sea, they are all as thoroughly hidden from sight as mummies.

The danger is soon over. The forts are now far astern. The proud flag of the Romanoffs has sunk behind the blowing fog wreaths. Ghazee has left his old life, his new foe (once a brother), and—his honor—far behind him. He is a deserter now; a traitor to be.

He is on his way—whither?

Nadya Vronsky's tear-stained cheeks rest on her pillows till late in the afternoon. A servant from the Turkish embassy brings a superb hot-house bouquet of flowers, priceless in the icy land of the Czar.

A tiny note tells her, "All is well. The boat has passed Cronstadt. Expect me this evening at dinner."

The sage Mustapha desires to be conspicuously absent should Ghazee be sent for. There may be no inquiry at the Legation, yet he lingers. The faultlessly dressed countess, reassured at heart, is at last seated at dinner. No news yet! The placid diplomat arrives, whispering, as he kisses her hand:

"Adjutants looking for Prince Ghazee at his house and club."

Mustapha smiles, however, blandly. The ring has done its work.

Neither hostess nor the now happy guest can understand the lightning quickness of this discovery. They know not Gortschakoff's intention.

While they are discussing the sterlets and Chablis, two grave-faced men are seated in Ahmed Schamyl's quarters.

Paul Platoff lingered not when morning roused him.

In memory of his resolution of the night before,

he sought his brother Ivan, who was always close to the person of the mighty Gortschakoff.

Venerable and antique diplomat, he, swift to act, was yet a patient listener.

Platoff had not regained his quarters in relief, when, over a dish of tea and a cigarette, Prince Gortschakoff formed his sudden plans. He discovered a pressing need for the services of Colonel Ghazee Schamyl, on a special mission to Tashkend, under a strong escort.

"I fancy the escort I will give him will prevent this craven scoundrel from wandering off to the Golden Horn, unless the dead can walk," ruminates the grim old prince, as he receives his colleague the war minister. A special list of confidential officers being conned over, Colonel Iranoff is sent for on a gallop. He receives some instructions at the war office which startle him. Yet he opens not his round Tartar eyes a whit. It is the Czar who speaks, with sacred order.

Platoff's long shot has done its work. "Thank my stars! I have saved Ahmed the shame of denouncing his brother," he whispers to himself on drill.

Platoff inspects his hardy troops in barracks. He smiles to see their rosy cheeks, straw-colored beards, and thorough sturdy Russian air.

"Glory to the Czar! No mountain devils here—half Turk, half Kurd!

"I am not afraid of treason in my battery."

Platoff is right, for the Turkish leaden hail may mow his stalwart gunners down. They will die, to a man, for the White Czar.

Ahmed Schamyl serves his guest at dinner with the scrupulous politeness of his mountain race.

"Brave in battle," "eloquent in assembly," are great titles in Circassia. But he who is the "most hospitable" wears the brightest crown of all. . .

At last the servants depart. Platoff hears the story of the parting of the brothers, on the snowy square.

"Had it been any man but my father's son, he would not have left that spot alive," is the gloomy conclusion of the dark giant, whose hand drops nervously on the heavy silver hilt of his belt dagger.

"And now, Paul, tell *me* of the day. I have purposely avoided the club. Even on the Nevsky I have not ventured. Is there more disgrace?"

Schamyl's eyes seek the answer in the steady gaze of Paul.

"Prince, I was told, late this afternoon, by Ivan, that a special secret expedition toward Tashkend was ordered—Iranoff with six sotnias of Don Cossacks, two light guns, and your brother in charge of the mission!"

Schamyl's wonder leaves him speechless.

"The adjutants have searched for Prince Ghazee at his house, in vain."

Prudent Paul says nothing of his own velvet hand and Gortschakoff's intention.

"What answer at his house?" huskily demands Ahmed.

"The maître d'hotel replied that Prince Ghazee went to the club from the ball last night.

"His carriage waited its turn and was sent home

by his order. He never reached the Yacht Club. He has not been found yet!"

There is a cold ring in Platoff's voice which cuts the young listener. A deserter!—Ghazee!

"Then he has fled!" Schamyl almost screams.

Paul bows his head.

"But where, how, with whose help?" the loyal prince demands anxiously.

"That we must leave to the Third Section, I fear, Ahmed," is the pitying answer of the captain.

"Schamyl's heir a proscribed fugitive," resumes the prince.

"You know, Prince, that in three days, on the summons formally left at his house, he will be reported to the Czar as a deserter."

"And I have not been questioned!" Schamyl murmurs.

"No, Major! your position is a delicate one. I doubt if you will be personally examined. There will be no general publicity.

"Ivan told me the Foreign office and Interior Ministry had telegraphed the usual orders in this case to all frontiers and ambassadors."

"Where shall I see Ghazee again, Paul? On the scaffold?" Ahmed groans.

"Prince, I think Ghazee will be surrounded with a thousand Kurdish devils; if you meet him, . . . it will be on the battle-field."

Schamyl lifts wearied eyes to his friend.

"And in the clubs—among the regiments" (his eyes are flashing). "Oh, for some foolish tattling victim!"

"Schamyl, you must notice no one. There will

be no slurs upon *you*—but you cannot defend the absent.

"No man could go out with you in such a cause. Loyalty forbids!"

Paul is deeply moved. "Magna est veritas!"

"You are right, my friend," Schamyl gloomily answers. "The eldest son of Sultan Schamyl is now a deserter and a traitor. I must bear this burden silently."

Platoff has one comforting conclusion. "Ghazee could not get away out of Russia without previous arrangement, help, and watchful friends. *If* he has been smuggled out, it points only to the Ottoman Legation. They cannot be questioned too harshly, for their whole 'personnel' will soon leave. This scandal will be swallowed up soon in the wild excitements of the war."

"By heavens! I'll beard that sly devil Mustapha in his den!" Ahmed springs to his feet.

"That is what you shall not do! The gravest displeasure of the Czar would punish your imprudent action.

"Wait for the battle-field, Ahmed, and bring home a Pacha's standard. You must shun your brother's quondam friend, Nadya Vronsky. Cherchez la femme. It is ever so. She is only Ghazee's tool. He bends to no other influence!

"Avoid the circle of his intimates."

"You are right, Paul! I rely on you for news. But, if I am relieved from my regiment, I will blow my brains out on parade. I will not stand open disgrace."

Ahmed is exalted to a nervous tension of madness. His mood is as high as the frowning Caucasus peaks.

"My comrade! Believe me, you *must* trust to the delicacy of our soldier Emperor. Promise me you will let me guide you in this."

Paul's voice quivers. The strong man's heart is moved to its core.

"Platoff, you have my word. Let us take a look at the Neva." Ahmed submits.

In ten minutes the friends are racing along the river drive. The cares of the day drift away in the mad rush of the steeds.

While the artillery captain sees Ahmed gently softening down from his excited mood, there was weaving of the darkest webs over Nadya Vronsky's board—at the tête-à-tête.

Mustapha's silken voice unravelled the tangled threads of the intrigues of the princely deserter.

"As you go to Constantinople, you must know all. Countess, I promised Ghazee the Armenian cavalry command. There are some private matters to be discussed yet at the Porte.

"Without haste, you must shortly leave, via Vienna, and take the railway to the Bosporus.

"*We* may receive our passports any moment! Gortschakoff, Schovaloff, Oubrey, and that arch devil Nicolas Ignatief are ready to light the mine."

"Can I be of no more use here?" the fair intriguante whispers, for even the stone walls have ears of acutest power on the Neva.

· Mustapha drains the forbidden glass. He smiles.

"Chère amie, you have performed wonders. You know what the Council will do for you on the

Golden Horn. Yet, *now*, every one knows that Vronsky did not bring back a Russian at heart, as his marital prize from the Danube! Your wonderful talent has marked you here too openly."

"And at Constantinople shall I rejoin Ghazee?" She is eager.

"I fear not, Nadya," replies Mustapha, beaming over his glass, feasting his eyes upon the "shapely silver shoulders" of the Turkish secret "moucharde."

"Ghazee will be climbing the crests of Daghestan or toiling over the Kasbek range before you arrive.

"He is to foment discord and raise a secret counter feud against these Russian dogs.

"Perfect in knowledge of the Caucasus gorges, able in cunning disguise, he will sneak over the present lines scathless. *But* he must go in varying guises, to outwit that Armenian devil Loris Melikoff. You cannot join him there.

"I have even begged him not to go to Tiflis: Melikoff would not stop to call out a firing party, if he were caught. The nearest Cossack's rifle would end the days of Ghazee.

"You will be sent back to the Principalities, I presume." Mustapha gloats over his bird in the net.

"I would brave any risk to go to Ghazee in Armenia. Please use your influence for me, Mustapha," the white-faced beauty pleads to the suave, insinuating Turk.

"Chère Comtesse," Mustapha rejoins, in his oily manner, edging his chair nearer the eager woman, "*he* won't miss you. He has sworn on his father's amulet to conquer and lead away to his harem the beautiful Princess Maritza of Tiflis. You know her family hold his old domains now. . . . Be reasonable, Nadya, do not rage now." He pauses. Mustapha has a scheme which includes the white Countess Vronsky in his own dove-cot, by the myrtle-fringed shores of Istambol.

"Why seeks he this border woman? Tell me, why?" Her lips are bitten till they bleed.

"Ah, my beauty!" slowly answers Mustapha (while his bold dark eyes rove over her charms), "he has in his stony heart, besides the devil of 'desire,' that giant Moloch 'revenge.'

"He swears now he will force her yet to hold his stirrup before his troops, for she flouted him when he met her here last winter."

"And he lied to me, the cold-hearted devil!" Nadya Vronsky harshly mutters.

"Ah! Fair lady, he then did tell you, his heart was yours alone!"

Mustapha leans back, enjoying her agony. This episode gives a real zest to a delicate repast. This is the wine of life!

"You remember, Nadya, the Duke in *Rigoletto*. One beauty in his straining arms, and the discarded one dying without, to the sound of their happy laughter. It is delicious to see a woman of the world, like you, touched at heart!"

"I swear by the God who made me, I will have my revenge!" the excited woman cries.

"Bah! Dear Countess, there are many other budding beauties in Georgia. It is the Land of Roses. . . . The fairest women in the Seraglio are those queenly Georgians.

"Now, be reasonable. Let *me* advise you. Ghazee has no feeling. *You* should know one better who is nearer you than this sullen mountaineer."

Mustapha complacently gazes on his vraisemblance in the mirror.

The white countess fixes her sapphire eyes on him with a glare as stony as Polaris shining on the lonely ice floes of an Arctic sea.

"You think I am in your power! You would drag me at your chariot wheels! I am a woman who chooses yet her own path." This hard mood of Nadya is defiance to the death.

Mustapha bows quietly as he rolls his cigarette. "I *know* you to be the most adorable of your sex. Possibly you are a little short-sighted. *I* never threaten. It is better to allow full head to a fiery steed. You *will* go your own way! Do so, ma belle! *I* ask you to Constantinople! You prefer—"

"My own way!"

The woman's voice is hard and dry.

"It leads to Siberia!" complacently murmurs Mustapha. He throws a letter carelessly on the table. The paper rustles nervously in her trembling hands. A deathly chill strikes her to the heart. The missive falls on the table. She bows her head. "You will abandon me?" her voice falters now.

"Never!" cheerfully rejoins Mustapha, as he trifles with a "pousse-café."

"When I opened that letter from the foreign office, I realized that they want a scapegoat to cover Ghazee's desertion. I am asked if you are under Turkish protection. As Vronsky's childless widow, you can waive your marriage change of citizenship."

Mustapha beams like a father on the white countess. He cheerfully rambles along.

"There were some little irregularities in the ceremony, n'est-ce pas, ma belle?

"No permission of the Emperor.

"No Greek Church baptism.

"No production of your papers."

Nadya mutely nods her head.

"Then, bella figlia, you are safe. It is a polite hint from Gortschakoff to avoid an immediate diplomatic rupture over Ghazee, by sending you out under my papers.

"I will do so, if you wish. The beau monde will imagine a love escapade of Schamyl the Circassian. You know the headlong way of that reckless man here. Disappearance; two months of bliss; a missing lady; Italy; glimpses of the blue Mediterranean through silvery olive branches; the wanderer's return; the ashes of time drifted over the burning lava of love. An old, old story here——"

Nadya glares at the mocking sybarite. "Why" (he laughs with a gurgling chuckle), "they will think *your* blue eyes drew the wild prince from his duty." She is sobbing now.

"Go now!" (he says with decision). "It is your only safety. Otherwise, if you decline my protection, you will be dragged before these cold Slavic brutes. They will visit Ghazee's defection on your defenceless head.

"Admit your Russian allegiance and you are

lost. I can now protect you. I will, if *you* see the world through my eyes."

Mustapha leans back in comfort. He has limed his bird.

Nadya thinks of the watchful, scarred-face Nubian eunuchs (cimeter in hand) at the stone gates of Osmanli harems. Dante's line flashes across her mind.

" Lasciate ogni speranza voi ch' entrate."

Still, a seraglio on the Bosporus is *not Siberia*.

One flutter of the wings yet. The bird struggles in the net.

"But—my character!" Her eyes are streaming now.

"Sapristi! My beauty!" carelessly remarks Mustapha. "Character is merely comparative. *You* will do very well on the Bosporus. Beauty is the 'sine qua non' there."

CHAPTER III.

IN THE CAVALRY SCHOOL.—CALLED BY GORTSCHAKOFF.—DIMITRI'S DOOM.—IN THE GOLDEN HORN.

Two days after her submission to Mustapha's logic, Nadya Vronsky steps wearily from her sleigh to leave Russia. The Moscow station once again.

Unattended save by her maid, she drives to the depot, leaving her apartment à l'improviste. Only her "batterie de toilette," jewels, and small belongings are in her luggage. She is waiting to dash quietly past Moscow, Warsaw, and Vienna. Anywhere! As for her establishment, goods, and last but not least "debts," the victorious Mustapha quietly says:

" Je m'en charge de tout."

The "dvornik" has orders to obey Mustapha's man of affairs, who will close up Mme. Vronsky's personal matters. Alas for him!

Gloomy is the morning. In the bustling groups a society friend here touches a hat, there a lady acquaintance smiles—no one suspects her departure.

Lonely enough, without escort, her flitting unheralded by " visites d'adieu," leaving no snow-storm of P. P. C. cards for the careless " one thousand " of the " gilded circle," the countess stares sadly at the environs of Petersburg as she rolls away.

" Triste!" It is only when comfortably reclining in her stateroom, that she reviews the past week; then there flashes over her mind the social effect of her flight.

The "maimed rites" of society will cause clamor! Sly Mustapha appeared not at the station. Her passports, funds, and instructions, quietly furnished by him, enable her to be at ease. She is well provided.

Yet Nadya Vronsky has left her good name behind her forever.

The clattering viper tongues of " les dames du haut monde " will dwell with cold sneers on her singular taste in selecting the brutal Ghazee as her Abelard.

"Lightly they'll speak of the spirit that's gone."

Puppet of policy! Victim of wily Mustapha!

Scapegoat for Gortschakoff's diplomatic unreadiness openly to disgrace Ghazee! "Quien sabe!"

She is only "rushing onward in the car of destiny."

Will she be followed, dogged, watched? Do the Russians hope to locate Ghazee through her presence?

Ah, no! There is no present answer. Only that this "way out" is absolutely necessary to save her. Constantinople, perhaps! Siberia, never!

Her aching head falls on her pillow. The monotonous click-click of the wheels brings sleep to her eyes. In restless dreams she wanders in the land of freedom—the future. Ghazee is by her side, and—and he is kind.

Waywardness of the heart of woman! Clinging to the impossible—dreaming of the unattainable!

Mustapha's dupe flies southward! He, busied with heightening diplomatic entanglements, gives only a thought to his bird of passage.

"She saved me an official explanation; she will be useful down there, and 'not bad looking'—no, not at all." (He purrs softly to himself.)

It is the time for the sword to cut the silken tangles of diplomatic lying. Mustapha's ciphers tell him the "conference" will fail. It is no longer at Constantinople a question of what will bring on the struggle, only when! It will come!

The Porte, *wise if slow*, adroit in intrigue, stubborn in resistance, is aware that for each slight concession wary Ignatief will push forward an insolent new demand; that behind him is the world-worn Gortschakoff, soaked with the fiery spirit essence of " highest Russian aggression." " Voilà tout ! "

Behind the two stands warlike Alexander (who has Catherine's policy in his heart's blood), sword in hand.

The gray masses of the Russian legions gather from thousands of haunts (grim wolves of the North), gnashing their teeth, pressing, toward the Danube and the Caucasus. " Cadmus teeth ! "

" War," muses Mustapha, " is the application of brute force (in organization) to problems not to be solved by human reason." He expatiates.

" It is mingled desire and expediency which swing the double-handed sword of conquest.

" *My* work is nearly over. Let the uniformed fools use powder and ball. *I* will have a season of rest.

" Pleasant hours can be passed by the groves of the Dardanelles; ah, yes, if the ' white countess ' does not go into ' heroics.'

" But I'll find a way to tame that falcon."

Ahmed Schamyl sternly attaches himself to the routine of his profession, day by day.

Petersburg (like all the other great cities of Russia) is now a camp, a mustering place, and a grand school of instruction—how to get cheaply shot.

All these last months, in droves, the shock-headed, blue-eyed, stalwart Russians have been drawn in by myriads to learn one end of a gun from the other.

Gymnastics, drill, exercise, all the preparations of the army (from its squads, companies, regiments, divisions, to its unwieldy corps d'armée) are unceasing.

Supplies, the devilish enginery of war, herds of cattle, and mounts for the troops are ruthlessly scraped together for the great campaign. Moloch grins and sharpens his sickle.

Your war is a huge consumer of necessaries, and with mad license, unbridled luxury, human passion runs riot; its awful course sweeps along, blasting, burning, destroying.

Blood and crime, wassail and madness, attend it. The wild-eyed Maenads are in ecstasies. Cosmopolitan human harpies, male and female, flock behind the crimson stains of the bloody feet of military glory. V'la la gloire! " Ça ira."

In the riding-school of St. Petersburg the model battalions of officers are receiving the final touches of their preparation to meet the Turkish cavalry.

An unrivalled swordsman, a horseman of classic elegance, quick, active, in the flower of youth, Ahmed Schamyl is second in command of this instruction of the "élite of the élite."

As he reins up his superb steed in the centre of the hall, giving his battalion a rest (while Mustapha ponders over his impending departure), Prince Schamyl sees his friend Captain Platoff dash up, mounted, to the far entrance. An orderly salutes, brings him a message for one word's conference.

Galloping over, leaving his cavaliers at a rest, Ahmed swings from the saddle.

Paul whispers a word or two in his ear.

Schamyl's face grows marble in its pallor. "An

aide-de-camp is on his way with orders for Major Ahmed Schamyl."

Brother Ivan's quickness has forewarned Paul.

There is no time to be lost.

"Remember your pledge to me," Paul whispers. "On your honor, no excitement!"

"I will obey you, Paul—only, if it is dishonor, I will not live."

He signals for his horse. The group of generals are entering the distant arch for their morning inspection.

"All is well yet, only Ghazee's departure and disgrace is now public."

Vaulting into his saddle, Prince Ahmed sweeps into the centre of the hall, brings his knightly riders to a " salute," and awaits orders.

It is a gallant sight. The "expectancy and rose of the fair state" are here, sabre in hand, saluting the grim chiefs, who are to send them all whirling on the turbaned foe, in that last mad ride, where Death is the goal.

Russia's best blood flows as freely on the battlefield as the rush of the icy waters of Neva, in the spring floods, sweeping to the sea.

Hassan, the scarred Circassian, standing by his master's second horse, casts adoring eyes on his chief. The unsubdued old warrior curses deeply, as he recognizes Gourko, Lazareff, Skobeloff, and others of the men who are to throw the gray coats on the Turkish lines in the iron game of war. Giaour devils!

Hassan will follow *his* master through battle smoke; but, were it not for the young prince, his aged hand would swing a sabre on the other side.

An officer leaves the gilded throng when the salute is acknowledged, and advances to Schamyl.

He hands him an order. The prince glances at it, turns to his mounted adjutant, gives him the order, and sits motionless as the adjutant rides out and reads it.

Every officer burns to read the secret meaning between its lines.

"SPECIAL ORDERS OF THE DAY.

"Major Prince Ahmed Schamyl is relieved from duty with the 'Model Battalion,' and will report forthwith to the General Commanding for instructions."

There is silence; when the words naming his successor are heard, that officer rides out from the ranks and assumes command.

Schamyl's hand drops to his pistol butt.

Now is the time to escape infamy!

"Blood pays all debts!"

And yet his promise to Paul ties him down! He will wait! In the very presence of fierce old Gourko (to whom he must report), he will avenge himself on cruel Fate. He will not live to be a discarded, dishonored man!

Riding over to the circle of generals, he dismounts and sends his horses out to await him.

Stepping up to the officer who brought the mandate, Prince Schamyl salutes and asks him when and where he shall report.

PRINCE SCHAMYL'S WOOING.　49

Exchanging a few words with the chief of staff, the officer bids Schamyl report for orders at once to General Gourko, who is the centre of the official galaxy. He is also commandant general of St. Petersburg.

Prince Ahmed walks up and salutes the stern old warrior, who dreams not yet of the fresh laurel wreaths waiting for him in the Balkan passes.

This simple formula over, Gourko growls (with a slight softening of his ursine inflections), " Pray remain with us, Prince. Breakfast with me this morning. I will give you your instructions personally."

The blood surges away from Ahmed's heart. It flows back. He draws a breath of relief.

This welcome—before the glittering circle—tells him that even iron Fate has its pleasant surprises!

Soldier as he is, Schamyl knows that some high purpose has claimed him—not an official disgrace. So open, so brilliant, so public, the selection is a bit of neat military flattery.

" The Russian bear can tap delicately with his iron paws."

Falling in with the train, after the " salût de ceremonie," Ahmed wonders how the brief duties of the morning can drag along. Minutes are hours to him now! What *are* his orders?

All things have an end, even morning drills. In a half hour, the coterie of " ranking chiefs " is discussing a splendid repast in the officers' club attached. The privilege of " entertaining their superiors " is freely extended to the swell " messes " of Petersburg.

After the coffee and cigars, Schamyl, seated with

the leading staff officers, receives a nod from the general. Approaching, he seats himself in a chair indicated by the old chief. All eyes are turned on him!

The moment has cóme!

Gourko is in excellent humor. The wines and meats appeased the critical gastronome; for Gourko is as fond of eating as of fighting, and much more delicate in the first.

"Major, I have been directed to send you to Prince Gortschakoff (personally) for a special and detached service. You had better see him at once. I am sorry I may not see you on the Danube, but you will find plenty of service where you are going.

"If you go to Armenia, we may meet in Constantinople. I hope so. I wish you every good fortune, for the minister of war told me you had been selected on account of the trust the Emperor has in your loyalty and knowledge of the Caucasus.

"A glass of wine, Major. You had better report at once."

Ahmed Schamyl has already faced his man at ten paces, when his life depended on the trigger finger. His nerve never failed him yet; but the wine-glass trembles in his hand as he touches the general's cup.

He rises, bows, and, saluting his friends, leaves the room.

His ears are ringing with Gourko's words: "The Emperor's trust in *his* loyalty!"

"*His* knowledge of the Caucasus."

Great heavens! There could be no more public way of setting a seal on any foolish canard of the moment.

For the great Emperor's words reach far. In society, in the clubs, through the army, the Czar's trust is a golden star lighting his way.

As Schamyl sweeps down the broad streets on his way to the ministry, Hassan clatters heavily in his rear. The young major has sworn to himself that his head, heart, and hand shall never fail the princely sovereign who has so openly trusted his yet untried loyalty.

He will keep his pistol bullets for the Turkish enemies of the aged Czar Alexander.

Prince Gortschakoff's cabinet in the Foreign office is a place of studious retirement. Dignity and repose reign in these halls of thought.

Massed books of references, maps of the political worlds of the *past*, *present*, and *future*, serried portfolios of papers (each clause a state secret), and the wires of the Czar tying this sanctum to the far ends of the earth, are the weapons in reserve here.

Grave-faced secretaries, alert guardians, and stern sentinels watch over the archives of the huge empire of the Romanoffs.

At a table, littered with the débris of toil, aged Gortschakoff scans the translations of General Ignatief's ciphers. . . .

Three men to-day hold the destiny of Russia in their hands. The Czar is the child of autocracy; Gortschakoff, a hero of countless diplomatic battles, the son of Russia's old genius; and Nicolas Ignatief, resolute, aspiring, accomplished, an embodiment of the polished Tartar of the nineteenth century—this is the great triumvirate.

An attendant announces Major Schamyl. The prince takes up a précis not larger than a visiting card.

His nod admits the young soldier.

"Be seated, Major," he observes in a gentle voice. Gortschakoff's beardless face is as refined as any marquis of the "veille Roche."

Ahmed's pulses are throbbing. This parchment-faced sphinx would give him an order to go to his death, without a change of inflection.

The premier observes his visitor narrowly.

"I desire you, Major, to prepare to leave instantly for Odessa. You have been selected for special duty, under the personal orders of General Ignatief at Constantinople. A gunboat will convey you to the Bosporus. You will not leave the vessel until sent for by the general. He will have news of your arrival. You will go ashore and confer with him at night. Conceal your identity. Avoid uniform."

Ahmed's bow acknowledges his understanding of these directions.

"You will be attached to the foreign bureau until hostilities open (should they occur). My secretary will bring you to your quarters an advance sum allotted to you. General Ignatief will supply any needs. You are not to speak of your mission, of your destination, to any one, even here. Absolute secrecy is required.

"Make every preparation for a long stay. You will not return here till the crisis is over, or the campaign finished. I give you no instructions here. General Ignatief will direct you in all. Report your arrival at Odessa to me, through the commanding general. He will give the gunboat its orders.

"When can you leave?"

Gortschakoff pauses, his cold gray eye fixed on the youth.

"Prince, I shall take the next train."

"Good," simply says the old premier. He rises. It is a dismissal.

He holds out his hand.

"Prince Schamyl, the Emperor trusts you. I hope you will have an audience on your return. I believe that our gracious Emperor will be satisfied with you. I am charged by him to say that he regards *you* as a Russian officer and a loyal subject. You may leave your family honor in his hands."

Ahmed bows over the aged man's hands, whose finger tips he touches. The exquisite courtesy of the old premier has won his heart. He withdraws.

While the young warrior bounds down the stairs, his armed heels ringing loudly in the silent halls, old Gortschakoff seats himself.

"A gallant fellow," he mutters. "Ah, I was young once!"

The days when the great Nicholas leaned on him sweep back from the mists of the buried years. In his old age, he is the Richelieu of another Czar, for Russia draws the sword in fight once more. The cannon will roar around the Euxine again.

Gortschakoff sighs as he wonders whether the fattened ravens of the fields will be the only gainers by the struggle.

Folding his arms behind him, the old man walks

to a wall-map of Europe. His gaze is riveted on the speck marked Constantinople.

"Ah! if England—if England—" His revery is broken—another visitor!

He seats himself. He has forgotten Prince Schamyl already, for he has sent him forth to life or death.

"In the name of the Czar."

Straight as a line can be traced, Ahmed gallops to his quarters. His heart bounds in his bosom. Hassan is off toward the barracks with a card to Paul.

"Come instantly to me; I leave in an hour!"

Before Platoff's sleigh draws up, Schamyl's preparations are half made. The messenger from the foreign office arrives and leaves the sum of twenty thousand roubles in notes. He bows as he says, "This is a personal allowance for your individual expenses; only give me a memorandum, your Highness."

As he leaves, Paul Platoff bursts into the room. A few words to Hassan cause him to join the body-servant in packing. En route!

It needs only Ahmed's happy eyes to tell Paul all is well.

As the friends seat themselves, Ahmed cries:

"Paul, I give my life to the Emperor! I am going at once. I cannot tell you where. It is a trust and an honor. I go from the Moscow station on the next train. I leave my horses to you. Take them to the field. You can trust Kara, the black, with your life. I leave my dvornik here. I want my campaign baggage sent by the Volga railroad to

Vladikaukas. Let the man go with it and wait my orders there by telegraph. There is nothing else. Let him apply to you, and you settle everything."

Paul's eyes open wide as Ahmed dashes off an order on his bankers for Paul's use.

"Send my letters on as I telegraph.

"Now, dear old boy," cries Ahmed (with a glance at his watch), "we will break bread together. We shall not meet till the last shot is fired, I fear."

The repast is on the table. While the friends make a dash at the luncheon, Hassan appears.

"Do I go with his Highness?"

Ahmed starts. His instructions covered no other man. Well, he can send him back from Odessa.

"Get a sleigh for you and the baggage," Schamyl cries.

Before the Burgundy is emptied, Hassan's kit is made—a soldier's cloak, his saddle, wallets, the "chaska" of twenty years' service, his tobacco pouches, and his pistols.

Prince Schamyl's luggage and arms are packed so as to disguise their nature.

Five minutes suffice to start the retainer to the station.

Ahmed's dress is already changed. His heavy cloak with its sable collar, and otter turban, are those of the travelling noble. In a dark gray tunic and high boots, he looks the type of a wealthy traveller.

Pockets? Yes; the notes in his wallet, his staff-map, passports, revolver, and a couple of books to lighten the tedium of the ride past Moscow and down the Kherson.

It is time to leave. One glass at parting. Paul's mind flies back to Ghazee. They drain one cup to the "Rose of Tiflis." There are smiles of meaning.

Ahmed gives a few orders to his bewildered man of affairs. Thank heaven, Paul can close up the details!

They are off! As the snow is spurned away by the steeds, Paul says, "Ahmed, I divine your path. May it lead you to Tiflis. Beware of Ghazee's subtle deviltry. Watch over Princess Maritza. God help her if she ever fell in the power of your brother! His plans include her future in some yet unhatched scheme."

Ahmed hurriedly says: " I thank you, Paul. You shall hear my news by telegraph and letter. Keep me advised of everything.

"You will watch over my name!"

Paul presses his hand. "Leave that to me. All know your standing since the orders of this morning. Before night every pretty woman in Petersburg will know that you breakfasted with Gourko. That is enough. We need no newspapers here while we have the ladies."

Paul's laugh rings out gayly. His friend goes in the path of honor.

Slipping through the throng, tickets are quickly purchased. A glance at Schamyl's passport makes the railway official open his dull eyes. It is an imperial special passport of the highest grade, handed him by Gortschakoff's secretary.

There is ten minutes in the stateroom before leaving. Schamyl "en mufti" would set every tongue to wagging if recognized. On the long stone platforms merry laughter, careless chatter, sighs and sobs mingle.

The Moscow station is like the wide, wide world—a place of incessant meetings and partings. Joy and sadness wandering hand in hand—the one blind, the other halting sadly in useless sorrow.

Schamyl and Platoff review their comradeship in a few last glances as they gaze fondly on each other. This will be no holiday campaign. Russian honors are won in the red whirl of battle. They will chase the bubble reputation on varied fields, and far from each other.

Still it is "cor unum, viæ diversæ." Clanging bells tell of the parting hour. Last words are in order. Ahmed's voice trembles.

"Paul, you must go soon. If I never come back, remember you have been my only brother. I will tell you yet of my quest. Be brave, fortunate, happy! Come back a general."

Platoff's eyes glisten as unearthly shrieks of the whistle announce the starting.

"Ahmed! friend and brother! May God guard you! Beware of Ghazee's treachery. I wait for *your* glory.

"Prince of the Caucasus, stand always for the Czar."

A last embrace! Paul dashes off the train, stumbling over a man clambering in. As he darts past, Prince Schamyl throws the door shut. It was Dimitri, the Greek arch-villain and pander, spy of Ghazee!

With a scream the train tears away in full swing.

Ahmed dares not show himself to watch Platoff straining his eyes after the retreating vans.

Who set the Greek on his track? This conjecture busied Ahmed. Was he returning to the Levant on some secret mission of the deserter, or merely fleeing the wrath of the police?

Call it safety watch, intuition, or chicanery. It was a master stroke of the sly Mustapha to set Dimitri to dog the movements of the Circassian.

A hurried secret report of Ahmed's departure sufficed to suggest to the Ottoman Iago the plan of dogging Ahmed to the end of the journey.

Schamyl remembers the injunction of Gortschakoff. He leaves not the car till Moscow is reached. A sight of his passport causes the train guard to supply all his wants en voyage, and leave him alone in his stateroom. All obey the Czar!

Darkness and wintry chill wrap Moscow as the train rushes in. Hassan has orders not to approach his master until Odessa is reached, and even there to wait with the unmarked luggage till sent for from headquarters.

An hour's stay at Moscow decides Ahmed to venture out in the darkness for exercise after his evening meal in the compartment. Muffling up, he descends, and, passing out of the station, breasts the wintry winds.

Glorious draughts of ozone fill his lungs. Tramping up and down with the zest of a mountaineer, his thoughts wander to this mysterious quest.

Ah! the train bell recalls him. Carelessly swinging around, his face covered to the eyes from the icy blast, as he crosses the dark lane to enter the station he receives a stab full in the breast. Treachery!

It staggers him! With a nervous clutch, he grasps at a dark form, which flees away down the long, outer street of the station. He dares not fire his pistol. It would betray his identity. Bewildered, he presses his hand to his breast. Yes, his clothes are cut! He dashes into the station and regains his compartment.

He is not hurt. Locking his door he examines his tunic—slashed over the heart! He smiles, in vacant wonder, as he draws out his tough campaign map case. The assassin's knife has split the strong leather. The folded map alone saved him.

The train is now rolling on. A cowardly cut, indeed. "What motive?" "Robbery?" "No!" "Revenge?" Schamyl has no blood feud. "Assassination?" "Why?" Ah, the swinging stroke recalls the work of Levantine bravos.

"Was that dark spectre Dimitri?"

Perhaps. Yet he must make no outcry. His sacred mission! Examining his heavy revolver, he slings it around his neck and shoulder with a cord —a friend in need.

The door fastenings are right.

Lynx-eyed must be the villain who will now catch Schamyl off his guard. He remembers that he bears the Emperor's orders. Defeat is dishonor.

Calling the guard, a man is posted at the end of the car to watch the compartment on peril of his life. A glimpse at the imperial passport insures faithfulness. The White Czar speaks in its magic lines.

Two days later Ahmed throws himself into a

carriage at Odessa. In ten minutes he is with the general commanding. An officer is sent to the station for Hassan and the baggage. They drive direct to the quay, where the government despatch boat *Seevoutch* has full steam up. Prince Schamyl's telegraphic report to Gortschakoff is sent from the general's headquarters. It is followed by the official despatch that the saucy *Seevoutch* is out of the harbor. Her last boats and stragglers were putting off for the vessel as the general's aide escorted Schamyl to the cutter waiting for him. He is muffled in a huge boat cloak.

Schamyl has a cabin assigned him by the commander, who has received his instructions.

Dashing out into the Euxine, the swift gun-boat tosses the spray high in air. Night falls. The glorious white stars sweep over the dark blue vault above. The prince walks the deck late; his brow is fanned by the breeze blowing down from the giant mountains of his youth.

Leaning over the low bulwarks, he watches the phosphorescent waves break in showers of yellow diamonds.

Onward, out into the mystic night and the hush of the sea, the quivering ocean rover ever speeds toward the eternal sea gates of the empire of the East.

Schamyl dreams of the pine-crested slopes of the Caucasus, the overhanging mountains of the north, and the bowers of Tiflis. Will he, indeed, see the spirited beauty of Georgia once more?

Ah! Paul's warning. His brother Ghazee! What deviltry is following the fugitive in his wanderings?

Schamyl doubts not that Ghazee will lurk along the border to aid the Ottoman hordes. A squall strikes the plunging vessel. Breaking in gusts of rain, it floods the decks.

Flashes of blue lightning tear across the now blackening sky. Groping back along the deserted deck, Ahmed stumbles against a man, who lurches heavily against him, as the ship rises to the buffeting waves.

In an instant, a pair of sinewy arms are round his waist; bending under him, the stranger with a quick turn has Ahmed half over the rail.

One wild swing of the vessel makes the struggling scoundrel slip. No word save a muttered curse escapes his lips. Is he a madman?

In an instant, the young Circassian, by a giant effort, bodily hurls the assailant over into the boiling surge. A flash of lightning shows him the distorted face of Dimitri the Greek. He sinks, with a wild howl, half uttered. The storm-driven boat, sweeping over the foam, leaves the drowning wretch far astern.

Prince Schamyl staggers into the cabin. Summoning the commander, the ship is searched. Ahmed reveals only his official order of supreme command, handed him by the general at Odessa.

Nothing is known save that the unknown slunk on board with the baggage boats. He was thought to be a legation servant.

Hassan, roused now, sleeps like a dog, crouched before his master's door, sabre in hand.

Schamyl recognizes his brother's subtle work in the midnight stab and the deadly grapple on the deck. It is the curse of the Sultan's amulet. Sleeping in uneasy dreams, when he wakes it is under the fringing cypresses of the Seraglio Point on the Golden Horn.

CHAPTER IV.

THE WHITE COUNTESS'S BOUDOIR.—WITH GENERAL IGNATIEF IN CONSTANTINOPLE.—WHERE IS YOUR BROTHER?—ON THE BRIDGE OF KARA-KEIN.

Pacing a long room overlooking the Seraglio Point, Nadya Vronsky crushes a telegram in her clinched hand. Constantinople brings her love-torn bosom no peace. "Fool and dolt! I can make no meaning of this. Where is Ghazee?"

Throwing herself on a couch, she tries to decipher the veiled despatch of Dimitri.

For nearly two years the wily Greek has been the Figaro of her lover Ghazee.

While Ghazee calmly ran the round of pleasure, Dimitri saw the countess in her highest exaltation, in the abasement of her sorrow, and the weakness of impotent rage. He has all his master's social secrets.

Though never lifting his eyes to the beautiful image before him, Dimitri's heart is yet on fire.

He wonders if Ghazee knows the unquenchable flame of love which glows in that woman's marble heart.

Stone to all else, she is mere wax to Ghazee, melting at his touch.

For long months the greedy Greek has privately sold the gossip of his brutal master's movements to the one woman who loves him. Her argus eye follows his path by day and night.

When he clutched the crisp hundred-rouble notes Nadya threw at him in their last interview he would not tell her he was paid twice as well as she could pay him to disguise Ghazee's movements.

Mustapha, with diplomatic acumen, reasoned out the policy of the Russian government.

One princely brother should find the other. A private feud between them might remove the Mohammedan aspirant to the Armenian crown. The fugitive Guardsman! The Russian deserter!

Mustapha the ambassador—a Moslem of the faith of the Sunis—burns with shame to know that the great Sultan, who now rides to St. Sophia in splendor, is the son of a Christian Armenian woman.

Mustapha was in Constantinople when Sultan Abdul-Aziz, after a fearful night of storm and struggle, lay in his royal pleasure rooms, stark and stiff, yielding up his life to a pair of sharp scissors in the hands of a ferocious Nubian eunuch. The purple marks of fingers on his throat were never seen. His veins were said to have been opened—a suggested suicide.

The fearful butchery of three cabinet ministers at Constantinople was not all in all explained by the hanging of the desperate Circassian Major, who killed nine men in all before a bayonet in his spine paralyzed him.

The Softa's riot of mad thousands, wild with frantic rage; dull Sultan Murad's election to the throne of Turkey, and his early deposition—all these dark events Mustapha well knew were the work of that Russian prince of deceivers, Nicolas Ignatief.

Yet now, Sultan Abdul Hamid—the son of an Armenian Christian beauty—wields the sabre of Solyman, and is lord of the Bosporus.

He is Ghazee Schamyl's best friend. Even the "Sheik ul Islam" has fallen before Ignatief's intrigues. To-day even the great statesman Midhat Pacha, Grand Vizier, is an exile in disgrace.

Ignatief, under a strong guard of Russian marines, laughs at the storms of Istambol and the wreck of thrones. It is his diplomatic "métier."

Mustapha's advices prove that the new Sultan and Prince Ghazee Schamyl are close friends. They are both Armenians. So are Melikoff, Lazareff, and the throng of Russian generals in Asia Minor—Armenians all.

In chattering fear, he cannot leave to Nadya Vronsky the power to sell Ghazee's secrets to Ignatief.

Dimitri—the all observing—has sold the confidence of the White Countess to Mustapha. A double traitor.

The ambassador smiles as he thinks she dwells in his palace at Istambol, yet knows not of Ghazee's near presence.

Dimitri, on the track of Ahmed, in his flight south despatches to Nadya Vronsky that the younger son of the great rebel goes to Odessa.

It is a Moscow telegram the countess dreams over. Where is Ghazee? Prince Ahmed is coming. Will he, too, join his brother in the Caucasus?

Cooped up in a golden palace, the countess ponders. From Odessa a second telegram clears up a part of the puzzle.

"The bird comes on the *Seevoutch* despatch. I fly also. His mate lost." Then Ghazee is not tracked by Dimitri. But the Greek will find him—must find him!

To bribe the watchers at the gate to set spies to give her warning of the arrival of any Russian cruiser, is any easy conclusion for the love-sick woman. Ghazee is still missing. His brother must surely know.

Dimitri—servant, thief, and spy—has sent her his friend at Constantinople—his "alter ego"—to aid until he can reap the golden harvest alone.

While the despatches lie idle in her lap, Nadya's heart beats time by dragging seconds. Her jewels —her very all—she will give Dimitri to discover to her Ghazee's abiding-place.

For her only safety, her only means of avoiding the golden barriers, making her cage a prison, is to leave Constantinople under Ghazee's sheltering arm.

From her windows she can see the whole sweep of the Golden Horn. No Russian flag greets her eyes.

Long in the watches of a weary night she eyes the narrow inlet.

Before the song-bird takes up the nightingale's refrain, as morning smiles over the Dardanelles, her trusty spy—Dimitri's friend—eager and excited, tells her that the *Seevoutch* tosses on the waves below the Karakein bridge.

Ahmed Schamyl is on board, for the crafty Greek

as a fruit pedler has visited the gunboat. He knows the young prince by Dimitri's sketch. Alas! Dimitri will never finish his report.

A Maltese sailor gives the spy the whispered story of a midnight encounter.

The White Countess, with lightning mind, takes her desperate resolve—to see Ahmed; to find his heart; to gain news of Ghazee.

And how? Any pretext will do.

Ah! He must surely report at the Russian embassy. Penning a few lines, she wraps them in a handful of gold.

"Follow this man. Give him this paper unobserved, and return to me."

The Greek is gone.

She dare not go to the Embassy, she may be watched. Ignatief's people might repulse her. Life itself may be her dreadful forfeit, if Mustapha should suspect treachery. And Russian vengeance!

Schamyl would never come to her. In the heart of Istambol, he would be tracked. He would fear an ambush.

As she ponders (while the messenger tells her of Dimitri's death), her eye sweeps over the bridge. There, below the barrier, the delicate spars and dainty beauty of the *Seevoutch* attract a crowd on the Karakein bridge.

Why not there, in that place? Every one can go there. With a woman's inspiration she asks Ahmed to meet her there at midnight.

It is this request her messenger bears. For as she looks in the glass, as the beauty of her imaged self smiles back on her, she says softly:

"He is only a man. He will tell me all. I will have news of my lover from the one man who can pardon my love—his own brother." . . .

Schamyl is on deck when morning breaks over the cypress-lined shores of the Bosporus, and the anchor rattles down in the Golden Horn. It is a day of fate.

The *Seevoutch* swings quietly in the silent waters of the lovely inlet.

Schamyl knows well these classic banks. He dares not feast his eyes from the deck upon the panorama of the world's most splendid harbor. He must wait in hiding. Ahmed grimly smiles as he looks at the slashed tunic. That coward stab at Moscow is now avenged.

When Dimitri sank " with the bubbling cry of the strong swimmer in his agony," he carried all his dark secrets to the black depths of the Euxine.

Schamyl cannot show himself until Ignatief's messenger comes to call him to the soldier diplomat's presence.

The Greek may have telegraphed from Moscow, in cipher, to the Moslems of Constantinople.

Ahmed gazes from the cabin port-holes at the white-walled houses of great Scutari; on the fragrant gardens of Seraglio Point; peerless " Istambol," the crowned city of the Crescent; Pera and Galatea to the north cluster thickly; there in the Russian embassy the master mind battles for the Czar and holds sway over the shifting balances of peace and war.

Old Byzantium and classic Chalcedon were once great cities here, before the mild-eyed Nazarene smote the gods of Greece with that pallid finger, at whose touch the graceful idols of the classic ages fell.

From this vantage-point Grecian civilization spread in centuries past to the shores of the Black Sea.

It is the centre of the old world of creeds and empires. A few beggarly hundreds of miles embrace, in a small triangle, the birthplaces of Christ our Lord; of the giant Machiavel of earth, Mohammed; and the fiery Othman, who from Biledzik, in Anatolia, sallied forth to found an empire destined to wrap the world in flame.

Schamyl knows now that in the scenes of his youth, where Persia, Turkey, and Russia meet under the shadows of Ararat, a new crusade will soon throw the sons of the Cross against the turbaned children of the Crescent.

As the Circassian frets (waiting for night), the breeze which fans his brows blows over the mingled dust of Goth and Greek, Saracen and Crusader. It sweeps over the graves of the unnumbered clans who met in fight beside these sculptured shores of Marmora.

His report to General Ignatief is despatched by an orderly; Schamyl idly watches the thousand slender caiques darting rapidly over the blue waters.

Up and down the old bridge and its fellow, the Karakein (joining the splendid groves of Istambol to modera Pera), a ceaseless throng of wayfarers presses across the Golden Horn.

Schamyl sees the line of carriages bearing the Moslem aristocracy on softest cushions, while the foot passengers envy the proud Pacha or dainty harem beauty (gauze veiled) with her velvety dark eyes.

A boat flying the Russian flag approaches. Orders at last!

The deck officer (who has grasped the idea that Schamyl is a " personage ") announces the dragoman of the Russian Embassy.

"Admit him!" briefly commands the prince. Shawled and turbaned, cimeter at belt, silver-headed staff in hand, the important official enters.

He bows low, and presents a letter silently. Ahmed tears it open.

It is a note from Count Ignatief, stating that the steam launch of the Embassy will be alongside, at eight o'clock in the evening, with a trusted officer to escort him to the count's residence.

"Say to his Excellency, I await the honor of his reception, and shall be ready."

(The note states that a verbal answer only is required.)

Schamyl raises his eyes to the dragoman, who is scanning his features curiously.

He cries, "What! Tarnaieff?"

"The same, your Highness!" He grasps the hand of Prince Schamyl eagerly. A comrade of Circassia.

" Sit down, my old friend. How do you come to masquerade in this costume?"

Tarnaieff accepts the cigars and wines offered by the prince. Noblesse oblige.

"When we finished our hunt in the Caucasus, Prince, *you* returned to St. Petersburg, *I* made a thorough reconnaissance of the Caucasus.

"I wished to know all our frontier passes. General Melikoff detached me from my regiment (on secret service) for a year.

"A Circassian Guardsman may not make a good dragoman; but I have been at Erzeroum, with our consul in that station, for six months or more."

Schamyl eyes his comrade curiously. Tarnaieff is a dashing Armenian.

Just the dare-devil to carry out Loris Melikoff's secret plans.

"Now, Tarnaieff, what was your *real* duty at Erzeroum?" queries Ahmed.

Schamyl knows ambition goads on Loris Melikoff. The keen Armenian general has sworn that he will be governor-general of the Trans-Caucasus, and some day lead an army over the Arpa Tchai.

His hawk eye catches the rising war-cloud.

Melikoff swears the White Czar shall have the quadrilateral forts—Batoum, Ardahan, Kars, and Erzeroum! Visions of a royal province at his feet; an army under his baton; and—and why may he not be the Emperor's chief aide-de-camp?

It is an epoch of many rising stars. Skobeleff's red planet of war gleams in right ascension.

Melikoff knows the Czar *must* have the road to Persia and the East.

For the Russian octopus throws out its feelers toward Merv, Samarcand, the Indian frontier, the Chinese border, the shores of the Black and Caspian.

Soon a steel line will creep from the Urals toward Irkutsk and the Trans-Baikal. Russia in Europe will be joined to the Amoor regions, and

Vladivostock, the gate of the East, be bound to the heart of Muscovy with magic rails.

Court, cabinet, and camp are thrilled with this well-judged plan, to fight Turkey on the Danube; but Russia must take and hold Asia Minor, and the gates of India.

This campaign talk is a lengthy one.

"Prince Schamyl," slowly replies Tarnaieff, "I can trust the Lord of the Caucasus. I have made sketches of all the Turkish works at Ardahan, Bayazid, Kars, and Erzeroum. Melikoff is ready to cross the frontier!

"Of course, you know, Ignatief will coldly juggle till we are ready. As soon as our troops can move, we will fight.

"The conference is, even now, a failure."

"How did you come here, Tarnaieff?" asks the prince, his eyes half closed. The panorama of a long war in the valleys of the Araxes and the Kara passes before his eyes.

"You knew Colonel Kondukoff?" Tarnaieff rejoins.

"Very well!" sententiously replies Schamyl.

"He was a valuable officer, from his knowledge of every inch of ground from Batoum to Sinope, from Trebizond to the Caspian."

"Well!" interrupts Schamyl.

"He has deserted us and joined the Turks, under the name of Moussa Pacha; he is raising a force of renegade Circassians and Kurds to ravage the border!"

"The black-hearted scoundrel," cries Schamyl.

Tarnaieff resumes:

"General Melikoff wants him traced up, and especially those flocking to him. I was sent here to act under Ignatief's orders; of course, as soon as war is declared, I hope to rejoin Melikoff's staff. He fears internal trouble in Circassia."

"Why?" anxiously queries Schamyl.

"Prince" (the dragoman lowers his voice), "we have lost fifteen officers in a month, by desertion! They have slipped (one by one) over the borders to the Turks. There is some more potent charm than this thick-headed Kondukoff at work. He is, thank God, so stupid, he cannot harm us much in the field. If we catch him, we will hang him in his regimental square, the false dog!"

Schamyl's cheeks are burning red. This secret devil is " Ghazee " his brother.

Does Ignatief know? Does Tarnaieff suspect?

Tarnaieff rises.

"I must go now, Prince! I will come with the launch and a dozen trusty men here to-night. By the way, Count Ignatief has one valuable hint as to the insurrection in our rear."

Schamyl starts.

"You remember Suleiman Effendi, our gallant hunting companion?"

"Yes, yes!" cries Schamyl, impatiently.

"He was sent on to Petersburg as military attaché. He has returned."

Schamyl nods.

"He is to have a frontier brigade, under the title of 'Mehemed Pacha.' He is a gallant fellow and a good soldier!"

"Certainly," Schamyl interjects.

"General Ignatief tells me that Suleiman is to move along and try our lines, coöperating with those cut-throat bands under Moussa Pacha the renegade. Their object is to keep up a disaffection among the Abkhasians and Circassians in our rear.

"When I fully understand General Ignatief's ideas, I am to stay to the last: then take the field against these spies and rebels."

Tarnaieff salutes; he turns to go. "See here, Tarnaieff," slowly says Ahmed, "I want to have a private hour with you after I have done with General Ignatief. I think I may be sent away suddenly. I rely on *you* for a personal service."

"With all my heart," answers the dragoman, whose twelve sturdy rowers are soon bending to their oars, throwing high the diamond sparkles of the Golden Horn.

Prince Ahmed paces his cabin rooms like a caged tiger, as the long afternoon wears away. Shall he tell Count Ignatief *all* he knows and fears?

In the throng pouring over the bridges are eager eyes watching the dainty *Seevoutch*.

Russian adroitness may meet its match in a chain linking Mustapha the diplomat, Ghazee his devilish brother, and the "White Countess," to Kondukoff and the warlike Suleiman.

Ahmed recognizes in this desertion the work of Ghazee. Present gold, attractive promises of rank, and the most subtle flattery have carried men who know *too much* into the ranks of the Sultan.

"Is Ghazee in Constantinople, or some other hostile conspirator on his own track?"

When the stars swing up from the far eastern

land of the fire worshippers, Schamyl throws a heavy boat cloak around himself, as the whistle of the steam launch sounds alongside. His revolver is ready in his pocket. He slings his trusty Circassian dagger at his tunic belt. It is the "sine quâ non."

It makes no noise. Swinging down the companion way, young Schamyl goes to the presence of the great soldier ambassador.

Tarnaieff bows in silence as the swift launch steams to the shore. In five minutes the Pera boat landing is reached. "Cæsar has burned his ships."

Lightly jumping ashore at the foot of Karakein bridge, Ahmed enters a waiting carriage.

Tarnaieff lingers to bid the launch await his return. He whispers to Ahmed as the horses spring away: "We can take a little run in the launch later, and be entirely alone."

Up the street, where forgotten armies have trodden for centuries past, and defiled by the famous cross-roads, the carriage dashes. It stops at the Russian Embassy, opposite the Hotel d'Angleterre. Here, at the Municipality house, Russia, Turkey, and England meet, in social opposition, but tied by fate in a knot only to be cut by the sword.

The Embassy windows are darkened. Tarnaieff bids Prince Ahmed follow him. Through a side door the prince enters that superb residence, which is Russia, though its walls are in Turkey.

Here the hatching of plots, the weaving of snares, the daily diplomatic tangle, is guided by the ablest dissimulator of the century, Nicolas Ignatief.

A grave-faced lackey bows low. He conducts

Schamyl to the private study of the ambassador. Opening the door he announces, "Prince Ahmed Schamyl."

The young soldier enters. He bends his stately head as he sees, beside the man of the hour, his gracious and beautiful wife.

With consummate courtesy, General Ignatief presents Prince Ahmed to the delicate lady, who lost no prestige as a Galitzin heiress when she gave her hand in wedlock to Count Nicolas Ignatief.

Serene, blonde in beauty, with the exquisite manners of "a duchess," Madame la Comtesse Ignatief places the young man instantly at his ease.

Ahmed has not forgotten his graceful early lessons of the Page School. While he presents his personal homage to the distinguished châtelaine, he studies the great man before him.

In the uniform of a general, with the aiguillettes and crown-bearing epaulettes of an imperial aide-de-camp, Ignatief shows the thorough soldier in his well-set frame and perfect self-control.

A high forehead, crowned with thick, long black locks, with piercing, deep dark eyes; a drooping, pointed Tartar mustache, and a smooth shaven face which shows the professional smile of the arch-Jesuit or the duellist "en garde"—Ignatief is a man of strange appearance.

His ready, mobile smile can stiffen into the set decision of a man who would send battalions calmly into a hell of fire, or charm with its winning frankness.

When his roving, bold black eyes have finished a survey of the youthful warrior, Madame Ignatief rises.

Schamyl springs to the door. He is rewarded with a smile which is doubly beautiful from its rareness. It is the alpenglow.

The Countess Ignatief's smiles are precious even in Russia, that land of most bewitching ladies.

Seating himself at a nod, Prince Ahmed awaits the general's pleasure.

"Where is your brother?" the ambassador asks, as sharply as a rifle shot.

"I cannot tell you, general," Ahmed frankly answers. He is paralyzed at this thrust.

Ignatief leans back in his chair. His eyes are half closed. . . .

"Tell me of his departure, Prince," he continues in an ordinary tone.

Schamyl briefly reports the facts as to Ghazee's disappearance.

"You have had no communication with him?"

"None at all," rejoins Ahmed, proudly.

"Tell me of your trip!" Ignatief is studying the ceiling intently.

Schamyl describes his voyage. He tells of the attack at Moscow, the weird scene on the deck of the *Scevoutch*.

His brief report is soon over. "*Finit opus!*"

Ignatief muses. .

"It is as I feared. They *know* of your secret voyage. Nothing is sacred in St. Petersburg. There are spies everywhere . . . even here."

The count is talking to himself. He rouses.

"Prince Schamyl, I intended to keep you here until I could explain the grave duties which will be intrusted to you. I do not wish to pain you. The influence of your brother 'Ghazee' may be annoying to us in Asia Minor. I see he has already tried to have you assassinated. Now I shall send you at once to Kertsch, on the *Seevoutch*.

"She will sail at daylight. Go from there by rail to Vladikaukas and join General Melikoff at Tiflis.

"I will send Tarnaieff over with full details when I leave here. An imperial courier can come across before the war.

"I have prepared a despatch, which I give you now. It is in a cipher which Loris Melikoff alone knows."

General Ignatief hands Ahmed a sealed packet, addressed officially to Count Loris Melikoff.

Schamyl bows as he receives it. A trust!

"My young friend" (calmly continues Ignatief), "I know your mystic land. When I left Moscow and put my first uniform on, I served in desperate mountain warfare against your great father.

"I saw Sultan Schamyl come down from his great eyrie at Gunib, leading you by the hand, when he surrendered to Prince Baryatinsky.

"Stirring days," muses Ignatief. "They made Baryatinsky a prince and field marshal, and *me*—a soldier.

"Thirty years' warfare. Two hundred thousand lives were laid down to subdue your warlike father and to gain us the silver-crested line of the Caucasus.

"When 'Jamal Eddin,' your brother (now long dead), was delivered up by your noble father, in a truce, two great armies in array watched over the scene.

"You see what we gave in blood and toilsome years to get the Caucasus?"

Ahmed bows. His eyes are roving over the great study, with its myriad books, its piles of maps, its pyramids of labored papers. The count is a man of the pen as well as the sword, a very hard fighter and a much harder student.

"Prince," continues Ignatief, "your royal father kept his word when he surrendered to us. You know the late Emperor was princely in his undefiled honor. It rests with you alone to keep the family name white!

"As soon as I have made a tour of the European capitals, I shall rejoin the Emperor at Kischereff. Prince Dolgourouki and myself will attend him to the field as special aides."

Schamyl's eyes sparkle. The eagle of the Caucasus scents human blood!

"These immovable Turks will refuse all wise concessions. Gortschakoff will then define our position in a logical circular letter to the powers. We will instantly attack the Turk."

Ignatief rests. His glittering eyes are fixed on the young soldier.

"The Turks are lost in their own quarrels. We incite these disturbances, for we *must* have Asia Minor as far as the Euphrates! You will find the Grand Duke Nicholas at Tiflis when you arrive. Among the leading generals are our very best frontier soldiers—Melikoff, Heimann, Lazareff, Komaroff, Count Grabbe, and Tergukassoff. But it rests alone with *you* to counteract your mad brother Ghazee's influence. To us he is merely a deserter. To you, a deadly enemy—a would-be assassin!

"The Emperor looks to *you*, loyal and true, to combat the schemes of 'Ghazee,' Kondukoff, Mehemed Pacha, and that black-hearted Kurd '*Ismail Pacha,' the Vali of Erzeroum.*

"They will spread treason and insurrection silently in our rear."

"Do you anticipate hostile foreign influence, General?" Ahmed queries.

"Hardly," replies Ignatief. "France and England helped your father in his last struggling years. Only a few resolute men like Captain Burnaby, Baker Pacha, Hobart Pacha, and Sir Arnold Kemball are trying to open the eyes of the English!— Fat-witted and too rich!

"They are too slow, these dogged islanders," sneers the count.

He rises. Stepping to an ebony escritoire, he hands to Prince Ahmed a magnificent Tcherkess dagger. "Prince," the old ambassador says, "your warrior father gave me this blade on the sad day of Gunib. Take it back. *You* go to the storied land of guerilla war, to impending death, to the land of the old Vendetta, to the land of the mystic fire worshipper, the land of savage witchery.

"May your fate be fortunate! I am authorized by the Emperor to say that he trusts you to the very death! Beware of sly Moslem wiles—shun the lurking assassin! If you are in sudden danger, destroy your despatches. Let them not leave your person for a moment!

"At Kertsch *you* can take a nominal guard—a picked escort.

"Now, Prince, beware of your wily brother! YOUR life is valuable to the Czar, for *you* alone shall lead the loyal Circassians in this war!"

Ignatief concludes. It is a gracious congé.

Prince Schamyl presses the silver-shafted dagger to his lips.

"I swear fealty, to the death, on this sacred emblem! The Czar holds Schamyl's honor!"

The stern general's face softens. He rings a silver bell.

A servant bears in the never-absent wine of the Muscovite. Ahmed's lips barely touch the crystal glass. As the general drinks he pledges, with a smile, to Schamyl:

"To our next meeting in Constantinople in the hour of victory! To the cross on St. Sophia!"

A heavy boom shakes the casements. Prince Schamyl springs to the window. There, a few cable lengths away, swings on the sea a huge black sea monster.

Another gun! It is the stern voice of England.

"What is that, General?" the Circassian queries with anxiety.

Ignatief's voice shakes slightly.

"*It is the English despatch boat saluting the Sultan!* This voice of the starlit night is an omen of evil import to the White Czar."

England's rough barkers growling a hoarse tribute to the *crescent flag of the Moslem!*

Schamyl springs lightly down the marble stairs, his nerves tingling with the anti-climax. The great steel cannon of the queen of the sea disputed boldly the ambassador's prophecy over the wine. "No thoroughfare yet."

Passing out, the carriage lights meet his eyes. With foot on the step the footman salutes and says: "Major Tarnaieff will join you instantly, Prince." As the servant speeds to call his companion Schamyl lights his cigarette. A swift-footed passer-by thrusts a paper into his open hand, and rapidly turns the corner of the Embassy.

Ahmed springs like a deer to the dark crossing. Many mingled forms, in all costumes of the day, are pressing toward the bridges in a huddle. The quest is useless.

Tarnaieff joins him as he endeavors to scan the mysterious billet. A second thought: What hostile eyes may now be fixed on him? He enters the coupé.

Tarnaieff closes the door sharply. In a few minutes the two friends are at the landing. The panting horses rest.

Muffled up well, Ahmed descends to the cabin of the launch. The disguised dragoman is about to give the signal for leaving the strand.

"Wait!" Ahmed cries. "Look here, Tarnaieff. The billet of the unknown is simple enough. 'Meet me alone at midnight, in the middle of the Karakein bridge. The life of the Rose of Tiflis is in your hands.'"

"A trap!" Tarnaieff snarls. "An enemy's device!"

Schamyl's eyes are fixed upon the signature— "Nadya Vronsky."

Ahmed ponders. The "White Countess" here. Mustapha's tool. Ghazee's fair devotee.

Then Ghazee himself is not far off.

Tarnaieff watches the young soldier. "You are not mad enough, Prince, to fall into this snare?"

Schamyl hears him not. He gazes on the lonely bridge intently. Launches and caïques innumerable crowd the glassy Golden Horn. His plan is instantly made.

"To the ship!" he commands.

The little steamer throbs to the twisting screw. On the passage Tarnaieff cries:

"It would be madness. I have orders for the vessel to leave an hour before daybreak for Kertsch —under your directions. The ship's company will be inspected, the boat searched for intruders. I am to go to Kertsch with you and report back your departure—by special train—to Tiflis."

Ahmed answers briefly. His mind is dwelling on the picture of the Diana-like Maritza. Those love-lit eyes shine on him once again. The soldier's blood is throbbing in every pulse as he recalls those drooping lashes, when she simply said, at their parting:

"Mon cher Prince. Au revoir à Tiflis!"

Fairest of the maids in the land of Prometheus and Cadmus! The armed men are now springing up around her.

Born on those classic shores, where, on a lovely island of the coast, Aurora and her dazzling train swept along in the dance of the Hours, in the old golden days—a daughter of the fabled Amazons— scion of the great prophetess "Thoulme," mistress of all weird mystery—Maritza de Deshkalin is now the reigning queen of his lawful patrimony in the Caucasus.

Her innocent life in danger! Is it a bold invention of the Vronsky? Who knows?

Can he meet a woman whom it were madness to trust? His honor! His oath on his father's dagger fresh on his lips. Ahmed's love combats his duty.

No soft daughter of luxury is the beauteous Georgian. Spirited and brave is she—a scion of that noble race which held the defiles of the Caucasus against the invincible Alexander.

Pompey's legions recoiled before her warrior forefathers. Attila, Tamerlane, and Genghis Khan swerved aside from the fierce mountaineers, who battled to the death under the shining crests of Kazbek and Ararat.

The haughty Persian and even the merciless Turk failed to subdue her martial ancestors.

Platoff's warning flashes to his mind. Is it a plot of the leaden-eyed Ghazee?

His head says, No! His heart cries, Yes! Love is prophetic.

For the sweet Rose of Tiflis, he will keep the dangerous midnight tryst.

Schamyl sees the glittering stars hanging high over the eastern skies, where the giant slopes of the Caucasus buttress the Czar's blood-bought domains.

These sparkling lights of night speak to him of Maritza, only Maritza.

Tarnaieff raves when Schamyl tells him his decision.

"I will take a boat with a dozen well-armed men,

and a couple of rope ladders. We will row to the Seraglio Point. When we have gone well above the bridge, we will then drift down. You and I can go along the bridge. *You* follow me, a few hundred feet away. If there is treachery, I will fire my pistol. The men will be at hand. We can drop into the boat and return to the vessel."

"Are you mad, Schamyl?" Tarnaieff cries. "I will not go with you, Prince. What can you say to your commander?"

Circassian blood brooks no checking. Schamyl says, in a chilling tone:

"All right, Tarnaieff, I'll go alone. *You* can wait here at the ship."

His friend bounds to his feet. Ahmed's words cut him like a whip-lash.

"Schamyl, I will not abandon you. I am yours to the death. But you are taking a fearful risk, my old comrade."

"We will take the risks together, then, Tarnaieff," Ahmed says affectionately, for his loyal friend's prudence alone held him back.

The preparations for the expedition are soon made. Schamyl's despatches remain on board. Hassan insists on tumbling into the boat. He scents danger.

At eleven the low cutter glides away to the gardens of Seraglio Point.

Even at this late hour, boats are darting over the waters. Twinkling lights on the anchored ships are mirrored with the trembling stars.

Under the bows of the English despatch boat, the armed boat speeds toward those bowers, whence dome and minaret, spire and arcade, rise faintly lined against the blue vault.

From the thickets, the perfumed breeze wafts the thrilling plaint of the nightingale.

Schamyl bears at his waist his father's dagger; a belt under his cloak also carries his army revolver.

To his ardent and impulsive soul, the plash of the oars, the birds' song, the sighing of the winds, repeat only that magic word—" Maritza."

Tarnaieff, in the hour of waiting, has told him all the diplomatic secrets of the day. They are to be companions in the coming war, until perhaps a shell, perchance a Turkish cimeter, may divorce them forever. Both are food for Turkish powder.

Hassan eyes his master like a wolf hound. He is once more "en Turque," his normal guise.

Strong arms propel them far up the stream, then drifting slowly along the strand, after a few whispered words, Schamyl springs ashore. Hassan gravely breasts the throng and wends sullenly along the bridge to his post, which is to be a hundred yards beyond the middle of the bridge. He is to conceal himself, and keep guard.

Schamyl loiters along, scanning the passers-by. He hears the click of the oars, as the boat speeds along, to station itself under the central span, in hiding.

Tarnaieff, on the other walk, lingers and smokes his cigar. He follows the tall form of the prince.

Ahmed's every faculty is strained. Casting his eyes uneasily around, he sees behind him the great dome of St. Sophia hovering between heaven and earth. Will the Greek cross rise there ever?

The thousand lights on the three varied shores twinkle lazily. Down the Bosporus, moving red and green lanterns show the track of swift packets.

Reaching the middle of the bridge, it lacks but five minutes of twelve. The belated stragglers are few. Loosening his revolver, with his belt-dagger in his left hand, Ahmed stands on the middle of the roadway. His heart is beating fast. Nothing in sight. No sound save the indistinct murmurs of the shores, where a million wait for the coming day. It is rash to be here. Hark! Clear and sweet, from the anchored ships the sound of eight bells strikes his ear. The boom of a distant heavy bell intones midnight. Where is Nadya?

Is it the roll of a vehicle? Yes! Swiftly, from the Istambôl bank, a double carriage approaches.

Tarnaieff, lurking along the eastern rail of the bridge, stands motionless.

The carriage soon halts. Some one is coming. Ahmed's heart is beating high. It is surely a woman. At a distance of ten paces a servant follows.

Schamyl scorns to show suspicion. As the woman approaches, he advances on guard. A white gauze veil covers the unknown features. She need not speak. The springy stride, the dainty bearing, are those of a European. No dumpy, over-fed harem beauty—this sombre witch of the night, whose white veil gleams like silver.

She pauses; with a quick movement of her arm, the attendant halts.

"Major Schamyl?" Her voice is broken and agitated.

"At your service, madame," calmly replies the prince. His keen eyes search her face.

She drops the gauze scarf a moment.

"Madame la Comtesse Vronsky?" he bows low. "Pray be brief, madame. You sent for me?"

"I did. Your brother plans the capture, ruin, or death of Maritza de Deshkalin! Look to her! His agents are everywhere. Tiflis is swarming with spies. Georgia is filled with his minions. I care not for this war of tyrants! But I know *his* dark purpose. The would-be Pacha of Georgia craves the Rose of Tiflis for his harem queen. If Ghazee leads the Turks to the heart of Georgia, she is lost. Let her leave Tiflis. She is only safe in Petersburg. Watch over her!"

"Madame, your motive?" Ahmed coldly murmurs. He muses. He is off his guard.

She throws aside her veil, and clasps her bosom with her nervous hands, flashing with gems.

"I have stolen away, at the risk of my life, to tell you this. Gold unlocks even the guarded gates of Istambôl! The road which leads him to her, takes him far from me. I love Ghazee! For God's sake, tell me where he is!" She is sobbing now.

She lifts her head—to cry: "Save yourself!" With a wild scream, Nadya Vronsky falls senseless at Schamyl's feet. He turns his head. Two writhing, struggling forms are behind him. *One* breaks away before he dare fire, and flees wildly up the bridge. He drops his revolver on its cord sling. Who is it lying there prone?

Ahmed is bending over old Hassan, whose heavy breathing proves his suffering.

Ah! Warm blood? Yes! From his side a stream trickles over Ahmed's fingers.

Tarnaieff has now raised the woman. The silent attendant springs to his side. While they seek to lift the fair burden and bear it to the carriage, the clatter of horses' feet dies away along the causeway.

Ahmed need not blow his boatswain's whistle, a half dozen stalwart fellows clamber over the low bridge parapet. That woman's scream has brought the sailors up.

The coxswain calls for a coil of rope. Old Hassan is lowered into the cutter.

Schamyl's presence of mind returns.

"Leave four men here! Row to the ship! Have the surgeon instantly dress this man's wounds! Return at once to the foot of the bridge where we landed! Give way strong!"—he cries. The boat is already sweeping toward the gunboat.

Side by side with Tarnaieff, Schamyl, aided by the four men, bears Nadya Vronsky to the carriage. There is something clutched in his hand which poor Hassan grasped in his stiffened fingers. Who was the assassin?

While Tarnaieff pours a little brandy from his flask down the fainting woman's throat, Schamyl looks at the object he retains.

The carriage lamp shows him Sultan Schamyl's amulet. It was Ghazee the deserter!

"You lured me to my death, you she-devil," he grimly says, as the woman opens her eyes. She is trembling like a leaf. . . .

"Drive on slowly," he commands in Turkish.

The servant mounts the box. By the side of the carriage the four sailors tread, pistol in hand.

Nadya Vronsky's hand clasps his. He throws it off.

"As God is my judge," she moans, "I knew nothing of this. I saw the man stealing toward you, and the flash of a knife. The other man sprang out and grasped him. I knew no more. I feared it was murder.

"I wished to warn you against Ghazee, and save that poor girl from his clutches."

"Liar and traitress! It was Ghazee who attacked me," Schamyl cries.

"I am lost! Mustapha has played me false. Ghazee will kill me!" moans Nadya Vronsky, and sinks senseless on the cushions.

Driving slowly to the bridge head, Schamyl aids to revive the frightened woman. Halting in the shadows of the overhanging cypress groves, she whispers:

"For my life, leave me now, at once! I am well. I must regain my home. Follow me not, on your honor. Prince, I have risked my life for you to-night. The harem walls tell no tales. Quick, quick! May God protect you! Beware of Ghazee!"

Schamyl's foot is hardly on the ground, with Tarnaieff by his side, when the carriage dashes away at headlong speed. The servant has entered, throwing the door to with a crash.

Silently the party regain the boat. Leaping high out of the water, the bows cut the flashing ripples of the inlet.

Seated in the steamer cabin, Prince Schamyl

listens to the surgeon's report. The wound is deep and serious. Hassan is very weak from loss of blood. He must not be disturbed.

It is half-past one. The anxious commander suggests immediate departure.

Schamyl consents.

In a half hour, while Ahmed and Tarnaieff discuss a bowl of vodki punch, the dainty *Seevoutch* is tossing aside the dashing spray of the strait, as she drives into the teeth of the northeast gale, headed for Kertsch.

Beside Schamyl lies his father's amulet, and below decks his old henchman groans under Ghazee's stab.

BOOK II.

The Deserter.—Cross Against Crescent.

CHAPTER V.

A STORMY INTERVIEW.—THE ROSE OF TIFLIS.
—SCHAMYL'S QUEST.—THE WHITE CROSS OF
THE GRAND DUKE.

FLYING steeds, panting and foam flecked, sweep into the court-yard of Mustapha Pacha's palace in Istambôl. The carriage stops with a crash. The Countess is half led, half dragged out. Nadya Vronsky passes the outer guard in silence. Her attendant roughly urges her along. He grumbles:

"Lady, I have earned your gold. If this night ride be ever known to Mustapha Pacha, I will be bastinadoed and sent to the trenches; he never forgives."

With haggard eyes the woman watches him as they hurry through the silent corridors to her rooms.

"And myself?" she hoarsely whispers. "Myself, good Abdallah!"

The man gloats over her delicate beauty. He eyes her askance. Drawing his hand over his throat, significantly, he growls, "Down there, with the others gone before!"

He sweeps his arm toward where the moonlight shimmers on the deep, silent waters of the Golden Horn.

Shaken and unnerved the White Countess throws herself on a divan as the servant closes her room doors.

"Stay, Abdallah." She fears to be alone. Any pretext to keep him. He can be paid. Ghazee may soon wreak another's vengeance on her if he is in his mad hour.

"I will give you gold—more gold. Seal your lips. Let no one know. Stay now on watch in the corridors. If any one comes, give me warning."

"Good!" grunts the slave, now master of another harem secret. "This fair Frankish woman has gold and jewels of price." He bows and leaves. In a few moments he returns.

"Drink this cordial," he says. "You are weak."

The potion he gives her restores her shattered self-control. Her brain is once more at work. How to turn Ghazee's fury—how to defend herself against Mustapha's vengeance!

The clatter of hoofs resounds in the court. Yes, yes, Ghazee has ridden over the other bridge! Abdallah glides down the corridor.

If he has corrupted the harem slaves, he was forewarned of her visit at night.

Does he suspect treason or an intrigue? Nadya shudders, for she knows many a servant has had his teeth dashed out by a blow of Ghazee's dagger shaft for a mere word.

This man, who had laughed and gayly breakfasted at her house an hour after killing poor Oliviera, the Portuguese attaché, is coming to call her to account.

"The fool leaped in the air and spoiled his beauty as he fell when I shot him. I told him I would kill him with no trouble." Ghazee Schamyl gloated over his wine, on the poor boy's dying agony.

"I never liked his pretty face," he sneered.

With frightened haste Abdallah rushes into the room.

"The Prince Ghazee comes! Furious!"

He glides around the corridor into a window recess. Ghazee has bribed all the higher servants of the harem. They fear the desperate Circassian. With an imperious toss of the curtains of the portal, the maddened deserter strides into the room.

Nadya Vronsky's face is buried in her hands.

He drags her by the wrists to a window. "I want all your story now. One lie, and I will throw you out and break that white neck. It is not far to the shore."

He growls like a wounded bear.

"What deviltry were you plotting? Telling all you know to that Slav cur, Ignatief?

"Speak! I will throttle you, if you don't find words."

Her heart bounds under her silken gown madly. She is on the brink of her grave.

"Ghazee! It was love for you led me to risk my life."

He snarls. "Love! A likely tale! You lie!"

"I found out where you were. I watched your messengers hanging around the quay. I had a report from a spy at Odessa that Dimitri was following that Giaour slave, my brother, here.

"I watched him. My men saw your messenger in waiting. I read your billet. I would have killed that young fool, but for the old wretch who has a taste of my dagger. My trap was to catch him, through you.

"Now I will settle with you." He throws himself on her.

Clasping him around the knees, the frightened woman begs for mercy.

"I wanted to see you—you alone! Oh! take me away from here. Anywhere, but with you. Mustapha will kill me when he comes, if you leave me.

"These slaves will tell him all. He may even harm you. I will tell you news." And she gives him the story of Dimitri's death—of Mustapha's under-plots against him.

Ghazee throws her off. He muses. "Sit there," he growls. "Answer me.

"Does that fool Ahmed know my plans?"

"No!" she falters.

He glares at her in silence.

Ambition goads him to a brother's murder for that glittering coronet of Armenia.

"I will take you along. If you have given Ahmed any news which will reach Ignatief, I will have you thrown to the wild Kurds as a camp follower.

"You may be of some use to me at Kars. I will have some woman's work for you there. If you are wise, you will obey me strictly. If you play me false, you may come back here to have Mustapha work his will on you. I will send him a cipher that I have taken you along. These slaves are in my pay. They will be silent. If you are sensible, I may send you back here to watch the palace intrigues. Mustapha is a deep schemer, but I must keep his friendship. You might spy on him for me here."

Nadya Vronsky throws herself on her knees before him. "I swear to you, Ghazee, I will follow your orders in life and death. I love you! You know my past. I will die for you—with you!

"Take me away from here. The very air breathes murder! I loathe these slaves! I shall go mad here!" She is sobbing wildly.

"Get up! No hysterics! You may yet be the friend of the Princess of Armenia."

He walks the floor.

"It is true! Mustapha hates Armenians. This fool has an influence over him," he muses and speaks.

"I wish to draw off that Georgian tribe who follow the girl Princess of Tiflis. She must be treated well. You may help to amuse her."

"And you will make her your wife," Nadya murmurs.

"One of them," Ghazee briefly adds. "My faith allows me several. *You* will do for *one*. Don't forget my caution. Serve me and watch my interests, for your life hangs on your fidelity!"

The next day Mustapha's harem has lost one tenant, for the White Countess is on the deck of a Turkish steamer with Ghazee sailing toward Trebizond. His troops wait him at Kars.

While the *Seevoutch* dashes northward through the silent night, Schamyl and Tarnaieff unravel the seeming mystery of the attack.

Ghazee must have succeeded in reaching the Bosporus to confer with the immobile masters of Muhktar Pacha and the great Osman. These great leaders now watch the Turkish lines in Asia and Europe.

A "holy war" will be proclaimed by frantic Dervish and sly Ulema. The hated Russ will be attacked (in front and rear) in Asia Minor, and withstood along the Danube.

Tarnaieff is ignorant of the social tableaux presented in the shifting kaleidoscopic salons of St. Petersburg.

He, however, instantly divines the policy of Ghazee. Nadya Vronsky, Mustapha's spy, must be watched until the Turkish legation leaves St. Petersburg. The ambassador's "honor" is at stake.

Ghazee's enormous wealth and his secret connections at Constantinople make it easy for him to watch, by his spies, the Russian Embassy at the "four corners."

Ghazee had discovered his brother's arrival.

The friends sit late over the flowing vodki bowl (for the breeze wails coldly from the north). They agree that Mustapha has secretly advised Ghazee to watch every movement of the impulsive "White Countess." *She* might play the famous "double cross," and give Ignatief news of vital importance. Russian gold is as heavy as Turkish.

Strange, mysterious philtre of love! Burning

human madness! Unreasoning desire to attain the unreachable! Nadya Vronsky's only motive is a frenzied woman's jealousy.

Her *two masters* basely think she slaves with unsleeping cunning for gold alone.

It is to them the sparkling, invincible yellow stream of the coveted dross which passes through the finest diplomatic nets—burning, cutting, breaking down.

Nadya Vronsky shuddered when she left her gilded prison walls at Istambôl to meet Schamyl.

She knows well many fair women's faces have drifted upturned on the deep waters of the Bosporus. A scream, a plunge—dark forms watching the sinking victim, as a white robe flashes once or twice on the merciless waters! Silence, and a few broadening circles.

The leafy groves of Seraglio Point could whisper tales of murder chilling the blood.

Dissimulation and death reign over these beautiful harem bowers, whose fragrant boughs sweep to the ground loaded with the rich fruitage of orange and pomegranate. There, in the silent glades, the bird of night sings over the graves of the forgotten and hapless victims of lust's fury or deadly intrigue!

Ghazee's gold had easily corrupted the messengers of the White Countess. Slaves sell their very soul.

It was indeed his design to cut the succession to the coveted coronet of the Caucasus with the blow intended for a brother's heart.

When morning dawns, the two friends stand by Hassan's bedside. The tough old servitor is able to thank Schamyl with his dog-like eyes. When questioned, he turns his face to the wall and whispers: "The great master." He knew well whose hand guided the knife. He fears Ghazee's awful curse.

There is no danger of a grave result. The heavy blade fortunately slipped and turned on a rib.

The boat races along over the curling billows of the Black Sea. Tarnaieff is glad to be relieved of the responsibility of his princely friend, who bears the precious despatches. No more escapades.

Schamyl listens impatiently to the many warnings of his comrade. He cuts them all short.

"Tarnaieff, I go now direct to Tiflis. After last night, I shall show Ghazee no mercy! He cannot reach Tiflis as soon as I will—even if it were not a desperate quest for a Russian deserter, whose life would pay the forfeit at once.

"If we meet on the field, there will be no quarter. I would not he dies by my hand, but I shall strike home and spare not!"

Thirty-six hours more brings the low hills and mud huts of straggling Kertsch up from the horizon. Hassan is able to hobble ashore.

The commander grins with joy as his mysterious charge leaves the ship's side. He fain would have no further mishap with this too important personage.

An officer of the staff, warned by telegraph, salutes Schamyl. In an hour the special train is puffing at the depot. The general in command will waive any formal visit.

Ahmed's orders are to proceed forthwith. In

the second car of the little train, a sergeant and half a dozen Cossacks of the Ataman Regiment of the Don, are a ready body-guard. They wait the beck and call of their lieutenant (a hawk-eyed youth), who reports to Schamyl, as guide, guard, and companion.

Tarnaieff glances toward the rolling yellow hills rising up to the east and north—the first spurs of the grand Caucasus.

"We shall meet, my Prince, and lead a charge together on those rascals over there! Au revoir at Tiflis."

Wringing Ahmed's hand, the gallant young Armenian watches the train dart away.

In a half-hour, the *Seevoutch* skims like a swallow toward the lovely harbor of the glowing south, where inscrutable Ignatief is now preparing for his last " coup de théâtre," of breaking off all relations. His " promenade en diplomat " of the capitals awaits him. War is only waiting for the snows to melt.

Then the truncheon of the mighty White Czar, lord of a hundred tribes, will be thrown down for a murderous war.

"Au revoir at Tiflis!" Yes, these words haunt Schamyl as the light train flies over the bare plains of the southern steppes.

His heart beats lightly. Every revolution of the wheels bears him nearer to sweet " Maritza." Fleet are the panther feet of love. The plains fly by unheeded. Home of the Crim Tartars and the Don Cossacks—old lands trampled under the charger's feet of the " Golden Band," the " White Horde," and the savage Scythians.

On the grassy hillocks the mounted Cossack watches his herds. In a month, the signal cry will rally the wildest riders of the world, under the blue and white cross. Their lances will shine on the Armenian plains.

Hassan is gaining hourly. He grimly smiles, as he realizes he will see again the holy land of the Tcherkess—the defiles of his own rugged Daghestan, and the fruity bowers of lovely Georgia.

Morning comes, after a wild rushing night, racing over the rough foot-hills.

Schamyl refreshes himself en route. Save for fuel and water, there are no stops.

Fast are the Czar's riders. Like lightning his august mandates are borne through storm and stress.

Afar in the south, a silver cone now rises glistening in the vast sea of the grassy prairie, swept by the icy breeze for countless miles.

Hassan struggles to his elbow. He faintly calls Schamyl. Pointing a feeble finger he murmurs, "Dsching Padishah," "the Great Spirit;" for it is indeed the mystic Elburz peak towering over eighteen thousand feet to heaven.

Anon, Kazbek lifts its rugged mass sixteen thousand feet in air, world-famed Ararat rises in this awful trinity of rose-tinted, silvery snow mountains.

Pagan and Persian, Gheber and wild Moslem, fiery Armenian clinging to the Cross, and scattered Kurdish devil-worshippers—all find inspiration in these awful monuments of God's sculpture.

Now the sunlight breaks upon a thousand lower

silver-sheathed mountain peaks. It is the snow king's citadel. The train flies along at fifty miles an hour.

Below the snow line, dark purple masses of mist roll away. There in witching beauty lie the heavily wooded ranges of the second mountains.

Giant oaks, cedars, bloodwood, and taxus crown these misty hills, where the savage wolf, the bounding deer, and tusked boar are lords of the hill.

In among the gorges and defiles the road twists and turns.

For thirty years Russia poured its devoted soldiers into the gloomy fastnesses of the forests now spreading their savage grandeur around—a graveyard of armies.

Rich valleys, deep defiles, and splendid river canyons open into the heart of the Caucasus.

Five millions of half-subdued liegemen of the Czar roam over the two hundred thousand square miles of the great Caucasus range. The Kuban railway is one of five great military routes joining Russia and Asia Minor.

Four hundred miles from Kertsch to Baku, the great chain sweeps, breaking in Daghestan into huge hills, seven and eight thousand feet in air.

Schamyl's heart beats proudly, as, far toward the rising sun, he sees the sharp peaks hanging over distant "Gunib," where the Lion of Daghestan held so long his mountain eyrie, undefiled.

Through these gorges, for a generation, the oft-defeated armies of the Czar plodded to their death under Jermoloff, Paskiewitch, Von Rosen, Grabbe, Mouravieff, and Woronzoff.

After the devoted gray-clad Russians had watered every acre of this mystic land with their heart's blood, the gallant Baryatinsky reduced, one by one, the great fortresses of nature—these strongholds which foiled even desperate armies led by a Czar in person.

Schamyl is in revery as the train sweeps past the queerly decorated and palisaded wooded houses. Flocks and herds are everywhere. In the long stretches of forest, the box, fig, pomegranate, and wild pear enrich the shrubbery.

Perfumed branches of laurel and myrtle, with the azalea, arbutus, wild roses, and violets, will make this a paradise when the spring sun bids the blossoms open.

Buffalo and wild horses and the giant elk abound here in the meadows.

Above, on the crested heights, the gazelle, chamois, and silver moufflon gaze at the meaner world below.

In and out the rock-ribbed gorges, the little train twists. On these northern slopes, the bear, wolf, jackal, and tiger stray. The mighty aurochs wanders sullenly in the glen. Pheasants whirr from tree to tree. They wait the richest season of the year, when the plum, apple, peach, and pear trees bend and groan under their precious burdens.

There is no land like the Caucasus. Its magic panorama of daring, witching beauty is wild and lonely in unearthly loveliness.

Huge granite and basalt masses lie around, scattered by the Titans of old in their play. Far above towers the mount where Prometheus in agony, bound to the rocks, was the sport of the gods on old Kasbek's seamy sides.

The "sacred fires of Baku" still burn in their holy wells, adored here by the last of the dreamy Persian clan of Ghebers.

This is the land of hospitality, of beauty, of impassioned oratory, of wild tradition, of freedom!

Stepping stones to God's freest vaults of ether are these romantic peaks.

Around them the world has grown old and worn. They mock to-day the dozen conquests of great Constantinople, lying over against them at the outlet of the Black Sea, a mere lake at their feet.

Fiery Tcherkess, wild children of Daghestan, and the devilish Kurd are here unchanged and unchangeable as the rocks under their feet.

Everything in this romantic morning land speaks to Schamyl of his warrior father, the weird seer and sultan of the sword.

Rushing along the splendidly constructed road, Schamyl, in the heart of the mountains (while his engine is changed), telegraphs Platoff at Petersburg to send all to Tiflis, where the next day's sun will greet him.

Hewed out of the mountain sides, the superb main road (a triumph of modern engineering) leads from the Volga to the great fortress of Vladikaukas, the gate of the Caucasus, holding with steel-mouthed cannon the grand pass of Dariel.

By five railroads the Czar can throw troops and supplies to far Baku, or rapidly reinforce Tiflis and Goomri, the great border stronghold on the Kara, now Russianized as "Alexandropol."

There is a wonderful genius in these ample provisions to hold communication for even the greatest of modern armies. The Czar's flag is planted on the Persian borders of the Caspian, as well as fluttering defiance along the great Turkish frontiers, facing Kars, Bayazid, and Erzeroum.

Ahmed listlessly tries a game of vingt et un with his wild-eyed escort officer.

He is a mere thing to swing a sword on! Relapsing into moody silence, Schamyl watches the play of the sunset glories among the purpling hills.

Through the silent glories of the starlit night, with the wild voices of the singing pines wailing above, onward ever, there is neither stop nor rest!

Gratefully does Schamyl leave his swaying despatch-car when the warm mountain spring sun of morning sparkles on the white crests at Vladikaukas.

Out of the embrace of the black mountains the little escort speeds into the rich beauty of the heart of Georgia. For Ahmed has two hundred miles of a ride to finish his journey. Three days' travel ends it. He must first report. Then will it be " au revoir " at Tiflis? The ardent Circassian thinks less of the fiery Melikoff than of the darling woman's face whose sweetness and passion haunt his waking hours— whose unrivalled beauty gilds his dreams at night!

Crowds of soldiers and guards throng the streets at Tiflis. Creeping out from under a high mountain range into the fertile plains of the Kura, the military causeway enters the Georgian capital on the river bank, five hundred feet only above the Euxine level.

While Schamyl heartily greets an old friend of

the Guards, now an aide of General Melikoff, he is bidden to join the general at breakfast. Ahmed leaves the care of his wounded servant and luggage to the escort officer.

The despatches!—A soldierly welcome from the glittering circle of the staff is waiting Schamyl, whose quarters are assigned already. His own despatch by military telegraph has arrived.

Huge parks of artillery, mountainous piles of shot, shell, and munitions are littered around the town. Sentinels and guards stalk everywhere. As Schamyl drives through the old quarters of Tiflis, he notes the town of a hundred thousand is temporarily almost doubled in size. Every possible accumulation of stores gluts the magazines. In the Asiatic half of the capital, the mingling of varied colors and diverse types is strangely bizarre. Armenians (hollow chested and mournful eyed), noble Georgians (type of the Caucasian race), sly-looking Persians, stolid Russians, unkempt Cossacks, bustling Germans, outlandish Kurds, and humbled Jews pour along the ways.

Ponies, camels, chargers, tamed buffalo, and wild-eyed mountain cattle throng the narrow streets, whence shouts and yells arise in Babel-like confusion.

The stone and mud walled houses rise no higher than two stories, with bosky gardens fronting on the rushing Kura or "Blackwater."

The heavy forts and outworks are strongly garrisoned, for Tiflis is the central nucleus of the army of Trans-Caucasus, a hundred and fifty thousand strong to be.

Though stifling hot in summer, and icy cold in

winter, Tiflis has its social charms. It is now throbbing with the life of the semi-regal Governor-General's court.

As the carriage sweeps over to the luxurious modern Russian quarter on the great square, a superb band is playing witching Strauss waltzes before the palace of General Melikoff.

The yellow and black double eagle of the imperial standard floats lazily on the palace. The Grand Duke Michael is here to superintend the military pageantry of hurling a hundred thousand men on the turbaned foe. Calm Gortschakoff is even now inditing "protocols," which in their artful wording are more bitter than myrrh to the Turk.

Thrilling along the talking wire a simple message—

"Cross!"—will soon bring the fateful forward movement toward Constantinople.

In this early January sun the square is alive with officers, ladies, and all the entourage of a great headquarters. A restless impatience thrills the community. Towering in air, the old cathedral disdains the meaner mosque and the clustering Armenian convents.

An air of brisk gayety haunts Tiflis—the Paris of Asia Minor. The grand ducal palace, a splendid opera-house, with clubs and hotels à la mode, are monuments of the luxury of the city of provincial government. Fifty-four empty churches attest the fierce rivalry of different warring faiths. Good seed wasted on the stoniest soil. They are empty ever. The opera bouffe and cafés chantant are crowded with the epauletted pride of Russia.

Viennese dancers, Hungarian gypsies (their eyes as black as sloes), and all the wandering flotsam and jetsam of Continental womanhood minister to that morbid craving for amusement, which is a reflex of the war fever.

Wine flows and gold rattles. Laugh and wild jest, with thunders of applause, greet the merry tricks of the fair sirens. Vive la bagatelle!

In the suburbs long lines of stalwart soldiery parade between their winter huts. In bazaar and by street, the treasures of Aleppo, Samarcand, Damascus, Teheran, and the unrivalled metal work and embroideries of the Orient tempt the unwary.

Pearls of Ormuz, sapphires of Ceylon, azure turquoises of magic virtue are displayed in heaps, with the jewels, amber, and filigree so beloved by the Moslem.

While Schamyl's carriage parts the throng in the square, he recognizes, here and there, a defiant, lithe Circassian, moving with that air of indescribable haughtiness which has given rise to the proverb, when a swelling port is exhibited:

"He is either a commanding general or a Circassian of the Guard."

Jealous and quick in quarrel, as keen eyed as the mountain hawks circling in the thin ether, the Circassian is the king of men in his majestic bearing.

At the threshold of the grand ducal palace, the sentinels present to the aiguillettes of the aide.

In five minutes Schamyl stands before General Loris Melikoff, "the coming man."

Alert, robust, thin lipped, with cold, steady, deep

searching eyes, the Armenian general lifts his eyes from his map.

"Prince Schamyl, you are attached to my staff. General Dragmiroff will give you your orders. You have despatches from General Ignatief?"

Schamyl bows as he hands the Czar's wily champion the sealed packet.

The man who is to lead into the field a Grand Duke (as military mentor) tears open the papers.

Heedless of Schamyl, standing "at attention," Melikoff devours the cipher.

"This must go to the Grand Duke. You will breakfast with me."

He nods carelessly, and, grasping his sabre, strides out of the room, followed by two enormous Siberian hounds.

In three hours Schamyl has made himself "au fait" with the racy gossip of Tiflis. His simple ménage as a soldier is in order. A couple of huge palace rooms are his, an orderly at his disposal, and his seat at the staff table assigned.

At the breakfast hour he is presented to the Grand Duke Michael, who is affability itself. Schamyl is "en régle."

"Ah, Schamyl, you are the man we want! Just reported! Let me see. Are you well mounted?" The Grand Duke chats over his wine.

Schamyl briefly reports the reason of his arrival without chargers.

"Get some good mounts. I am going to send you on a general tour, with a couple of sotnias of the Guard Cossacks. Your old regiment may come to us later."

When the glittering "mess" breaks up, Schamyl,

with one or two friends, passes his day in choosing a couple of animals worthy of the Centaur he is. A long price does not frighten him. "In Eastern countries the steed often bears the master in life and death dashes."

Despatches and mail from Platoff tell him of mobilization. His man and heavy goods wait him at the border. He telegraphs for the maître d'hotel and his reserve luggage.

Paul writes:

"I go with the horse artillery to the Danube. My battery is in splendid order. Nothing here but war talk.

- "By the way, the Turkish Embassy leaves here in a few days.

"Write me to my corps headquarters as soon as we move. Till then, here, I await your news impatiently. My compliments to the lovely Princess Maritza!"

Ah, yes! the lady of Georgia! While Schamyl gallops his new steeds a half-hour or so in the suburbs to try their paces, he carelessly asks his fellow-aide, Gronoff, where the Princess Maritza may be found.

"She is with the Lazareffs and Argutins at their palace here. You remember, Nina Lazareff and Tia Argutin were at the Catherine Institute with the Princess."

Well does Schamyl remember the lovely trio, called the "Three Graces" by their fond girl associates of the royal institute.

"There is their palace over there by the Kura in those great gardens!"

Gronoff indicates its white façade with his whip, as they swing their steeds homeward.

"There is great fun up there now. General Lazareff has no less a visitor than the Lady Fatima, the daughter of Ismail Pacha, the vali of Erzeroum. She has been at the schools here, and will soon be sent home under an escort of honor. A wild, untamable hawk is that Kurdish princess! Just as dangerous as a young tiger!

"Prince, you will see all the famous beauties at the grand ball which General Melikoff gives to the Grand Duke in a few days. We can show you as pretty a ball-room here as at the Cercle de Noblesse in Petersburg."

Schamyl gives his charger the rein. There is no reason why he should disguise any longer his handsome proportions en mufti. Yet, he must wait.

The next day crawls along until the afternoon. The morning brings his man and luggage.

There is a spice of military coquetry in the care with which Ahmed dons all the bravery of his picturesque uniform. A little billet, in answer to his own, tells him that the Princess Maritza will see him with pleasure.

When the carriage sweeps up to the portals of the Lazareff mansion, Schamyl eagerly enters the salon.

Duty causes him to linger with his lips on the hand of Madame Lazareff—"grande dame" and a kindly friend.

Raising his eyes, he sees at her side, with her lovely laughing companions, the lady of his dreams, the belle of belles—sweet Maritza.

"You have not forgotten me, I trust, Princess,"

he murmurs, as her splendid eyes are fixed upon him.

"Mon Prince! It was 'au revoir at Tiflis!'—n'est-ce pas? Fate brings us together in the Caucasus, on the eve of a terrible war, I fear!"

Her wistful voice thrills him with its exquisite music.

In a half-hour the bevy of graces have taken the young Guardsman into their fairy junta. The grand ball is the topic dear to the hearts of these budding beauties of Tiflis. Ahmed does not lose a moment to claim the honor of the mazurka at the fête.

It is granted. Love's madness chains him.

Wandering in the great gardens, where delicate leaves already speak of spring—their slopes sweeping down to the willow-shaded banks of the swift Kura—Ahmed walks alone with the young princess. Stretching far away over the bleak southern stony valley are three highways leading to the Turkish frontier.

On the other side, huge masses of Turks are ready to reach, in three days, the lines where the Moslem cavalry even now picket the border.

In the gardens Schamyl meets a tall veiled lady, followed by two attendants. It is the young Princess Fatima. When Ahmed greets her, in her native Turkish, he can only see two dark eyes glittering like basilisks. Though an adept in Russian and French, the Lady Fatima prefers her own dialect.

"I knew your brother, the great Prince Ghazee," she sharply says, eying Schamyl's Russian uniform askance.

Ahmed starts.

"Indeed, Princess! Where did you meet him?"

"He visited my father last year at Erzeroum. They are very great friends."

Schamyl finds *this* conversation awkward. Then Ghazee has laid his secret snares long in advance of the coming conflict. For Ismail Pacha is the hardest task-master and coldest brute even among the rapacious pachas of Asia Minor. Fit associate of a renegade traitor!

"Where is your brother? I liked him very much," the Kurdish princess demands.

"I do not know," Ahmed replies, at random. He catches a swift glance from the Princess Maritza. His brother's shame is now known to all!

"He is a great warrior! He is a Moslem," the Kurd says proudly, as she turns away. "I hate the Giaour and the Russ!"

"A strange being," Ahmed says, to break the awkward silence. His companion's eyes are downcast. She pities him.

"She is very strange," Maritza replies. "She talks always of your brother Ghazee. I feared Prince Ghazee always. He is cold and haughty."

Schamyl checks his speech. Shall he warn *her* now? No! At the ball he can talk. He will not alarm this gentle girl yet. He will talk with the Lazareffs. She should go! Yet, love!

As they stroll back to the mansion, Maritza tells him all her girlish budget of news:

"We have had a great panic here at Tiflis, until the main body of the troops came. It is only three days' march to the frontier. Bands of Kurdish horse have overrun the border. They live by plunder only. And, Prince, there have been many desertions of men and officers all along our line from Goomri to Baku."

"Will *you* remain here, Princess?" queries Schamyl.

"Unless Madame Lazareff goes into Russia when the general takes the field. The Abkhasians are very restless along the Black Sea around Poti. They are treacherous. But, if the troops cross over to the Araxes and the Euphrates, we will stay here, Prince—unless—"

"Unless what, Maritza?" Schamyl speaks eagerly. He drops into anxious fondness.

"They say," the girl falters, "that your brother Ghazee will stir up a great revolt among the Circassians. Then, it would not be safe here. He is feared by all. We women would all have to go beyond the Caucasus."

"You know of his dishonor, Princess?" Ahmed asks, his cheeks burning.

"Yes, we all do! His secret agents and spies swarm from sea to sea now. He has connections with all the disaffected. I hear General Lazareff often talk of him. They have already executed some of his agents."

Schamyl cannot linger now. When the conventional visit has been already far prolonged, he takes his departure.

Was it a faint returning pressure of the hand he felt, as he said adieu to the Rose of Tiflis?

Standing in the rich salon, her exquisitely moulded form draped in fleecy cashmere of the rarest Persian looms; her necklace of pearls, no whiter than the swan-like throat—a dark-eyed goddess with features of the rarest mould, Maritza de Deshkalin is as fair a daughter of Pontus as ever graced this morning land of loveliest women. In these later days, a truant young Greek nymph—a dream of beauty.

For two long hours next day, Ahmed toils with General Melikoff over plans and maps. He receives a list of telegraph stations, a route covering several hundreds of miles, and instructions too important for any but a commander's own lips. Schamyl hears calmly of his desperate quest. He is to visit the whole frontier secretly, to pursue and break up knots of malcontents; a warrant under the Grand Duke's seal authorizes him to use any garrisons and moving troops.

At each point he is to report in telegraphic cipher.

Above all, the capture of the arch-traitor Ghazee is to be sought, for crafty Melikoff has sounded the dark partnership of Ghazee and the bloody Kurdish Pacha at Erzeroum.

"I will watch these Abkhasians on the Euxine. I wish you to make sure of Daghestan and the line from Bayazid and Ardaban to Baku," Melikoff says earnestly.

"There is *no* reward you cannot claim of the Emperor if you prevent a general revolt in Daghestan and Circassia. As soon as the armies take the field, and the danger is past, you shall have a brigade of horse, Prince," promises Melikoff.

"Hold yourself in readiness to leave at night within two or three days. Lazareff has detailed two sotnias of picked Cossacks. Every man is a veteran. You will have a double set of officers to each troop. No one must know of your errand!"

Schamyl rejoices that his old retainer is now able for the saddle. For Hassan speaks every border dialect, he knows every nook and cranny of the Caucasus. Can the prince depend on his loyalty?

Schamyl swears the old sergeant, on the sacred amulet, to bear him faith in the campaign.

Hassan growls, "I will! The 'great master' shed my blood and would have killed you. He is accursed now! a son of Sheitan!"

Revenge is the one unfailing passion of the warlike Circassian. Hassan's side burns with his knitting wound.

Absolute secrecy is enjoined upon Schamyl. His heart fires him to go once more to the presence of the gracious woman whose lightest touch thrills his bounding pulses. He must see her before the ball— before the summons. For "boots and saddles" may sound any instant. Duty yields to love.

The war news swells on the rising gale. Ignatief is even now departing for his tour of the great capitals; the Russian Legation at Constantinople is closed. . . . He is with her once more.

Seated in the drawing-room at the Lazareffs, Ahmed tells Maritza that he may depart suddenly on secret duty.

With frankness he imparts to her Platoff's forebodings, the White Countess's warning, and bids her beware of dark Ghazee's snake-like treachery.

The beautiful dark eyes linger tenderly on him. Her voice is low and strangely sweet.

"Prince! your brother is not my friend. I know it. Last winter "—she checks herself.

Ghazee's suit was, then, *unsuccessful.* His heart bounds.

"I am an orphan ward of the Emperor! He would never permit me to marry a Moslem."

A strange light shines in Ahmed's eyes. He takes her trembling fair hand in his own.

"Princess, I leave you soon! Will you give me a little token that you will not forget me till I return? I may even go before the ball."

Maritza glances at Madame Lazareff. The good lady is intent upon the *Revue des Deux Mondes.*

Hastily drawing from her slender finger a great pigeon blood ruby ring, she drops it in his hand, and whispers:

"Wear this for my sake!"

Their eyes meet. In all the splendid depths of her dark glances he can read the shy self-defence of the proud girl's nature. She would not be too easily won. . . .' A princess in her own right! The châtelaine of these storied hills—a daughter of the gods!

"I will guard it with my life till I come back to you. I shall see you to-morrow."

Faint and soft as the chime of distant bells, her voice repeats, "To-morrow—Prince!"

As he rises she shows him a face whose burning blushes cannot mislead him. A rustle of her gown —the goddess has fled!

Murmuring a few commonplaces to Madame la Générale, Ahmed drives to the palace in a happy unconsciousness of time and place.

For Love's dainty sceptre has touched him. The Czar's soldier once, he is only *now* a slave in the service of Queen Maritza!

CHAPTER VI.

MISSING.—UNDER THE SHADOWS OF ARARAT.— A MOTHER'S MEMORY.

PRINCE SCHAMYL'S head tosses on his pillow all night. In his dreams, Ghazee drags the beloved Maritza down into the black waters of the Kura. He cannot hold her back. . . . Agony haunts his sleep. With a bound Ahmed springs to his feet.

Those hideous visions of the night fade away. Morning already! His orderly is knocking.

"Highness! This is immediate!" The soldier salutes.

He tears open Melikoff's hasty scrawl.

"Report at orderly hour. Haste!
                                    MELIKOFF."

Schamyl despatches a Spartan breakfast; old Hassan nimbly assorts the camp outfit.

"Ready for the road." Hassan hobbles away to inspect the animals. The veteran Moslem is good for a dozen raids yet.

As Loris Melikoff steps into his orderly room, the staff officer announces:

"General, Prince Schamyl in waiting!"

A satisfied gleam crosses the Armenian's cunning eyes. He is like the white general—Skobeleff. His staff officers must appear like sprites, and move with lightning speed.

Melikoff nods when Schamyl enters; the Grand Duke Michael is also at the table.

Their faces are grave.

"Major," Melikoff growls, "our signal officers report many beacon fires on the mountains to the north last night.

"Prince Tchavachavadze, lord of the Abkhasians, reports the signals also on the mountains behind us here. He is already miles away toward Poti and the Black Sea.

"We fear some dangerous uprising. I have sent your squadron of Cossacks off at daylight.

"One officer waits to guide you out at nightfall.

"His Highness wishes to keep your mission a secret. You will leave without a word to any one. You have your orders."

Melikoff twists a cigarette carelessly.

The Grand Duke Michael adds a few words:

"Prince Schamyl, the Emperor has given a division of cavalry to Tchavachavadze. He is the chief of all the Eastern tribes. The Princess Maritza is firmly attached to our gracious Empress. *She* is the last of the line of Georgia. *You* are now the chief of Circassia and Daghestan."

Schamyl bows in silence.

"We know well the importance of tradition with these uncertain Asiatics. Count Ignatief writes me that in Thibet, in Turkestan, in his years in China, he has met no nature as proud and defiant as your own people."

Schamyl's eager eyes rest on the Grand Duke.

He knows what the prince of the house of Romanoff would not dare to say. His heart beats wildly.

"I send you, Schamyl, with a stainless sword to hold your old altars and castles for the Emperor."

The Grand Duke detaches a great white cross from his bosom. Handing it to the young man, he says simply:

"My *Brother* gave it to me. Go now, my young friend!"

The subtle flattery of this great prince sets the soldier's heart on fire.

There are tears in Ahmed's eyes as he salutes.

Melikoff says, simply: "Send back a man to tell me of your first march. Telegraph direct for orders from every garrison."

Noblesse oblige. Ahmed's cheeks burn as he affixes the white cross to his breast. It may not be hidden, but he has not fairly earned it yet.

As he passes out of the ante-room, thronged with grizzled veterans, there is a hum of envy and astonishment. These princely youngsters rise so easily!

Reaching his quarters, Schamyl spends a restless hour in writing Platoff and in arranging his simple kit for the scout. His troops are away. He chafes for the road now. The music floating in from the square, where hardy battalions are exercising, reminds him of that grand ball which he cannot attend.

And Maritza is queen of hearts now!

He dares not visit her again so soon. Les convenances!

At dusk his horse's head will be turned toward Daghestan. He *may* not come back. There are swords as sharp as his own in those rugged hills. Shall he send a message—a letter? Whom can he trust?

As the lover ponders, Hassan gravely enters. All is ready.

With inspiration, Schamyl pens a brief note.

"Will the Princess Maritza ride this afternoon to the band practice?"

Hastily sealing it, he bids Hassan mount and bear it to the Lazareff mansion.

Schamyl tells him to ask for the Princess Maritza herself.

Clattering hoofs tell him the rider is on his way. Schamyl paces the room uneasily. From the windows he can see the wooded hills, rising four thousand feet in air, where last night the fires of treason glittered.

There already lurk the dastards in the rear who would give up their own native land to the Turk!

Ahmed remembers grimly that his own father was a Moslem of the Moslems; that a hundred and fifty thousand Circassians are even now, after two hundred years of warfare, fanatical sons of the Crescent, though clutched in the never relaxing grasp of the Eagle of the North!

Ghazee, the renegade, now wears the fez and turban of a Pacha in the Turkish ranks!

With a rush Hassan's charger reins up in the court. Love's messenger appears. His eyes are shining.

"I saw the lovely daughter of the morning, Highness!" Hassan announces, handing a billet to the Guardsman.

The note is brief, but precious.

"We ride at four this afternoon, in the square. Au revoir.
                                                    MARITZA."

Ahmed thanks his lucky stars that the general order has been given for pleasure parties not to cross the line of sentinels on the town limits. All the beauties of Tiflis ride in the great square.

For the black-hearted Kurds are abroad! Concealed by day (thieving and plundering only at night), their zone of rapine and murder unites the two opposing lines already.

"The day star spoke in my own language," proudly exclaims old Hassan.

"She is more fair than the moonlight on the waters!" The old messenger's heart is captured by her native graces.

He is gone.

Ahmed smiles at this poetical outburst of the cut-throat descendant of Hafiz.

Hassan's words haunt him. "She spoke to me in my own language!"

Ah! General Melikoff, love will ever find the way! Your orders will not be *literally* disobeyed!

When the line of carriages sweeps around the square in the afternoon, Prince Schamyl slowly rides past the procession. His new charger is a towering son of night. A white star blazes in his forehead. The Circassian silver trappings deck the noble steed, whose princely rider's face is haughty and unmoved.

All eyes gaze on the tall youth, whose heavy Tcherkess sabre swings easily from his jewelled belt. There's not a lovely Russian "aristocrate" in the line who does not glance kindly on the man whose white grand cross tells the story of the honors of the morning.

The mysterious freemasonry of garrison gossip has already spread abroad the singular distinction of the Prince of Daghestan.

Far up the line Schamyl recognizes the livery of the Lazareffs. Lovers' eyes are keen!

Dreamy, delicious music floats over the parade. Far away the course of the Kura divides the great valley beyond, on whose farther crest the Moslem foes are even now mustering. His own brother waits to cross swords with him there!

With the easy grace of a Bayard, Schamyl reins up his fretting horse beside the carriage.

"Place aux grandes dames!" The prince can hardly trust his voice, as he pays an homage "not altogether guileless" to Madame Lazareff—a beauty yet, a reigning belle once!

His bow to the young ladies brought his noble head to his charger's mane.

Madame la Générale smiles as she notes the highly prized decoration.

"Mon Prince! Je vous en félicite."

These moments are ages to Schamyl. He has now a fair excuse to address the young reigning beauties of Tiflis.

His French and Russian sound charmingly to the merry Nina and the bright Tia.

When he softly speaks to *Maritza*, it is in the beloved tongue of her childhood.

The eagle-eyed young prince knows he is beloved. For *she* has said it! Schamyl needs not wait for the seventh heaven. He is realizing it here on earth.

A wary glance from Madame Lazareff bids him restrain the sparkling eagerness of his eyes. Does she suspect their secret?

Even duennas know the language of love! And, in Russia, an emperor's orphan ward is sacred.

Around the parade, the cortége of rank and fashion creeps. These blessed moments fly all too soon. When Madame Lazareff draws her Persian shawl (a prince's ransom) around her, for the evening chill is falling, Schamyl knows the Fates are cutting the thread. The parting moment comes.

Raising his astrakhan shako artlessly, he presses to his lips the blood-red ruby ring.

Maritza is leaning forward slightly. Her glorious eyes dwell a moment on him with a tenderness which thrills to his bosom's core.

He is the "Prince Charming" who has come across her unvexed girlhood to lead her "over the hills and far away," out into the fairy land of love which wraps this work-a-day life in a glamour of enchantment.

She knows he cannot grace the stately ball of the Grand Duke. While she dances there her lover will be far on his way to the robber-haunted defiles of Daghestan, at the head of his troops.

With courteous salutation he greets the other ladies; in wheeling his charger, he brings that blood-red ruby ring once more to his lips.

Princess Maritza does not watch how grandly his black orloff dashes away, for there are shining mists of happy tears veiling the eyes of the fairest maid in Georgia. The dialogue in Georgian puzzles Madame Lazareff. Maritza's *heart* goes out with him on the dangerous quest, wherein he must earn the white cross already given by the Emperor's brother. The Czar alone can give away her *hand*.

Princess Maritza's fluttering heart prisons her new secret, as the carriage rolls along.

Her lover's praises are sounding in her ears. Schamyl " has builded more wisely than he knew " in his Grandisonian tenderness of manner to Madame Lazareff.

The bright twin stars, Nina and Tia, chatter in their heart-whole glee. They can freely rally Maritza, for they have not yet tasted the elixir of love.

One bright star hangs over the high northern hills, when Schamyl, followed by Hassan, dashes out of the eastern guard gate of Tiflis. His horse's feet sound sharply on the jagged stones. He is musing, dreaming of the fair girl who in her lonely room, sitting in the evening shadows, murmurs, "When shall I see him again?"

Four trusty Cossacks, with a corporal, are waiting at the first village. They left with the packs four hours ago. The three riders join them.

Winding down the willow-screened banks of the Kura, his escort officer at his side, Schamyl takes his place in front of the little squad.

The mechanical rise and fall of the horses' feet on the frosty road lulls him. His heavy hood hides his face. Once on the road, Ahmed is a soldier again. From these wooded bends of the Kura a lurking band of Kurds may dash out at any moment.

It is long after midnight when the camp of the squadron is reached.

Schamyl's heart bounds as he sees the stern riders, in bivouac, around their tethered steeds.

Sitting by the camp-fire, he realizes he has entered into the enjoyment of his patrimony—the empire of the sword!

Examining the carefully posted sentinels, with brief directions to his officers, the lover throws himself down to dream of Maritza, the dark-eyed, whose smile gilds even the darkness of the chill January night.

He has indicated a star on the Circassian's dial. When that bright spark reaches the western horizon, the squadron will sweep swiftly toward the gloomy hills hanging over Bayazid—the outer gates of Erzeroum.

When Hassan rouses Schamyl, with his coffee, the two "sotnias" are in arms. Gathered around the camp-fire, the eight officers greet their young commander.

Hassan and the orderly remain with the guard squad when Schamyl's breakfast is despatched. In a half-hour, they will overtake the command, with the pack animals.

Sweet is the sound of the singing bugle as the young chief rides to the head of his cavalcade.

A guide, a trusty sergeant, and three troopers lead the advance. The two sotnias, in column, tramp along, the hardy horses tossing their heads in the nipping morning air.

As the sun leaps out of the plains of Khorassan, Schamyl surveys his bold riders.

Trim, brawny horsemen, in short tunic and leather trousers, a warm cloak over their shoulders, and wearing rakish sheepskin caps, they are the pride of Russia, these dare-devil Tcherkess swordsmen!

Schamyl has ordered them to leave their lances behind. With a Berdan rifle in its leather case, two pistols, their belt-daggers, and the heavy razor-edged Circassian sword swinging noiselessly in its wooden sheath, they are armed to the teeth.

They stride along, riding easily, with knees high drawn up. Their neat-limbed chargers are as agile as mountain deer.

Accustomed to govern and direct themselves in fight, they neither give nor take quarter when they meet either of their deadly foes—the thievish Kurd or lumbering Bashi-bazouk.

In single fight they mow down the despised Turkish cavalry, or pick them off with unerring aim.

Proud are the Ataman riders that the Czarewitch is the titularly lord of the Don Cossacks! Mazeppa's mantle descends upon the eldest son of the Romanoffs.

It is to the uncorrupted fidelity of these warriors that the sacred body of the Emperor is confided. They are the inner ring around the imperial person.

"Preobajensky," "Cuirassier," nay, even the white "Garde à Cheval," must yield in personal devotion to these fierce children of the mountains and steppes.

Man and horse (blended in a double unit) camp, sleep, eat, and play together.

The faithful steed is a living bulwark as he drops

at a signal, his rider firing over him. Swimming like an otter, climbing like a mountain goat, dog-like in fidelity, the Cossack horse is his master's greatest treasure.

Along their line the magic word "Schamyl" is whispered. With sparkling eyes they follow the tall form of their new chief, who was cradled in the arms of the great sultan of the sword, the Imam of Circassia. Every childhood song, every wedding feast harangue, every legend of this wild, bookless nation, burns with praise to the mighty chieftain of Gunib.

It is his princely son who rides at their head, in the flush and glory of young manhood.

Schamyl communes with himself. He knows these rolling hills, these grand woods, these defiles where a few may hold a host at bay.

He will please the eagle-eyed Melikoff. When he has broken his next camp, sending back a report as ordered, he will strike boldly across the broken mountains, from the Kura to the Araxes, and reach Erivan (the last Russian stronghold) before Bayazid, on the open gorge of Erzeroum.

On this lonely way he will surely meet any wandering parties. He needs no map. The eagle of the Caucasus finds his way alone. Each boyish memory is a treasure now. Then, refitting, he will (by the mountain defiles) gain great Himri, the birthplace of his stern father.

If Ghazee is stealing along the lines, his spies will be busy in the heart of Daghestan.

Woe to that traitor if he meets this forlorn hope now sweeping along under Ahmed!

While from the heavy forest the small animals flee at their approach, herds of deer troop over the misty meadows. It is a land of silence and savage beauty.

At noon Ahmed halts his squadron beside a sparkling river.

Throwing himself down under a tree, the young major communes with his officers.

While Hassan (who scorns that another should serve his master) spreads the repast, Schamyl exchanges a few words with his subordinates.

An old gray-headed captain interests him—a captain at fifty.

"You have served here?" he asks.

"I know this region well, Prince! It was from these very mountains your father dashed down in 'forty-eight,' and captured our Russian Princess Orbelian, the general's wife."

Schamyl eyes the bristling peaks with interest.

"I was a boy soldier then, just joined. I was cut down trying to save the princess. I lay in the forest, unnoticed, and was brought in by the rescue party." The old captain sighs.

Ahmed's memory is strangely moved.

"The Princess Orbelian!" His father's noble captive. He wonders.

"Tell me the whole story," he directs. When the captain's brief recital is over, Ahmed remembers that the Russian Government gave up, in later years, his captive brother Jamal Eddin, in exchange for the Princess of Abkhasia and this lovely Princess Orbelian.

"Ah, Hassan *must* surely remember!" He signals

to the veteran who is bearing along his master's viands. Speaking in the tongue of his youth, he queries:

"Hassan, do you remember the Russian Princess Orbelian?"

The veteran drops his dishes, open-eyed. He mutters wildly, and proceeds to recover his scattered charge.

Schamyl sharply cries: "Well, can you speak?"

Hassan turns a frightened face on his master.

"My oath! The great sultan! No, I never speak of those old days of the great master. May Allah be my guide, I know not!"

When the cavalcade sweeps up toward the spiral height, from whence he will break away toward Erivan, Schamyl is haunted by the soldier's story as he rides.

"The Princess Orbelian!" He questions his servant again.

Hassan's obstinacy foils him. He will not speak.

As the wind sweeps through the lonely forests where his father's voice so often cheered the wild riders onward when they struck the Russian foe, Ahmed's boyhood comes back. Somewhere, in yonder sparkling mountain ranges, sleeps the gentle-eyed woman whom his fancy, born of an unloved boyhood, paints to him as a tender mother bending over her child.

The Princess Orbelian! She was seven long years in great Schamyl's eyrie.

The reins lie idle on his horse's neck. He forgets even the star-eyed Maritza to dream of the dear unknown (hidden from him by the mists of buried years), whose ears never lovingly heard him say "Mother."

Chill winds whistle over the rocky ridges at sundown, as Schamyl pickets his weary horses on the southern slope of lofty Mount Alacez, three days later.

Hassan's knowledge of the old Tcherkess trails enables the fiery major to gain unperceived this point, from which he can strike quickly in any direction.

Schamyl is happy at his good progress and unperceived march as he sweeps his glass over the wonderful panorama. In sending back his courier from the first day's bivouac, he has asked permission to leave a half sotnia, "en perdu," in the groves of Alacez. All is quiet so far here.

From his vantage ground to the north great "Goomri" hangs over the Araxes in warlike defiance to the Turk. It is the Russian frontier stronghold.

His nimble warriors have climbed out of the Kara valley; below him, to the southwest, lies the great Araxes River, whose northern branch, the "Arpa Tchai," is the hostile frontier.

Due west one hundred and fifty miles, Kars frowns under the Kara Dagh (only thirty miles from Goomri). It is the goal of General Loris Melikoff. His marshal's baton awaits him there. He has the Grand Duke's pledge.

Southwest the road sweeps up the valley of the broad Araxes toward populous Erzeroum, in its amphitheatre of cannon-crested hills.

Due south rises the awful mass of Ararat, undefiled by man's polluting foot, and a little to the west is the city of Bayazid, the third precious morsel for the maw of the Russian.

There, at Ararat, a man in a run of fifty yards can wander in Persia, Turkey, or Russia. It is the one giant corner post of Asia Minor.

Schamyl sighs to think that though his keen eye can sweep over the whole valley of the Arpa Tchai and the Araxes (fenced across by the great ridges of the Kara Dagh and Agra Dagh), it will take months to make that bloody march.

Fiery though Melikoff be, fast though his riders press to the front, it may take a year's time, and a hundred thousand lives, to grasp in the iron hand of Muscovy those three priceless jewels glittering under his feet—Kars, Bayazid, and Erzeroum.

Yet the White Czar *must* have them to fence, with their massy citadels, the flanks of his great strategic railway from Batoum to Baku. Batoum yet flies the crescent and star of the Ottoman. It is the fourth jewel of the quadilateral.

Eastward, lying under Russia's claws, are Merv, Khiva, Turkestan, Cashmere, and Khuldja.

Not in vain did wily Nicolas Ignatief toil for four years in the Asiatic Bureau of the Ministry of the Interior. His fertile brain has caught the enormous value of the Baku oil regions. The "sacred wells" of the fire worshipper will furnish fuel for hundreds of locomotives on the railroads of treeless Asia and its barren steppes.

Steamers, by the fifties, on the swift Volga and the Caspian Sea, will be propelled by these liquid riches wasted for long centuries.

Ignatief's keen mind has discerned the royal road of advance to Central Asia. The conqueror's sword must now carve out a line to keep the Turk at bay on the Euphrates.

Morning mists scarce roll away before Schamyl's pickets are sweeping (in dispersed knots) away on their searching raids.

So far hut and village, forest and dell, are unprofaned by the Kurdish struggle.

One platoon is to thread the border as far as "Goomri," reporting to him at Erivan by telegraph from that fort.

Another will search, in loose order, the wooded plains as far as the junction of the Araxes and Arpa Tchai, rallying at Erivan.

With the other forces, Schamyl spreads a line ten miles broad, flanking the main road to Erivan. There he will be able to telegraph Melikoff that the southern border is clear of marauders.

Strong bodies of horse are already picketed on the frontier from Ararat to the Caspian. With the Abkhasian cavalry on the Black Sea flank, and the Caspian troops to his left, Schamyl's duty is to guard inviolate the roads to Daghestan and his own wild Circassia.

Ahmed leaves the trusty old captain on Mount Alacez with orders to send each day a rider in to Erivan.

They will pass a daily vidette, returning from the stronghold, where that unrivalled tactician Tergukassoff is ready to seize Bayazid the moment that "protocols" and "Vienna conferences" are abandoned.

Schamyl has been over a week in the saddle when his jaded troopers ride into Erivan. .

To report to the fort major and despatch supplies to his troop left at Mount Alacez, is his first charge. To report *himself* to the commanding general and inform General Melikoff of his dispositions, is the second duty.

Bravely has Hassan, the mystic retainer, kept his sturdy roan at Schamyl's heels. The old swordsman seems all the better for his blood-letting. In vain has Schamyl urged him to speak of the Princess Orbelian.

" The great sultan sealed my lips when he died. The curse of Allah rests on the babbler."

Leaving his second in command to arrange the details of rationing his outposts and quartering his men, he lightly gallops over to the headquarters of the division commander.

As he swings himself out of the saddle, a staff officer hurriedly accosts him.

"You are to see the General without delay, Prince. Important orders await you!" he says, with an anxious face.

In five minutes Schamyl has made his brief report to Tergukassoff. What new anxiety? The chief's brow is gloomy. He tosses a telegraphic order to Ahmed. It is personally signed by Loris Melikoff.

Schamyl reads its few stern lines. He utters a cry like a wounded lion. The fatal words are burned into his brain. It is three days old!

"COMMANDING GENERAL AT ERIVAN :

" Send Major Schamyl with all his force to scout the Arpa River banks from Parnault and Assar, to meet our own force descending from Goomri. Princess Maritza and Lady Fatima were carried away last night from Lazareff's gardens. Kurds supposed to have descended river. Send him to report back from Goomri.

"MELIKOFF."

The general growls out : " I have sent out already four companies of Cossacks to scout from Ararat to Assar. They left in an hour after the news came. If you are able, you had better strike now for Assar, with a fresh half sotnia. I'll send an officer to lead your own men down to the river at Kizilkule to meet you there. I will station another company on the mountain. Can you start back now?"

Schamyl's eyes are blazing. He has already forgotten his fatigue. For Maritza's sake, anything!

"As soon as I get fresh horses, and my troops are ready, I will go, General," the prince gasps.

"Good!" growls Tergukassoff. "I should judge that Melikoff is not very happy over this. That young princess is the head of the Georgians now. These sneaking Turkish spies may have cajoled her away. It's a bad time. But what did they want to steal the Kurdish girl for also?"

Ahmed is about to speak. He masters himself. A spectre of Ghazee rises before him.

"Sit down and write your report to Melikoff. I will send the despatch on at once. I approve all you have done, Schamyl. You have made a good march!"

Ahmed blunders over his official lines, for his heart sinks within him. Maritza, the day-star, now in the power of the black-hearted Kurds, who spare neither the living nor the dead! His brain is on fire.

The general reads Schamyl's despatch.

Touching his bell for his adjutant, he simply says: "Carte blanche for Major Schamyl. He goes at once on 'special service.' Look here, Pashkoff, don't forget to give him a good dinner."

The busy commander kindly dismisses the restless young prince, who joins Pashkoff in the staff headquarters.

"Schamyl," says Pashkoff, an old Petersburg comrade, "I have a telegram here from Gronow to you. While I get your dinner up, read it, and tell me what you want."

Fresh horses and refreshment for his orderly and Hassan are Ahmed's first thoughts. He tears open Gronow's telegram.

"DEAR SCHAMYL: Madame Lazareff frantic! Princess was surprised walking in garden on the evening of the ball; undoubtedly carried off in boat, with Fatima. Object unknown. Ransom, perhaps. Kurds must have been hidden along river bank. Official telegrams from Turkish commanders. Nothing known by them. Some say Princess joins Turkish party. Will write you fully at Goomri. Answer this. I suspect treachery!

"GRONOW."

Ahmed's whirling brain will only permit him to telegraph Gronow:

"Despatch received. Start in half hour along river to Goomri. Troops in the field everywhere. Greeting.

"SCHAMYL."

Pashkoff with difficulty detains the young chief of the Caucasus long enough to swallow a few morsels and drain a bottle of Burgundy. Before the first star sparkles over blue Ararat, Prince Schamyl, on Pashkoff's best charger, is spurring ahead of his fresh Cossacks.

Hassan strains the pace of his big roan to keep up with Ahmed.

As they ride, they commune in the language of Daghestan.

Hassan has played the border guerilla in his younger years and is a master of every Kurdish artifice. The rugged henchman smacks his lips, for he knows the pack mule, urged along with the command, is loaded from Pashkoff's generous larder.

Their own command will cut over to Assar and be fresh to meet them there in two days. Schamyl rides out into the black night to glean from the villagers or friends along the river some news of the kidnapping party.

It is between Goomri and Assar that the enemy must have crossed from the Kura to the Arpa. It is the road to Erzeroum, the home of Fatima, also to Kars. That hideous night-dream comes back!

Great God! This is Ghazee's work!

CHAPTER VII.

TCHERKESS AGAINST KURD.—AN OLD FRIEND WITH A NEW NAME.

ONWARD, in the darkness of the lonely roads, Schamyl threads the path toward the meeting of the Arpa Tchai and the Araxes.

A quick road trot keeps the column awake. Schamyl's black follows the three shadowy forms in advance. His heart is on fire! On, on to the rescue!

They keep always within sight of the Cossack guide.

Turning now and then, Ahmed sees the spectral forms of his platoon.

Hassan takes *his* cat-naps in the saddle.

Before daylight the drowsy ferry-man at Chobankara passes them quickly over the north branch of the Araxes in two squads. *He* has seen no wandering Kurds. It is too near Erivan. Tergukassoff is a vigilant soldier and knows his outpost duty.

A long halt at noon, at the main crossing of the Araxes, enables Schamyl to snatch a rest, while the hardy Cossack ponies nip the tender shooting leaves and munch daintily their grain.

When Hassan rouses him, with his coffee, the exhausted leader rubs his eyes. Blessed sleep has brought oblivion of that gnawing pain at his heart.

Yes, he is *here* in the heart of Anatolia. His wild horsemen are ready for the road. Far to the south the savage crests of the Jula Gadek fence off the Turks, with their snowy barriers.

Springing again into the saddle, Schamyl rides on to Kullink. If he reaches that town at night, he will be ninety miles from Erivan.

There is a military telegraph there. He can despatch to the commanders of the four river garrisons between Assar and the main fortress of Goomri.

As he rides with bowed head, in silence, Ahmed studies the situation.

It would be impossible to transport two ladies in litter or carriage past Goomri over the border without suspicion. The river is closely picketed from

Goomri down to Assar by the troops of both armies.

Any floating boat would be fired on from both sides, if suspicious.

Besides, at this season, the travel must be slow, with two young girls unused to fatigue.

The air is sharp enough even now to try the patience of even a Circassian scout.

Down the wild Kura (by boat), concealing themselves by day, floating with the five-mile current at night—a hundred miles—would be the easiest way to escape the Russian outposts of Tiflis. Then across the valley, travelling at night, hiding by day, to the Arpa Tchai at Kizilkule. From there the rushing current would swiftly take a well-guided party to the Kurdish villages of the impregnable Kara Dagh.

When rested, a dash of three days would suffice to reach Erzeroum.

Some one has planned this raid who knows every foot of Anatolia! Is it the devil Ghazee?

The weary prince groans as he rides along. A thousand desperate expedients flit over his mind. A quest to Erzeroum! Useless! He cannot disguise his face and form. For Kurdish eyes are the sharpest in the world.

Where Fatima appears, there will be news of the lost Rose of Tiflis! The Kurds will never harm Fatima, Ismail's favorite daughter. She is their "queen"!

What if the wily old scoundrel Ismail made his daughter play a deep part in this scheme? He will dissemble and lie. Shut up in the Pacha's household, Fatima cannot be reached. Even were she, Schamyl remembers her snaky words : " I hate the Giaour and the Russ!"

His sinking heart tells him Maritza will not be taken to Erzeroum.

Though the Kurds are "called out," though their lances bristle along the Arpa Tchai, war is not yet declared. Intercourse is indeed cut off, but there is no means of using military force in this chase.

His instructions are to bring on no conflict, save with some armed party of raiders. Spies he may arrest and bring in.

It is ten o'clock when the column straggles into Kullink. Schamyl blesses Tergukassoff for the plenary order given him by the adjutant.

While the escort officer places the men at their ease for the night, Ahmed is at the telegraph. Despatch after despatch forces the operator to protest vainly. The lover's mind is too quick for his fingers!

The major is an anxious man as he listens to the rattle of the magic key.

Hassan throws Ahmed's blanket roll down on a rude couch in the office. Squatted on the floor, he smokes à la Turque. The lesson of the bridge is enough for the retainer. While Schamyl slumbers, Hassan fingers his sabre or feels his heavy Smith & Wesson at the slightest noise. He is "on guard." No more treachery! The brief answers to Schamyl are soon read. No news! Every scouting party reports no sign of fugitives.

Ordering his men in the saddle an hour before dawn, Schamyl forgets all his woes in a dreamless slumber. His own and only love blesses his dreams. By noon next day Kulpi is reached. The garrison commander has official reports urging every activity. Nothing yet!

Sending a dozen men to ride across the country to Parnault and scout the river bank to Assar, the major cheers them with relief there, for his own men will await him.

Bending to the right (in a three hours' smart trot), the command draws up at the État-Major in Assar. Crossing the Araxes, Schamyl learns that the river front is now swarming with the irregular Turkish cavalry and the Kurdish thieves.

A company is on picket at the ferry. Their officer tells Schamyl there have been disturbances the whole week along the lower river.

Prince Schamyl (seated at ease with the colonel commanding at Assar) finds that he has been forced to draw in his outposts along the river to prevent bringing on an irregular warfare.

Schamyl is a happy man when he sees at nightfall his own men ride in from Erivan in good order. Tossing his head, the gallant black charger is ready for his master once more.

A telegram announcing his platoon up the river, in rendezvous at Goomri, is answered with orders to join his main body at Kizilkule from the mountain.

Long and late Schamyl discusses the grave situation with the colonel. His orders are imperative to search the river from its junction to Goomri.

It will take a strong force to move there with safety now.

The cautious colonel hesitates until the plans arrived at are sanctioned from Erivan. Schamyl displays his positive order from Loris Melikoff. Every one bustles at Melikoff's beck and call.

At the gray of dawn, three strong companies of picked cavalry wait on the parade for the prince. A couple of light mountain "galloper" guns are also ready for the road.

Tergukassoff's despatch sanctions all these risks.

The post-commander sends a steady old lieutenant-colonel to bring this force back when Schamyl reaches his own troops rallied at Kizilkule.

Directing the main body due north to the great bend at the foot of the Kara Dagh, Schamyl sends a company to scout the river bank. They will join the main body at the old crossing under the frowning peaks where the Kurdish robber chiefs still hold their mountain eyries in the very teeth of the Russian garrison.

It is late in the afternoon when the battalion is abreast of the point of the Kara Dagh.

Born with the border chief's instinct, Ahmed leaves the main road, and leading his silent riders into a valley (to the north) he bivouacs the men in cover.

A half company in rear are stretched in a picket line to the river, with orders to send into camp the scouting party from the banks.

Leaving the lieutenant-colonel in command, Ahmed, riding to a high knoll, sends out a half company in a fan-like chain of videttes covering five miles. Riding on their lines (three hundred yards apart), these men can stop any wanderers of the night.

Two or three small squads occupy salient points, ready to gallop to the sound of firing.

Schamyl knows that the unusual activity along the river banks may drive any raiders to swing low down toward the Kara Dagh.

His net is spread. By a little camp-fire, hidden by a rocky cleft, Ahmed listens to Hassan's tales of the old border days of warfare.

Sleep comes not to his eyelids. He must finish this quest. *One* deserter has brought a stain upon his family name. To endeavor to pierce the Turkish lines in search of Maritza *now* would be madness. No! he will report from Goomri, and ask General Melikoff to order him into Tiflis. *Then*, when the war begins, he will take the advance and cut his way to where his darling love is hidden from him. That is best.

Bidding Hassan watch, Schamyl tries to sleep a few hours. There is silence in the camp. Only a charger's neigh, or the foot of a sentinel slipping on the grass, disturbs the sleep of two hundred men. The river patrol is in. All quiet on its low banks.

Schamyl awakes as Hassan's hand is slipped over his mouth. The old man motions for silence. Springing to his feet, Ahmed grasps his sabre and revolver.

"Come, master," whispers the old sergeant. He climbs a little knoll. Pointing to a few flaming points of light on the Kara Dagh, he softly says: "The Kurds are talking to their friends."

Prince Schamyl rubs his eyes. These are surely

stars twinkling over the crests of the lofty range. In a few words he sneers at the old man's suspicions.

"They are on the peaks, miles apart from each other. *You* have slept four hours. *I* crept up and watched them. They never move. They are *fires*. The Kurds are coming back from this side."

It is even so. They would not signal if their men were on *their* side of the river.

Lightly as a mountain deer, Ahmed springs down the knoll. Awakening the officers, they return and join Hassan, who stands grimly surveying the enemy's lights.

The veteran lieutenant-colonel slowly says:

"It wants two hours of day. They always cross back just before daylight. They are either signalling our presence or warning their friends up the river."

"Get the men under arms in half an hour, colonel. We will be ready for any alarm."

The field officer rouses his adjutant. In ten minutes the Cossacks are silently moving among their horses. Dark, double shadows in the faint, thin light of the fading stars make man and horse take on unearthly forms.

Hassan stands ready with the noble black tugging at his rein; his own horse is patient.

The Cossack's witchery has conquered him already. He points his fox-like ears.

Schamyl drains a draught of Pashkoff's good brandy from his flask.

Ha! a sharp, snapping shot a half mile away. Half his men are already in their saddles. Another, another! It is now the heavy ring of the Berdans.

A faint sound of distant yells floats on the silent night. Shot follows shot.

The men are motionless as rocks. The colonel is at his side.

"Lead one troop and follow me. I will take the first." Springing on the black, whose back quivers under him as the high-blooded charger gathers for a bound, Schamyl calls out as he whirls to the front: "Only the sword; no firing till orders!" A guide and fierce Hassan range alongside of the young prince, whose first field is this one under the black shadows of the Kara Dagh.

Leading his men steadily, he rides down into a long valley, at the head of which confused firing and yells prove that the Kurds have broken his thin picket lines and are hastening toward the river. On for Maritza! His heart thirsts for vengeance.

Behind him, the cold daylight begins to streak the eastern skies. The sloping valley stretches two miles to the ford, under cover of the overhanging cliffs across the river.

A regular ringing crack of rifles tells Ahmed his pickets are following the main body of the raiders, and teasing them.

Schamyl raises his sword. The column halts. Five minutes now to breathe the horses and men. The colonel rides up.

The young leader falters not.

No; the light of battle flashes in the dark eyes of Ahmed. Revenge for Maritza!

"Colonel, send half a company to cut them off from the river and open a rifle fire. *You* follow with the rest of your sotnia, and charge them home with the sword. *I* will attack them here in flank. Wait my signal."

It is high time! Seven hundred yards away a band of scattered horsemen are pricking toward the river, in wild confusion.

Schamyl waves his sword, the rifle platoon dashes down the slope, racing for the bank.

Leisurely the old colonel leads his half company down, at a slow trot. Every bright blade is out. The excited men see their hereditary enemies. Only the Sioux and Pawnee can close in as deadly a grapple as Tcherkess and Kurd. War to the knife!

Quarter! It is an idle by-word. Mercy is forgotten! Leaning forward, his " chaska " double-knotted to his wrist, Ahmed settles his shoulder revolver-string, and watches for the main body. He wheels his men into a loose line.

There they come! Breaking out of the underbrush, pack animals are dashing along. A mass of yelling riders crowds down the valley. Several hundreds press along in the mad race for life.

Old Hassan's blade is bare!

Schamyl presses the panting sides of the black. Like a whirlwind he dashes down the slope. His last sharp order to the company leaders is to follow the mass and charge through it, wheeling and riding back.

Three minutes after, with a wild " Hurrah! " the Tcherkess strike the turbaned invaders.

In the front, the ring of the Berdans knells the death of the foremost fugitives.

Hassan is hard by Schamyl, as the fleet black tears his way through the frightened huddle.

Schamyl sees a huge rider in his front. Something flashes. It is a long flintlock pistol. Dropping his point, he feels through his heavy blade the sickening yielding of soft flesh. He is ten yards away as the Kurd drops from his saddle. His hands are wet with warm blood. The tiger in him is loose! It is a mad five minutes of frantic struggle.

He strikes for Maritza!

Encumbered with their lances and long, useless guns, exhausted and breathless, the Kurds, wrapped in floating draperies, make no real stand against the Tcherkess.

Breaking up in little knots over the plain, they now struggle toward the river.

Revolvers begin to ring out where a resolute few couch their slender lances, as Schamyl's troopers pour in a deadly fire.

Whirling down the valley, pursuer and pursued near the river. The Kurds fight now like demons, for life.

Followed by Hassan, Schamyl charges on the heavier knots of fugitives, leading the wild-eyed Cossacks in their dashes at the strongest clusters.

He is sick of this slaughter. Over the valley the sunlight steals. The heavy blades glitter as they rise and fall.

A scattered train of the dead lies along the half mile of the flight.

Prince Ahmed casts the eye of a leader on the river bank. It is lined with his advance guard, whose Berdans are pouring in a deadly fire.

The "rally" has been sounded by his bugler. By sheer dint of survivorship, a frantic mass of fifty to seventy Moslems plunge into the long ripples of the swimming ford of the "Arpa."

As his men coolly pick off these tired swimmers in the stream, a useless hail of spent balls falls from the rocks of the Kara Dagh, opposite.

They are swarming now with hostile Kurds. The river resounds with their frantic yells!

All too feeble are the old carabines of the wild hill tribes. The balls fall short.

Yet their numbers are imposing. Prudence returns to Schamyl. Sounding again the "rally," he draws up all who will obey the call, in two formations, a hundred yards from the bank.

The colonel rides up to him with dripping sword.

"Take charge and watch the river now. Send down and stop all useless fire across the stream. For ammunition is precious; the tribes may attempt to revenge the surprise." Ahmed screams his orders.

Rattling down the slope, the light guns and the camp reserve join the two rallying sotnias.

Schamyl sends out a sergeant and ten men to collect his scattered troopers and bring in the riderless horses.

Dashing around the field, with dragging bridles, the Kurdish ponies are loaded with plunder, or buried under the huge peaked saddles of the enemy.

Schamyl's pickets are leisurely riding, in loose order, down the valley. Now and then the crack of a revolver or a sabre flash tells of the *coup de grâce* given to some foe, wounded yet living, or else hunted, unhurt, from a covert, to die in mad flight.

Scattered plunder covers the path of the sword.

With unscrupulous readiness the practical Tcherkess are already looting the dead.

Black browed and fierce, with drooping mustaches and tufted crown, the Kurds lie stiffened in every repulsive attitude of the battle-field.

Picking his way along, the noble black throws high his head in air on nearing the clumps of the dead. He scents the blood and trembles as he bends his royal head away.

Despatching a flanking squad to watch the river above and below the bend (from the heights), Ahmed rides over his first victorious field. He has lost but three killed and a few wounded.

His eye recognizes the path of his mad charge down the hill. The piles of dead begin there. The trampled earth, spurned by the charger's feet, shows the frantic rush of that race for life in the dam.

Yes! There, great among his fellows in death, lies the brawny Turk who fell beneath his own thrust in the charge.

A hundred and seventy Kurds lie silent in the half-mile of the struggle. Their dead are scattered far to where they first forced the picket lines to the north.

It was their vain belief that they had merely encountered a passing patrol at first.

Schamyl, in calmer mood now, is revolted at the awful work of the Circassian ". chaska." He rejoins his main body and finds a dozen or more straggling prisoners.

These he sends Hassan to question in their own tongue. A courier is spurring already back to Assar to report the smiting of the borderers.

Though war is not yet declared, no formal orders are needed. Tcherkess and Kurd are never at peace. Anybody of the enemy on the Russian side is fair game for the Cossack, whether they be soldiery or only predatory thieves.

Scattered along the fringes of the woods, the Cossacks are lighting their cooking fires. The handy plunder of the foe enriches their larders.

Directing his field officer to send out a detail and bring the arms and plunder in, Schamyl occupies a high knoll from whence he can view the whole river bank.

The horses are grazing alternately, with saddles on, a strong herd guard in charge of them—one company ready for action.

The two rifle guns command the ford. Schamyl does not wish to open fire across the Arpa Tchai unless forced to by a counter attack.

The prisoners, bound securely, are passed in review before the Prince of the Caucasus. Sullen, low-browed brutes are they, in the main. Among them is a poor wretch who howls his innocence, in Russian.

Calling up his officers, Schamyl seeks to see if any of them know of him.

"His huts, a few miles above the bend, were burned and plundered by the Kurds, and two or three of his companions killed. It is four hours' march away."

"Keep that man with us," Schamyl orders. He says, "We will march by your place. If you have lied, we will shoot you and leave you in the road for the wolves!"

The man solemnly protests his truthfulness.

"We shall see!" says Schamyl, grimly. "Colonel," he directs, "send these prisoners over to Assar, to your commander, with a sergeant's squad to drive in all the captured horses and collect the arms."

The old field officer nods assent. He grumbles: "You may as well shoot them here, as there! Erivan orders are to execute them forthwith."

"I am no butcher! I am a soldier," coldly says Schamyl.

Yes! by the token of his blood-stained blade and signal victory, the young eagle has fleshed his talons now.

As he despatches a mid-day repast, he waits for the marshalling of the command.

They must hasten up the winding Arpa, for it is two days' march to Kizilkule. He burns to report his combat to General Melikoff. One blow for Russia! The first!

An officer from the river picket dashes up, mounted.

"Highness, a body of regular Turkish cavalry and a white flag are at the head of the ford. What are your orders?"

Schamyl sends his old field officer, with one gun and the company on duty, to take post on the bank and cover the crossing of an officer with a white flag, who will meet the enemy's flag at the rapids and report the object.

No treachery for him. He calls for his horsemen to follow. The sound of wild outcries from the knot of prisoners diverts him now.

The Russian captive, whose hands have been loosened, is trying to throttle a hang-dog-looking Kurd, who essays vainly to protect himself.

"Ah! Villain! Son of a dog! You butchered my wife! You came in the boat, you devil!"

Schamyl is curious. "A boat! What boat? Explain!" he sternly commands, as the man is wrenched away from his victim.

"Highness!" he cries, falling on his knees, "my life be on my head if I lie! Four nights ago a boat with a party of Kurds came down the river in the night. I have lived in peace and long traded over the stream. My brothers and their wives lived with me.

"The boat party all landed, for they knew my huts. The party were from up the river, and had a lady with them. She was cold and sick. They made us serve them. My wife fed the stranger—a veiled Moslem.

"I feared them not. After daybreak they were warm and rested. The men all went to the boat with the woman. They pushed across the stream. Some went away with the lady. I saw horses ready. Five or six came back with the boatman. I liked it not! We tried to flee, and then to fight. My poor old wife was killed. The other women were carried away. All my brothers slain. Me they took away to guide them back from this last raid. This devil here was one! The other hill soldiers came down from the Kara Dagh. They burnt my house! Let me kill this beast!"

Schamyl's brow grows black. He is a true Circassian. He cries:

"Keep that man with us. Send the rest off to Assar.—If your story is true, you shall kill him on your own hearth-stone."

Revenge for blood is the first commandment in Daghestan.

Schamyl gallops swiftly to the bank where the white flag waves. He unslings his glasses.

Surely they are regular Turkish cavalry, in order. He instantly summons his whole force and the other gun to move up, in support, leaving only the camp guard on the field. He may have a serious engagement.

His second in command reports the return message.

The Turkish commander wishes to confer in person with the commanding officer. He begs permission for a party of Kurds to pass unarmed and carry away their dead.

"I will see him!" cries Ahmed. He may learn here of Maritza. If *she* has joined the Turks, it will be noised abroad with much flourish. May God grant it!

Riding into the stream, with his bugler carrying a white pennon (on a captured spear), Schamyl meets in mid-stream the officer, who is similarly guided.

The troops of both watch the meeting.

With a start Schamyl cries:

"Suleiman, my friend!"

"Prince, I am now Captain Mehemed Pacha," replies his late guest at the Uhlan mess. "How did *you* come here?"

Suleiman is astounded.

"By the same path of duty which led you," is Ahmed's softened reply. " Ride over with me, with a couple of your officers."

In a few moments two dark-eyed wearers of the fez salute the bold Circassian.

Riding up to a knoll, in full view of the troops on either side, Schamyl asks his second officer to join him.

He may not confer alone, even with a friendly enemy.

In five minutes the business is despatched. Schamyl agrees to withdraw his command to the heights to the west and allow some unarmed villagers to cross and bear away the bodies of the slain.

" I care not for this carrion. These Kurds are only thieves. My orders are to watch the river," says Suleiman. "These robbers crossed before my arrival."

In a half-hour a hundred swarthy wretches are bearing the Kurdish slain to the banks. Their women wail loudly at the other shore.

Suleiman agrees to leave the other bank with his force at once.

Ahmed eagerly asks if Suleiman came down from Erzeroum.

"I did not, Prince. I have moved down the interior valley from Kars, and have been scouting for three weeks along the river hills."

" Did you meet any parties on your road who passed up from here?"

His heart beats. Shall he tell him of the boat party? Duty forbids.

"Only a few horsemen convoying the Lady Fatima to her father at Erzeroum."

"Was she alone?" Ahmed queries, as he hides his anxious face by swinging his steed.

"Yes; she was in a mule litter. There was no other woman in the party. Ah, her father is a rare old scoundrel!"

Schamyl fears lest some straggling shot may embroil the horsemen lining the river banks. He says, with a glance of old-time friendship:

"Captain, we must part. I hope, if we meet in the field, you will remember that it is duty alone divides us. I shall be on Melikoff's staff."

Captain Mehemed rejoins with pride: "I will be with Mukhtar Pacha. I would not serve under the old Vali Ismail. He is a thief and coward!"

Schamyl rides down to the river with Suleiman. As they ford the waters at the parting, Schamyl whispers: "Where is Ghazee?"

"He is at Kars, Prince," Suleiman sadly answers. He knows the dark gulf of crime between the brothers.

"Suleiman," Schamyl says, "if I can serve you in any proper way, write me to the État-Major at Goomri."

Suleiman grasps his hand. "Old Abdallah, the jewel merchant in the bazar at Goomri, will convey a letter to me any time. Write me if I can do anything, for I fear we will have war in a few weeks. May Allah guide and guard you!"

They clasp hands in a soldier's farewell. With rare politeness Suleiman moves his men a few miles parallel on the Turkish bank, as Schamyl's column marches, led by the prisoner to the plundered huts.

Schamyl orders the two Cossacks leading the captive Kurd to keep him at the head of the line. As night approaches, the advance halts around the ruins of the poor prisoner's house. It is desolate and burned.

His tale is too true, for, as the troops draw up, two half-famished wretches crawl out of the bushes. They are the survivors of the dwellers at the little river station. One of them is well known to the guide.

Schamyl examines the crumbled ruins. The fugitives have dragged the bodies of the slain into the bushes. Schamyl directs a few men to cover them with the half-frozen sand. He will not leave his command here, exposed to a dash from the other side. Night is falling fast. The men need rest.

"Bring up that Kurd," he commands. He has ordered food and a flask of vodki to be thrown to the starving sufferers, who feared the return of the invaders and hid in the thickets.

As the Moslem is dragged forward, he loses heart. He cries, "*Amaun! Amaun!*" and besides, howling for quarter, frantically insists he will tell all. Hassan, in his border jargon, interprets the Kurd's plea.

"Stay!" orders Schamyl. "Send a couple of the guard here." They dismount and approach, with their pistols in hand.

"Hassan, tell him if he does not instantly tell us about the Lady Fatima, his brains will be blown out at once."

The frightened wretch volubly describes how, led by two men of higher station, the party of twenty

Kurds lay concealed a week in the river forests in front of Tiflis.

One of the men stole into Tiflis as a jewel pedler and communicated with the Lady Fatima. A dozen of the raiders brought the two ladies to the boat at nightfall. The Russky princess was bound and gagged. Down the " Kura," and over the hills to the " Arpa Tchai," they safely fled. The " Princess of the Russkys " was afterward well treated. *She* mourned unceasingly, but the Lady Fatima was cheerful.

Schamyl's heart is about to burst its bonds.

" And where is she now ? " he hoarsely demands.

" She was taken to Kars by the Alam road. The man Omar Effendi said she was worth a thousand purses in Kars for the great Pacha Ghazee. It is five days since she left the river below Kizilkule, where a carriage and a squad of zaphtiehs were in waiting. She was a beauty fit for the Padisha's harem."

Schamyl's face grows harder than flint. He orders the commander to lead the troops on. There is a good forest, with water and shelter on high ground, four miles farther.

The hardy victors of the morning fight file by, with pride in their dashing leader. A lieutenant and the rear platoon alone wait.

Schamyl speaks, in Russian, to the refugee:

" You and your friends can follow my men into camp. I will take you up to Kizilkule, and you shall be well treated. I leave you this man." Making a sign to his escort, he rides slowly away, leaving Hassan watching the howling murderer.

As he gains fifty yards, he *must* turn his head. There are three struggling forms around an awful shapeless thing lying prone on the ashes of that plundered home.

Hassan rejoins his master in a few minutes. The released prisoner is running at his stirrup. The other waifs follow at a dog trot. As Schamyl halts to question Hassan, the houseless wanderer hands back old Hassan's belt dagger, which seems to have fallen to the ground; or had he loaned it?

Prince Schamyl asks no questions. The dead Kurd is left alone, with his staring eyes upturned to the darkening heavens, to be food for the wolves.

In an hour the victors are bivouacked in comfort. Blazing fires shed their genial glow. A dozen recaptured kine have been slain, and their carcasses loaded on Kurdish ponies. It is a camp feast. While the keen-eyed sentinels and strong outlying pickets watch the lines, and the herd guards move gently among the hobbled steeds, the troopers sleep.

Schamyl, wrapped in his cloak, gazes into the watchfire, around which his gallant officers are feasting. His stricken heart is cold as stone in his bosom. What is victory? His love is a harem captive.

Maritza, queen of roses, in the power of Ghazee at Kars! Double-dyed, damned treason of the wild girl "Fatima"! Haste now to Kizilzule and Goomri. He will despatch direct to General Melikoff. He will reclaim the girl of the Turkish commander.

Mukhtar Pacha is no black fiend, but a high-souled Osmanli,

Ah! Deadly wiles of Ghazee! He may conceal the Rose of Tiflis and deny all knowledge.

As for Ismail of Erzeroum and his daughter, it were idle to believe their latest dying word. They are haters of the Russ!

The grand white stars swinging high over his first battle-field shine unpityingly on Schamyl, whose ruby ring speaks sadly of the vanished Rose.

He falls into broken dreams of her, with a last oath to high heaven, that even behind the walls of Kars he will find her yet. For Ghazee may not dare to press to the extreme his villany.

The Princess of Georgia is a great factor in the future of Armenia—even in captivity.

CHAPTER VIII.

ABDALLAH'S RUSE.—SCHAMYL'S SPY IN KARS.

Two days later the battalion sweeps proudly into Kizilkule. Schamyl has now fathomed the mystery.

The river was the line of retreat. Every hut on its banks has been examined. Another halting-place was found where the Lady Fatima came alone ashore. Her good-humored chatter with the obsequious escort proved the pleasure of the Kurdish princess in her pretended abduction. But the Rose of Tiflis is behind the walls of Kars.

Schamyl has been unable to control Hassan. Since the fight he spends his leisure in sorting a varied loot, secreted in his strangely swollen saddle holsters and valise.

A princely shawl, a priceless sword (he knows the old Damascus mark), a string or so of pearls, and rich jewels adorn him. A remarkable amelioration in the splendor of his horse gear also proves that Hassan has gleaned the red fields of Bellona to great profit.

Prince Schamyl thinks that his own sumpter animal looks strangely like the royal bay ridden by the Kurdish leader who fell under his sword.

And yet the work-a-day animal is also there, plodding along under a heavy pack. A sudden increase of live stock! "Hassan," the prince dryly says, "did we not have one pack-horse?"

"Praise be to Allah!" replies Hassan the unblushing. "We *now* have two!"

"What is he loaded with?"

"My baggage," gravely answers Hassan. "My lord rides far. I need many things."

Alas for Hassan's conscience! He is a self-elected general heir of many Kurds who are "not lost but gone before." Schamyl abandons this vain curiosity.

Hassan makes a very brave appearance at Kizilkule—a cross between a retired pacha and a wandering millionnaire of the bazaar.

Fit henchman for a Falstaff! He would have been a worthy member of General Jim Lane's Kansas cavalry regiment. Nature endows him with the greed of a New York alderman!

There is great joy in Kizilkule at the victory. Schamyl finds, at this outpost, his own squadron reunited. All his detachments are in.

By the talking wire, he reports to General Melikoff. He receives orders to push on to Goomri, and there take the road to Tiflis, after resting and refitting his own troopers.

It is a brave sight on the parade at Kizilkule when the Erzeroum troops defile past Schamyl's own chafing warriors, who envy them the glory of the fight.

They are homeward bound; a strong regiment with four guns now holds the " Kurds' crossing." The Erivan chief is awake to the wants of the hour.

As the brigade bands sound the Emperor's hymn, Schamyl passes his own Circassians along the lines of the garrison in review before the commanding general.

Proudly they defile at the walk and trot. On the third passage, there is but a tossing sea of steeds, dashing along at a full run. The Circassians are hidden, like Comanches, behind their animals. As they gallop by, they are greeted with the plaudits of the garrison ladies.

Evening shadows fall on Ahmèd's sturdy troopers, thirty miles toward Goomri, where stout General Komaroff holds that enormous river fortress, ready to fall upon Kars with his force. His horses and crowded troops are under the sweep of the bristling guns of the citadel. Before the daylight gilds the Aladja Dagh, the eager steeds are snuffing the morning air.

Hassan lingers at the town of Abduhraman, chaffering for the supplies dear to an old campaigner.

He overtakes Prince Schamyl with a rush.

"Highness," he breathlessly announces, for the

command is well past the town, "this is the nearest crossing-point for Kars. I have found the road of the day-star you seek. Come!" Ahmed drives the spurs into the plunging black. In five minutes, Schamyl reins up beside a ferryman's cottage. A lank Armenian youth, his eyes rolling in terror, is pushed forward.

He nervously eyes Ahmed's revolver as he talks.

"Last week I was at the ferry. Late at night a boat came down. I hailed it. A stranger gave me two gold pieces to run over the hills to Alam, and bring down the carriage waiting there for Omar Effendi. I reached there at daybreak, and came with it to the great rocks on the Arpa, below Bairain Kend. There I waited with it till night, and hailed the same boat on the river at the rocks. Omar Effendi, who gave me two more gold pieces, got in the carriage with a lady, who was fair as the stars on the moonlit river. I know it, for she dropped her hood. He had soldiers.

"I knew the other lady in the boat was the Princess Fatima. I ferried them over when they last went to Tiflis."

"And the boat?" Schamyl demands.

"Went down the river," the frightened boy answers, "with the other lady. They passed both the forts above in the night."

Schamyl tosses the lad a gold piece. He dashes up the river road, followed by Hassan.

Long that night, by the camp-fire, the eagle of the Caucasus talks with his sly old retainer.

It is but thirty miles from Goomri to Kars. Yet Schamyl may not hope to traverse it in months.

As he thinks of his pathway up the river, the words of Suleiman return to him.

"Hassan," he cries, "do you know old Abdallah, the jewel merchant at Goomri?"

"A wise Hadji; a rich Hadji. He has journeyed to the holy places." Hassan reverently uncovers, bowing to the east. This perfunctory reverence is like the genuflexion of the Calabrian banditti, and equal in sanctity, to the pious sign of the cross made before the Russian burglar will dare to break a lock—mechanical devotion.

"How long have you known him?" Schamyl queries.

"Many years, my lord. In his day he brought pearls from Ormuz, turquoises from Samarcand. I know he was trusted by the 'great master,' your father."

"We will see this man at Goomri," concludes Schamyl, as he closes his eyes.

"He is wise and powerful," answers Hassan.

A thousand twinkling lights surround the great border fortress of Goomri when Schamyl rides through the main gate in the shades of the next evening.

Crowded one on the other, great bodies of infantry, cavalry, and artillery crouch under the frowning walls, where a hundred Krupp guns protect the priceless military magazines of the White Czar.

Dismounting at Komaroff's headquarters, Schamyl is soon at his ease. His men are well bestowed without the walls. Hassan, with the chargers housed, makes merry in the courtyard.

There is pride in Prince Schamyl's glance when he reads the despatches waiting him.

Melikoff says briefly:

"Good! Report here at once with your command."

The Grand Duke Nicholas deigns to send a special telegram.

"Well done, my faithful Tcherkess! General Tergukassoff commends you. I renew my regards.
"NICHOLAS."

Tearing himself away from the merry bumpers of the mess, Ahmed finds the fame of his achievement has run on beyond him. It is the first blood of the coming campaign.

Doubt lingers no longer as to a bloody war. The Emperor is ready to leave Petersburg. Troops massed in Bessarabia wait but the word to cross the Danube. Melikoff is ready, and Ignatief travels through London, Paris, and Berlin wending toward Vienna. "La danse va commencer."

"What can I do for you, Prince?" heartily queries Komaroff, as Schamyl takes his leave.

The Circassian proposes to sleep in three days at Tiflis. He has a boon to ask of Melikoff.

Maritza's fate depends upon his brain, his own loyal heart, and—his sword.

"General, do you know Abdallah the jeweller?" the young lover respectfully asks.

"Very well. He is our best agent in the secret service at Kars, Erzeroum, and Trebizond. We permit him to remain here and guard his riches, untouched by Pacha or grinding Kaimakan. He is true to his word, able, and devoted to the Czar."

·

"I would like an hour with him on my private affairs," Schamyl answers.

Komaroff seals a card with his own signet ring.

"Show him that, major. If you want anything more, bring him to me."

The latticed second-story windows of Abdallah's spacious house are gayly lit up as Schamyl and Hassan leave their steeds in front with the orderly. A cross-legged old servitor rises and answers Hassan, who beats on the iron barred lower door with his dagger-shaft.

Sending up the general's card, Schamyl gazes on the dark shop, lit only by a swinging cresset. Here, the crafty Moslem will chaffer over a five rouble turquoise, or can hobble out and bring bowls of diamonds, pearls, and rubies from the gnome-like nooks of his masonry vaults.

A wise old Turk is Abdallah. At this calm hour of rest he disdains not the peaceful chibouque, the forbidden wine of the Giaour, or the blandishments of those docile beauties who peer slyly through the lattice of his harem, as the troops pass.

Abdallah has reached the comfortable age when a gentlemanly avarice and the care of his hardearned hoards make him conservative. He prefers the security and flowing stream of Russian gold at Goomri to the orthodox life of a subject of Abdul-Aziz. It is safer.

Grave in manner, ripe of years, he keeps his network of bazaar agents spread all over Anatolia. Public opinion in Turkey is made by the babble of the marts.

Abdallah exchanges his carefully culled secret

reports for the minted red gold of Russia—an information bureau, à la mode.

A well-fed Armenian Vicar of Bray is Abdallah. He has houses at Kars and Erzeroum; at Ardaban, Bayazid, and Trebizond also are branch dépôts of his political exchange and jewel business.

Mighty Mukhtar Pacha, soldier and governor, holding Asia Minor for the Sultan, might well tremble did he know of Tarnaieff's little dinners of the past year at Erzeroum, in Abdallah's walled mansion. The disguised dragoman, over the sparkling wine, gained whispered secrets, each worth a man's life, from needy Hassan Bey, the Turkish citadel commander. Abdallah's Turkish guineas paid Hassan Bey well for selling the plans of Erzeroum. Russia's secret service money rewarded Abdallah.

Now the Arpa Tchai is soon to run red with blood. Hassan Bey is the confidant of Mukhtar at Kars. There are *more* plans to sell.

The great Pacha Mukhtar forgets that old saw, "Like father, like son!" in making Hassan his confidant.

When Paskiewitch swept through Asia Minor in 1828, he wisely bought the fall of Varna from Hassan Bey's Judas father. It saved his troops.

Abdallah's flowing beard wags gravely as he scrutinizes the noble Schamyl.

In an inner room, hung with wondrous shawls and choicest arms, lit by crystal lamps, where lovely slaves bring the richest wines and fragrant Latakia, the jewel merchant listens to Schamyl's tale of hapless love.

Hassan, the swordsman, sits beyond the curtain.

He has greeted as an old friend the great merchant.

In the dialect of their youth, he tells Abdallah, Schamyl is now the black eagle of the Caucasus.

When coffee, served in golden cups, follows the wine, Abdallah, caressing the diamond circled black amber head of his narghilèh, slowly answers the impatient prince:

"Son of the great sultan, I will serve you. I knew your royal father. I know Ghazee, the man of stone."

Schamyl winces.

Abdallah calmly proceeds:

"The great Ferik-Pacha Melikoff must fight Mukhtar to the death in the valley of the Arpa before any siege. But the Russian eagle will fly over Kars. The city will be taken—Erzeroum also. It is written in the stars.

"Komaroff, your leader here, sends me his signet for you. It is enough.

"Son of Schamyl, I will tell you all. We have Osman Bey here now, who knows all the Frankish deviltry of war. He learned it in Europe. He is the right eye of the Russian general here. It was madness for the Turks to drive him into your service. He is the sworn brother of Hassan Bey, who is the favorite of Mukhtar. They were fellow students in Paris.

"Now, in my house in Kars, all our spies are safe. Hassan protects them! He is to have a mountain of gold from your Czar when we get Kars and Erzeroum.

"I have made all the ways smooth to send news.

For *your* people may not go and come. *My* servants have the eyes of the serpent.

"I will send your man into Kars; he can watch over the Princess Maritza, if she is there.

"But I would not try to rescue her till the city falls."

"Explain, Abdallah!" Schamyl cries.

"Ghazee Mohammed, your brother, has sent secret proclamations all through Daghestan and Circassia, that a holy war will be proclaimed.

"He thinks England will help the Turks. He has runners everywhere, bearing messages secretly. The Turkish government has given him a brigade. He will try to raise the Circassians with his friend Moussa Pacha, who was once Colonel 'Kondukoff,' you know."

Ahmed is impatient.

"Gently, my son!" chides Abdallah.

"Ghazee makes his headquarters now at Kars. He thinks he will see the Russians driven over the Caucasus. As Prince of the Tcherkess, he will remain here. The Abkasians will revolt. If he should hold and espouse the Rose of Tiflis, it would give him all the rights to Georgia and Circassia."

"True," Schamyl murmurs.

"He will treat the lady well, and conceal her in Kars. It is the safest place. He *must* keep in good relations with Constantinople to become the Pacha Viceroy of Armenia when the war is over. He would not dare to maltreat Princess Maritza. We will find her through Hassan Bey.

"Now, your man knows every border language. Hassan Bey will aid him. We will send him in with some countrymen. He can be a camel-driver. He speaks Persian."

"But how can he help the princess if a war begins?"

Schamyl is incredulous. His heart calls for action.

"Listen! The English insist upon the protection of the Armenian convents and churches. If we can only find where the lady is, Hassan can help us smuggle her into one of the Armenian convent-churches.

"Their priests are all married. The troops will not search the convents. She will be safe till we know where she is. She can disguise herself.

"When the city is taken, she can be at once found."

"But can she not be got out before?" Schamyl anxiously queries.

"I will have letters or a message for you if we find her. I fear Ghazee Mohammed might poison her! You must keep away. My son, Ghazee will watch *you*, not her! You must keep away. Be not rash."

The jewel merchant is right. While Schamyl thinks the scheme over, Hassan and Abdallah talk at length.

"Taib, Taib Kètir! *Very* good," says Abdallah. "Leave now, my son, your servitor with me. I will take care of his horse and his goods. He can come to me any time."

Schamyl offers Abdallah the use of money.

"Buckra! Buckra! Later, my son," replies the cunning old Moslem. "We will talk later."

In a half-hour, Schamyl has closed his conference

with Abdallah. A billet for Hassan to deliver says:

"Trust the bearer in all. He will tell what to do. Your lover till death.
"AHMED."

"My son, the stars are high toward the west. You go to Tiflis. I will see that Hassan Bey guards your man. You will come back here with the invading army. I will work silently in this cause. Let the man stay with me. He shall have money and all he wants in Kars. To Hassan Bey I will myself write, in Persian, by my own spy. He will send the Princess Maritza money for bribes, or any help he can. You can repay me later.

"But, if we endeavor to bring her off, Ghazee will poison her or send her away into the heart of Syria or farther Turkey. If she ventured out of Kars, the Kurds and spies spare neither the living nor the dead. They are the vultures of the battle-field. They even rob the Christian graves! They strip the dead.

"May Allah protect her! We will hide her in Kars. When the city falls we can send her at once to Russia, far away over the Caucasus.

"Tell the General Komaroff all. He will help me and send you the news. Now go, my son, and send your man back in the dark.

"No one must know where he is. There are Turkish spies even here!"

Ahmed promises Abdallah a princely reward for the safety of Maritza. The old sage is wise indeed. Ah! Osman Bey, the chief of the Intelligence

Bureau. He will get Komaroff's order for Osman's aid.

"I will send a message to Suleiman Mehemed Pacha. He will watch Ghazee's daily life and tell me of those around him. He is a true soldier, and my trusted friend."

Schamyl briefly informs Abdallah of their meeting.

"Good! I can send him your letter!"

Saluting the wise old negotiator, Schamyl rides to his troops at their camp. It is the best he can do.

Hassan prepares his entire luggage, and all the treasured relics of the Kurdish defeat. He must slip out of the camp and say "Good-by" to his master, for a time. He is strangely eager for this desperate service.

If discovered, he will be impaled alive, and left for the rock-ravens of the Kara-Dagh.

Schamyl, in plain words, gives Hassan his parting commands. He has told him what to do in every case—above all, not to risk the life of the princess, or to make any rash attempt to rescue her. Hassan Bey, for Abdallah's gold, will act when chance occurs. Schamyl begs Hassan to send out his news and any letters to Abdallah.

"And if the Master Ghazee should try to take her away from Kars?" Hassan queries.

Schamyl is silent. *He* cannot order the assassination of his *brother*.

Hassan answers for himself as they ride up to the dark square where Abdallah waits for Hassan.

"Highness," says Hassan, grimly, "your brother, the master, shed my blood. I am a Circassian. If he leaves Kars with the day-star, I can follow him for my revenge. It is my right."

Schamyl is silent. One last precaution! He hands Hassan a little scrawl to Suleiman Mehemed Pacha, his old friend.

"Should you be captured, Suleiman will help. You may tell him all, if you fall in his hands."

They are at Abdallah's gate. Prince Schamyl remembers the secret of his birth, locked in that rugged old breast. Only Ghazee and Hassan know.

He pleads with his old servitor. Hassan bows his head.

"May Allah judge me! I gave my oath to the dying. Should the dark angel's wing sweep over me, you will know then, but not till then."

The parting moment comes. Schamyl holds up the mystic amulet of his father.

Hassan kisses it humbly.

"Swear faith to the princess, Hassan," he solemnly says.

"I swear on the tomb of Mohammed," utters the old man.

He is gone. The courtyard gates, unbarred, hide him. Schamyl gallops to his troops; the twinkling stars hang over distant Kars, where his lost love, perhaps, watches for the help which comes not.

Before Komaroff has buckled on his sabre next morning for parade, Schamyl's squadron, sent in advance, is twenty miles toward Tiflis.

Ahmed's steed champs below. Three orderlies wait with him to overtake the column.

General Komaroff gives Prince Schamyl his latest despatches. To both the general and Osman Bey he imparts the secret of old Hassan's desperate venture.

"I will see that Abdallah and Hassan Bey, in Kars, have every aid my headquarters can give. Pray ask General Melikoff to send you to lead my advance, Prince," says the old fighter, as Schamyl bends low in thanks. . . .

The three days' march to Tiflis is a dream to Schamyl. Pricking sharply along the road, he heads his men cheerfully. Osman Bey, as chief of the Intelligence Department, can use every wire in the Trans-Caucasus. A few cipher words exchanged will enable Schamyl to hear of every movement. Now for Circassia! Then for the field! The sound of wedding-bells was never as welcome to eager groom as the first roar of Komaroff's cannon will be to fiery Ahmed.

When his splendid squadron swings into line on the square in front of the Grand Duke's palace, Schamyl dismounts, to be greeted by Gronoff with the enthusiasm of a brother of the sword.

"Breakfast with me. I have letters for you," he whispers. Schamyl's magic word "Despatches" gives him precedence over all the waiting generals of the garrison.

Loris Melikoff is not chary of his praise for Schamyl. "You will dine with the Grand Duke and myself, alone, this evening. To-morrow you go to Circassia and Daghestan!"

In a few words Melikoff tells him of the fruitless search for the Princess Maritza. Schamyl's reports alone indicate her presence in Kars. Melikoff pledges the whole secret service in her aid.

The Turkish commander as yet denies all knowledge of her. He even promises to aid!

Schamyl rejoins Gronoff. Seated in the luxurious mess-room, the grand square before the palace windows is a living picture.

February breezes move the budding leaves. Passing troops and all the bustle of an early war keep up a daily excitement.

Gronoff hands him a sheaf of letters—Paul Platoff, his brother officers of the Uhlans, Tarnaieff from Constantinople, and many others.

He tears open Tarnaieff's first, at the well-spread table covered with the dainties of Tiflis. It is soldierly in its brevity:

"DEAR SCHAMYL: I find from our secret service here that Countess Vronsky has joined Ghazee Schamyl in Asia Minor. She took the steamer to Trebizond. His brigade and Moussa Pacha's are at Kars. Look out for him! She is also dangerous. I think Mustapha was glad to get her away from Constantinople, for fear of Ignatief. I hold on here to the last. The embassy is shut. I join by Odessa and Sughum-Kale next month early. I am to see the commander in Bessarabia, and then report to Melikoff. Will hope to meet you on the staff.

"TARNAIEFF."

Platoff writes from the frozen mud of the Dobrudsha:

"Our artillery is here, all waiting for the signal. All your brother's estates, property, and goods are confiscated, and his commissions and titles cancelled. You are now Schamyl the chief! Beware of assassination.

"PLATOFF."

Thrusting the mass of unimportant matter into his tunic, Schamyl listens to Gronoff's description of the sorrows of the Lazareffs, and the two lovely friends of Maritza, the missing Rose.

"My dear Schamyl, there is a growing fear that Princess Maritza has joined the Turks. It is all we can do to keep the Abkhasians from open revolt. The official denial of the Turkish commander of her presence leaves us no means to force the search for her now. We must all wait."

Gronoff gives Schamyl the latest phase of the war news.

"Only waiting the signal! The Turks dally, and will not sign the protocol. St. Petersburg's cabinet waits but one word from the Emperor to issue its circular note to the powers. A second nod of the august imperator will throw four hundred thousand men on the foe!"

Schamyl hardly listens to Gronoff's gossip. His heart is in Kars with Maritza.

Nadya Vronsky, the "White Countess," there! Can he not use her jealousy in some way? He must warn Abdallah! Hassan Bey may watch the lovesick dupe of Ghazee. She will ferret out the hiding-place of the Rose. Can he trust her?

Schamyl's lip curls in a cynic sneer.

"Can we trust any one in this world?"

Schamyl's visit to Madame Lazareff wrings his heart with the old anxiety. Nina and Tia mourn for their beloved Maritza and refuse to be comforted.

Ahmed dares not trust himself in a long interview with Madame la Générale. His judgment tells him the fall of Kars will be the prelude to the real search for the Rose of Tiflis.

He dares not unfold a whisper of the awful intrigues tying Osman Bey to the willing traitor

Hassan Bey at Kars. The fate of the campaign depends upon that slender line tied in the golden knot of Abdallah's purse-strings.

Comforting the ladies with his belief that Maritza is too powerful a political prize to be grossly maltreated, he slowly regains the palace.

In these warm February days the willows by the Arpa Schai are straggling into green.

A zigzag line of red rifle-pits covers the winding river bank, and a double chain of sentinels prevents a coup de main. Alas! the pearl is stolen!

His Highness the Grand Duke Michael greets Schamyl warmly at the dinner.

When the circle of officers thins out, General Melikoff leads the way to his "bureau de travail."

Schamyl follows the Grand Duke. There is no one present save the factotum Gronoff.

A huge map of the Trans-Caucasus lies unrolled on a table.

Melikoff with care arranges a number of red and black flag-pins over the map.

In low tones the Grand Duke and his general confer.

At the end of half an hour, Gronoff has traced for Schamyl the route of his command upon a campaign map. He retires to prepare the order assigning Prince Schamyl to a moving column of picked troops.

"Prince," the general directs, "you will leave to-morrow with your present command. At each of the marked points in this list you will pick up two more sotnias. Your route will occupy two months. After you have moved through Circassia and Daghestan, you will march, clearing away any uprising, direct to Goomri.

"As you return, picking up the troops laid out on this route for you, you will arrive at Goomri with ten full squadrons. The army will be ready to cross, and I hope to see you lead the advance. It rests with his Highness to reward your services. Don't spare the sword with traitors! You have full power!"

Ahmed bows low in appreciation of the honor. His secret instructions are prepared. In parting the Grand Duke Michael says genially:

"Prince, you are rather young for a general!"

Is it a prophecy? It does not rouse the lover's heart. Beloved Maritza is his only thought.

Before the midnight bell booms from the old cathedral, a fleet courier is on his way to Goomri with a packet for Abdallah.

Schamyl has given old Hassan his scheme to discover the lost Rose of Tiflis. A jealous woman's wit is sharper than a keen-edged sword.

The White Countess may turn the tide in Maritza's fate.

By the light of the morning stars Schamyl sweeps away to the gorges of the Caucasus, to wander over the defiles of Daghestan. He will hunt out, with his merciless riders, the vermin spies crawling in the rear of the great army. It is now ready to spring over the Arpa Tchai, unstained for a score of years with the blood of warring enemies.

CHAPTER IX.

IN THE WOLF'S DEN.—KARS.—THE MESSAGE OF THE ROSE.—AHMED, MY LOVER!

A CAPTIVE woman gazes wistfully from a grated window in Moussa Pacha's superb headquarters at Kars.

Rising out of the bare Armenian plains, like a black ship on a desert shore, Kars bristles rudely, its rocky walls armed to the teeth. It lies under the overhanging citadel, on the Soghanly spur, the last stronghold of the Turks.

A thousand feet below the city, crowded on the western, southern, and eastern slopes of the steep mountain, flows the swift "Kars Tchai." Its deep gorge cleaves in twain this town, which is Persian, Turkish, or Russian, as fate ordains. Kars is the prey of the heaviest sword. Star forts and outworks dot the desert plains around it. Their parapets are piled with shot and shell.

Every engine of war, from the olden Ottoman bronze culverins to Krupp's masterpieces in rifled steel, is at hand to welcome the warlike Russ, whose own lair can be seen thirty miles away.

Princess Maritza's tear-stained eyes note the crowds of armed men, the groaning wains of military stores, the huddle of zaphtiehs, Kurds, deserters, renegades, and Bashibazouks. Solid battalions are embattled everywhere.

Forty thousand fierce Moslems listen daily to the muezzins' wailing cry from the slender minarets. The plains are covered with the growing Turkish host.

It is all so strange, so new, so wild! The proud

girl sees the far blue hills of her native Georgia pencilling the pale-green northern sky. It seems like a horrid dream, these three long weeks, since she was torn from the gardens of the Lazareff palace.

Since she entered the gloomy sally port, on the southern wall, she has been a close prisoner here, her brutal warden the detested Ghazee.

Every day the princely deserter renews his passionate arguments and prayers. She is deaf to all his entreaties. And even *he* dares not use force. He fears noble Mukhtar.

Her mind is fixed on the horrors of those hours when, muffled and bound, she floated down the dangerous Kura, under the very guns of Tiflis. Yet her wild captors, her savage companion (the Kurdish lady), were not unduly rough.

Lonely days in a frail river boat, hiding in the marshes by daylight, floating under the chill winter winds at night, brought to her only a dumb sense of suffering. Across the wintry plains of Anatolia to the valley of the broad Arpa Tchai, and by carriage to Kars, she was hurried with cold sternness, but no positive cruelty.

Omar Effendi but once in this journey showed his tiger claws. Muffled in a Turkish lady's bashlik and veil, she was driven quietly into Kars, with a significant hint as to any outcry.

A drawn dagger terrified her shaken soul.

Alone and a prisoner! She was betrayed by the mocking she-devil Fatima, who only answered her reproaches with the taunt at parting:

"You will be comfortable enough in Prince Ghazee's harem by and by."

Conducted to secluded rooms, where she is waited on by two stolid Turkish women, she fights off the dread thought ever gnawing at her heart:

"I may die here—alone—before I am freed."

For, though the Russian blue and white cross has twice waved from Kars' citadel, Paskiewitch's capture in 1828 was useless; the treaty of Adrianople gave it up again to the Crescent. In 1855 the Russian gained Kars once more, to lose it by the juggling treaty of Paris.

Now, between her loyal friends and her prison door are the bayonets of forty thousand sturdy Moslems in arms. Mukhtar will contest every inch of ground from the boundary line.

Clouds of recruits pour in every day to swell the ranks of Mukhtar's troops.

Her flesh creeps at the memory of Ghazee's slimy advances, as he gloated first over her helplessness. Her arrival inflamed his olden greedy passion. A lonely Rose indeed!

Solemnly has she sworn to him that her death will follow his renewal of a detested suit.

The daughter of the old Greek warrior princes has still the bearing of a goddess, though caged within these sad stone walls. Death before dishonor is written on her bright brow.

In vain Moussa Pacha diplomatically pleads the cause of the wily Ghazee. His voice falls unheeded on her ear.

"When I am again at Tiflis, when you are once more Colonel Kondukoff, I will listen to you; not till then."

The deserter renegade's cheeks redden under her bitter words. The days are wearing away into

March, the war cloud settles into overhanging blackness. Any day the crackling rifles may rain their death hail over the Arpa.

From her iron-barred windows she can see the roofs of the Armenian convents near by, surmounted by the cross. Oh, for one friend! never so humble, still a friend—and true!

The Christian population live in Kars on sufferance. Bereft of her money and jewels, only supplied with Turkish garb for her daily use, with no means of bribery, she is absolutely powerless.

Day after day drifts by. Leaning her pale, proud face against the casement, Maritza dreams of Ahmed, the soldierly brother of the cruel scoundrel who holds her in his net. Is he faithless? Is he— O God! is he dead?

Her abductor has never mentioned Prince Ahmed. Is it state policy? Is it as a hostage for the future, or to serve a mere caprice of the deserter who shines "en Pacha" now, that she is confined in these lonely mansion rooms with her watchful women attendants?

Ghazee Schamyl Pacha's daily visit brings her a fear of the worst of fates. The spring flowers are peeping out now on the slopes of the Kara Dagh.

Ghazee at last shows his true colors. He will plead no more. "Princess," he roughly says, "I have pointed out to you the advantages of a union of our houses. This holy war will wrap the Caucasus in fire and flame. Within a fortnight I shall go forth to the field with my troops to cut my way to Tiflis. Ismail Pacha, from Erzeroum, will invade Circassia with fifty thousand men. The Sultan will erect Georgia, Abkhasia, Circassia, and Daghestan into a vice-royalty. I ask you to share that throne with me. England is with us. We must succeed."

Maritza de Deshkalin's first answer is a contemptuous glance which cuts the renegade. She slowly says: "I swear to you, by my mother's grave, I will kill myself before I will be your bride! Wear your stolen crown alone."

"Ah, you will have time to think better of that! I will send you to the farthest castle in Kurdestan, and there give you time to think it over, while we bait the wolves with the Russian dogs." Schamyl Pacha's anger rises. "One week I give you now. Before then you will know how to answer me."

Maritza is mute. Unknown future horrors haunt her.

As Ghazee mounts his horse to ride to his brigade camp, he jostles a camel-driver at Moussa's door. Full on the back of the poor peasant falls Schamyl's koorbash, cutting to the quick. The howling man darts into the courtyard of the house.

Shaven and blackened, a coarse brown skull-cap on his head, a dirty caftan fluttering around his bare legs, his feet shod with rawhide sandals, only a wand in his hand—Hassan, the old borderer, howls under the lash of Ghazee. His old master rode him down without knowing him. A compliment to his disguise! A sore one!

Hassan is no more the gorgeous legatee of departed Kurds. Though his back smarts (the blood streaming freely from the sweep of the rhinoceros riding whip), there is a wild gleam of triumph in his glittering eyes.

His sworn revenge can *wait*. His triumph is near.

For, day by day, he has dogged Ghazee over Kars. In every visit within the town the watchful eyes of Hassan follow the proud pacha.

Sneaking at night into Hassan Bey's courtyard, the old Circassian, in the darkness of night, whispers to the staff officer his daily report.

With all Abdallah's gold, with Hassan Bey's complete knowledge of the town, no news of lost Maritza has yet reached the anxious Abdallah at Goomri. Even when the houses are listed, and the Christians are turned out to make room for troops, no trace of the hiding-place of the Rose of Tiflis is found.

Hassan conceals in his girdle the little strip of parchment with Prince Schamyl's greeting to his love.

Hassan has searched every bazaar and coffee-house. Not a whisper of the vanished Rose.

Hassan Bey, eager to hold Abdallah's favor, daily watches Moussa and Ghazee. No trace of the dark-eyed "day-star."

But now the Circassian has at last a clue. Several times a week he has followed Ghazee to Moussa's quarters. Long the pacha's charger stands in the court, and Moussa is not there. To wander over the silent mansion of Moussa is an impossibility for any humble servitor. What can he do? The day-star must be hidden there!

Leaning against the walls, jostled by the waiting crowd of attendants, a grim smile flickers over Hassan's face. He has a desperate plan.

He is a Turk of the Turks in his knowledge of customs. But one sacred sufferer cannot be turned from the Moslem door. Where even a holy pilgrim may not claim hospitality, the unfortunate fool may enter at will. God's wanderer, bereft of his senses, cannot be roughly treated under the crescent flag. He is free and guarded by the prophet's blessing.

Haste! haste! Hassan the camel-driver! In two hours a gaunt form wanders down the street, where Maritza hopelessly peers from the diamond-screened lattice of her prison.

Hanging jaw and rolling eye proclaim the sacred sufferer whom Allah has chastened.

Roaming at will, even the Pacha of Kars dare not maltreat this child of misery. Mixing with the scullions of the Turkish kitchen, he signs for a cup of water. It is offered in Mohammed's sacred name. Up the stairways, unopposed, the idiot wanders. There are no lattices on the rear of the mansion overlooking the dark river in its dismal gorge below. The side walls are blank. She must be on the front corridor. Fearlessly he wanders along.

Two rows of arabesque windows overlook the noisy street with its throng of passing soldiery.

Unnoticed by the guards, the sacred fool may pace to or fro. It is the black curse of Eblis to drive him from any Moslem's door.

One room after another does the fool wander through, his broken voice jibbering words from the Koran.

In the corridors he passes the loitering, dull-eyed women of the house. They pass in bated breath, for the awful spell of Allah's words is on them.

A heavy curtain swings before each door; with

a skinny hand, Hassan pushes aside the last one of the row.

Seated on the window bench, friendless and sorrowing, Princess Maritza turns her head.

Startled yet not dismayed—for Tiflis has also its wandering mollahs, its semi-frantic dervishes—she regards the intruder. He eyes her closely.

It is indeed the lost Lady of Tiflis—the Princess of Georgia! At the distant door, with timidity the attendants watch the progress of God's wandering visitor. He can do no harm.

As he approaches, Hassan murmurs a word or two of her native tongue. Maritza's cheek grows very pale. Seating himself on the floor, he intones a wild harangue of Turkish. In a low voice he whispers quickly the messages of Ahmed Schamyl.

Princess Maritza is herself once more. Hassan tears his gown. He rocks to and fro. He plays with pebbles and some bits of colored glass.

Dropping at her feet the little slip of parchment from his girdle, he raises his strained voice in a chant of Moslem praise.

Her flaming eyes are on him. The listless attendants wander in the corridors.

There is a gleam of joy on Maritza's face. In a few moments, she knows that the traitor Hassan Bey is a friend to the Russians. Abdallah's agency and Schamyl's wishes make her heart bound.

"Be calm and quiet, oh day-star!" Hassan interjects, in his praying. "I will be under your window, and can warn you in our *own* language. I go now to Hassan Bey. He will contrive the way to get you out of here. I watch over you night and day now."

Wildly swinging his arms, Hassan arises and paces slowly from the room. There is foam on his lips. Down the corridors, past the armed sabre-bearing eunuchs at the door, the poor fool wanders. He is soon lost in the wild throng outside. He bears a token.

Maritza can send no message; no word will she yet trust, save to give the messenger a red rose. The flowers are blooming now in the garden of the palace enclosure.

"To Ahmed, my lover, this rose," she whispers as the messenger departs with a little paper.

Hassan Bey sits pondering over the war telegrams in his headquarter room. A dark form stands in the doorway. The Circassian wanders past him into an inner room.

There is triumph in the eyes of the old spy. He tells his story. Keen-witted and subtle, Hassan Bey's plan is soon made. He has now found the bower whence Countess Nadya Vronsky watches uneasily Ghazee's movements now by day and night. Abdallah's letters give him her full history.

"Do you know this pale-faced puppet?" he questions of the old sergeant.

Well does the Circassian remember the élégante. The fair Countess Vronsky dashing along the Nevsky in her sleigh, or rolling through the leafy drives on the island, drew all eyes.

In his former attendance on Ghazee, he has learned to know the face of the lady whose wiles embroiled many a " preux chevalier " by the Neva.

"You await me here. I will see her. I propose to have her help the princess out of that wolf's den.

"You can watch, in your disguise, to-morrow morning until she arrives. I will have Prince Ghazee sent out on a reconnoissance for three days. The moment we can get Princess Maritza out, I will be at hand with a covered wagon. The great Armenian convent is the place for her. There are fifty nuns there. I will have a guard of my men on duty in a by street. When Ghazee returns, all traces of her will be lost."

Two hours later Ghazee Schamyl clatters out of the sally port, surrounded by a hundred Circassian deserters. Three or four renegade officers ride at his side. A sudden order sends him to inspect all the outposts. With a hurried good-by to Nadya Vronsky the burly, red-faced pacha sets his steed in motion for a whirling dash through the circling picket camps, fifty miles in extent.

Hassan Bey's potent touch sways Mukhtar's daily orders. A gallant chief! a faithless confidant!

Daintily down the main street of Kars, Hassan Bey, the citadel commander, curvets on his splendid gray Arab. European polish lightens his manners. He has mingled in the gilded circles of the Continent.

His jaunty uniform blazes with embroidery; his red fez surmounts a face of inscrutable repose.

As he throws the reins to an orderly, the obsequious attendants of the Hotel de Bêyrout announce his visit to Madame la Comtesse Vronsky.

A graceful Turkish costume becomes the lovely countess, whose fair complexion and light hair betray her masquerade.

Hassan Bey, with easy politeness, explains his object in calling.

"I have received letters concerning you, madame, of a private nature, from my friend Mustapha Bey, the chargé d'affaires at St. Petersburg. You know him?"

Nadya Vronsky's pale face is a shade paler. She inclines her fair head.

"I wished to speak with you on his behalf. I premise that this conversation must not be imparted to Schamyl Pacha."

"Why so?" the lady coldly asks.

"Because," Hassan answers, in his fluent French, "it would be very dangerous for you."

"Ah! you threaten—a woman!" her voice rings with a cutting sneer.

"Not so, madame! I only *warn*," quietly answers Hassan. "Pray pardon my directness. You have been a private Turkish agent at St. Petersburg. *I* am in charge of the secret service here. Several of the ablest representatives of this service have disappeared from time to time." There is an ominous hush.

Nadya Vronsky trembles at heart. She is no longer in the pale of even semi-civilization. In savage Kars, Mukhtar Pacha reigns as absolute dictator. Hassan Bey is his factotum.

"What do you wish of me?" she murmurs.

"Only this: Schamyl Pacha is deceiving you. He hides a sweet divinity whom he worships in the palace of Moussa Pacha. He has lied to you. He loves you not. He stole this woman, Princess Maritza, away from Tiflis, and now means to marry her.

"He is ambitious. He would sacrifice you to his

greed for power. For he would gain a crown through her."

Hassan Bey touches the right chord at last. Ahmed Schamyl's letter to Abdallah gives Hassan Bey the keynote of her stormy nature—an insane jealousy!

She is aroused. Her blue eyes blaze.

Hassan calmly continues. He assumes her perfect acquiescence. For the citadel commander is all powerful.

"Listen! I have sent Schamyl Pacha off on a three days' tour. To-morrow, at nine o'clock, you will go to Moussa Pacha's house. Take with you a couple of your attendant women. Let one of them put on two shawls and veils. I will ride into the courtyard of the house as you approach. I wish you to bring the Princess Maritza out of the house in the disguise of one of your servants. She will be warned.

"At the door of the mansion she will disappear. I pledge you that Schamyl will never see her again. I will be near you."

"I demand an explanation of this. I will not take these risks blindly," Nadya answers. Her nerve returns. What is his real object?

"Bah, madame! You are finical. No one will know who you are when veiled. *I* will protect you. Ghazee and Moussa are *both* Russian renegades. They are powerless here; we *use* and *despise* them.

"*You* are the last one he will suspect of knowing his dove's retreat." Hassan's sneer is coldly premeditated. She has fallen low enough—a betrayed mistress!

"And my reward?" she doubtfully asks.

"The confidence and protection of Mustapha Bey when Schamyl Pacha casts you off. He has a heart of stone."

"I will be there!" cries Countess Vronsky.

"Good!" exclaims Hassan. "I will extend to you every favor in the stormy days to come. Kars will be no paradise in this coming siege."

With morning's glimmering dawn Princess Maritza is at her window. When the attendants bring her food, she forces herself to eat. A wild excitement burns in her veins. The sun mounts in the east; its golden lances break on the crags of the Kara Dagh.

Hark! Beneath her window now rises the shrill sound of Moslem song—a wandering mollah.

Yes—beneath her casement the wild singer throws aloft his lean arms in prayer. It is her savior Hassan.

His eyes are fixed steadily upon her windows. When the street is silent a few words reach her.

Her heart beats wildly. The hour is at hand. In a half-hour her curtain is swung aside.

A veiled woman enters who speaks in Russian. Two Turkish maids follow her.

"Quick! Not a moment lost now. Wrap yourself and follow me."

The visitor throws her a shawl and heavy veil.

Maritza's knees give way.

"Courage, fool! I risk my life for you."

With a sweep of her own veil she shows the face of Nadya Vronsky. Maritza saw it last in Petersburg.

Bewildered, Maritza dons the heavy mantle, and twists the veil over her head. The maids linger in the room. Her form is swathed from head to foot. Now, for liberty and to Ahmed!"

Down the corridors, among the waiting suitors and idle officers who throng the crowded courtyard, the veiled lady passes, her servants straggling well behind. Moussa Pacha is away. No one regards *women* around the harem!

Princess Maritzka stands now in the street. Her heart beats wildly. By her side the mollah moves up closely. A covered wagon receives the vanishing form of her conductress. The servants separate and are lost in the throng. Down toward the narrow street on the river bank the insane dervish leads. A few steps bring her to the corner. In a curtained chariot she is quickly concealed. An officer and some troops block the street behind them. It is Hassan Bey!

"Drive on!" he yells, in Turkish.

By her side old Hassan sits, his eyes dancing with joy. He tells her of her destination.

The wagon rolls into the courtyard of the gloomy old Armenian convent.

Hassan springs out. A side door opens in the area.

The frightened girl is safe under the cross. It is a small room, where before a huge ebony and ivory crucifix a candle feebly burns.

The rumble of wheels tells of the departing chariot. Hassan stands by the door; a heavy dagger is gleaming in his hands. He is a crouching tiger.

As a door from the interior opens, a grave, bearded priest heavily treads over the stone-tiled floor.

"Hasten, my daughter; there is no time to

lose!" By his side is Hassan Bey, the citadel commandant.

A few words in French adjure her to implicitly obey the old priest. She knows now Abdallah's sly agent.

"I will send this old man daily to you, or the prior, to communicate. Thank me not, lady. I am acting for your friends at Tiflis. Keep my secret with your life. Both our heads are in danger!"

Hassan, the Circassian, whispers: "I will come to-morrow." He disappears by the court.

The Turkish staff officer is gone. With a kindly voice the bearded priest bids her follow him.

An hour later the splendid richness of Princess Maritza's hair is given up to the nun's shears.

A sombre religious robe and veil disguise her.

She is no longer the Rose of Tiflis.

"Sister Agatha" is the handsomest neophyte in the old nunnery. But even the nun's mantle cannot dull the richness of her eyes.

A quiet rest steals over her, for a spacious and well-furnished cell hides the once laughing Petersburg beauty from her baffled captor. The Armenian convent walls are inviolable, even in Turkey.

While Maritza dreams in peace of a princely, dark-eyed rider, pressing to his lips her ruby ring, her slumbers are only broken by the boom of the convent bell. But Nadya Vroñsky tosses upon sleepless pillows. Her master will return!

The awful wrath of Ghazee may crush her! His treachery proves to her that lips of love can lie in passion's wildest kisses! Ingrate!

Haughty Ghazee Pacha, galloping up the valley

from the Arpa-Tchai a day later, passes a humble donkey driver, belaboring a jaded animal.

No human eye can discern the deadly import to the proud city of the crescent of the papers hidden in the cushion's linings of the rude saddle.

The peasant wanders along to Goomri unchallenged. Poverty is his safeguard! The best!

Abdallah, seated in his den at Goomri, waits for the words penned by Maritza for the absent man, on whose finger flashes her ruby ring. Hassan bears a letter every word dear as a diamond to Schamyl.

Gloomy and lowering is the brow of Moussa Pacha, when he listens to Ghazee's frantic ravings. He bastinadoes his louts of domestics uselessly. The Rose has vanished in mystery.

Moussa was away on duty himself. The two serving-women are gone, none know whither. They did well to flee the vengeance of the murderous Ghazee.

Attracted by some fellow-servant's jabber—they had only returned to find Maritza's rooms empty.

Every guardsman, each swart eunuch, swears that no one passed the portals! The two refugees dare not openly complain. There is danger in their situation.

Fear of the mighty Mukhtar ties Ghazee's tongue. For the great Moslem general is a loyal soldier! Should he discover the princess in Kars, she would be openly held as a political prisoner of rank. Ghazee would then lose her forever.

Ghazee vainly sends his trusted renegade officers by day and night searching over the town. There is not a trace of the proud beauty—no sign of her bewitching loveliness.

If the earth had opened for her, the mystery were no greater. She is lost among a hundred thousand.

Countess Vronsky eyes askance the lowering brow of her careless lover. As each night settles down on Kars, its chill darkness seems to drag her down toward the chasm of the rushing Kars Tchai. An impending doom appals her. But Ghazee is only gloomily silent. He suspects nothing!

The days drag on wearily. Maritza, in seclusion, hugs to her heart the joyous news that her letters to her lover have safely reached Abdallah.

Faithful Hassan (once more the ragged camel-driver) haunts the courtyard of the monastery and convent.

A dozen times over he tells the glowing girl the stirring history of Ahmed's battle with the Kurds. Her pulse bounds with pride. She can wait with a patient heart. Her lover is a hero.

Hassan Bey comes not. An awful punishment hangs over his slightest misstep. He would die in the torments of the damned! His messages to Maritza are borne by the disguised Circassian.

On her knees, before the image of the dear Christ who died for us all, Maritza prays nightly for her champion.

A message from Abdallah tells her Ahmed Schamyl is now threading the wild defiles of Daghestan. It is Abdallah's sage advice to conceal her hiding-place even from the Russians until the army reaches Kars. For *then* the sword will set her free.

Free she is from the traitor—unless some fatal accident arrives.

Hassan cheers her daily with his presence. He

will stay to the last. Watching over her, he can slip out with Hassan Bey's help, and guide the rescuers to her place of refuge. The prior concurs in the evident wisdom of this. The sanctity of the convent is assured by treaty with the powers.

Before the first cannon's roar wakes the echoes on the Arpa Tchai, Princess Maritza prays daily for the success of the Russian arms. It is her salvation—that fluttering blue and white cross.

Far up in the awful chasms of the Caucasus, creeping below basalt cliffs, threading gloomy forests, scaling nature's battlements, Ahmed Schamyl sweeps along at the head of his warlike column. He has gazed once more upon lofty Gunib—eight thousand feet in air—his own mysterious birthplace.

His charger paws the earth where once the embattled Russian army received his father's last surrender. Aul Gunib is vacant now; only a few old crones linger there.

Far above on the cliff stands the "eagle's nest," within whose walls the smile of that lovely, dreamy vision of childhood—his mother—shone upon him in the years gone by. A nameless angel! The lovely valleys and dells are all silent. The frightened villagers avoid his troops. Silent women, shy children alone meet him. The men are buried in the forest to avoid conscription. They war only of their free will.

Onward to the great keep of Himri, where Sultan Schamyl lay for dead after its terrific storming by Grabbe, he sweeps through the budding glories of spring. Ball and blade could never kill charmed Schamyl.

Here " Khasi Mollah " died, whose mystic lore was his father's awful legacy. By a charm of the Kabala, Schamyl of the " shining veil," at this place, escaped again the red death. So swear the old survivors with bated breath.

A heap of gray ruins meets his eyes when the coursers measure four days' farther march. Here Sultan Schamyl—priest, magician, leader, general, and bravo—was the only one who left the burning tower alive. Hamsad Bey died there, under the vendetta of the Tcherkess. Schamyl took his honors.

Far and wide, Ahmed sweeps over the romantic land, where forty thousand horsemen once owned the sway of that great arch-rebel. The chief of thirty years' war, whose name he bears, has made these glades historic.

Prince Ahmed gathers in his train a few malcontents. He finds the hill-dwellers in trembling fear of that keen sword of war which smites both ways.

Yet no welcome waits his path. None of the children of the thousands who died for his royal father throng in to welcome the young prince of the land.

Is it the subtle influence of the Kurdish Free Masons, who date their mysteries back to ages before the days when the Assyrian scrolls were moulded?

Is it the Kurdish hatred of the Russian, or the illicit trade in the beautiful children of Circassia and Georgia, which holds the people away?

No; the Kurds are in both Russian and Turkish

pay. It is not local sympathy; for in 1864 all the Moslem Tcherkess crossed, the lines to Turkey, when the Russian flag was nailed to the mast. Over Circassia, in final conquest, the Christian faith triumphed.

Maps of Europe change; heroes live their brief day; but Russia never loses an inch of blood-bought ground. There is a strange silence, a cold unrest, in the lofty mountain homes of the only race on God's footstool to whom courage and beauty are a never-failing heritage.

Here, an Emperor of Russia vainly sued to gain the affections of these " dwellers of the mist," after a hereditary war of two hundred years had brought them to bay, but never to their knees.

The cherry blossoms hang over the path as Ahmed Schamyl rides in the land of his birth over his great father's fields. March gives way to fragrant April.

Long before Byzantium gave its name to new Rome, centuries before Istambôl changed the cross for the crescent, freedom reigned here on these sculptured mountain heights. God's own sunlight and the sacred Persian fires light yet the crests of the awful Circassian peaks. The barriers held by these peerless swords against " Timour " were only broken by the gallant, patient " children of the Czar "—the soldiers of destiny. The Man of Austerlitz foresaw the sweep of the men who humbly kneel before their white-robed priest when the battle opens. They sing the regimental hymns, proudly marching along to die for holy Russia. Devotees and docile heroes!

Only England sleeps, while the world is waking to the onward stride of all-conquering Russia.

Tiletti's towers rise before Prince Ahmed. There the Sultan escaped General Fesi by an artifice still staining the great Schamyl's honor. He surrendered and broke his oath, taking the field again. He had a "revelation" which justified his duplicity!

Over the field, where the bones of Count Ivilitsch's doomed regiments fell under the keen Tcherkess sword, and on to great Akhmulgo, the column wearily plods. There, on the heights above a new Mokanna, Sultan Schamyl's "silver veil" glittered on a servant's brow. The poor slave died a martyr; while the crafty old leader himself fled down the river in a boat, leaving hecatombs of dead. The victims of the Russian assault mutely attested his third great "miracle." His splendid court life of five years made Akhmulgo a dazzling palace. The bats flit through the crumbling windows now. Prince Ahmed asks not to see the gloomy keep wherein old Schamyl's own mother died, under his hand, by the lash. This mystic fraud, the awful barbarity, the foul ingratitude chills the bones of the son of the chief of the "Sûnis." Nature abhors the human monster who emulated Nero; yet Christian England and France sent money, swords of honor, and munitions of war to this man. His own aged mother died under his rhinoceros lash, as a martyr to Moslem superstition.

Dargo, with its gloomy history of a three years' siege, rises before him. General Grabbe, after the terrific battle in the dark, tangled woods there, returned to the Neva to answer the question of a Czar, borrowed from a Roman emperor's anguish, "Where are my legions?" And yet, stern Woronzoff finally drove Schamyl from these heights, under the pelting butchery of a desperate assault.

Over the broad plains of the "Kabardas" (where the countless Tcherkess horse once swept in pride, led by the Silver Veil), Ahmed Schamyl leads his watchful men to the river ford. Here two great armies witnessed the delivery of his brother "Jamal-Eddin" to the sultan after a long captivity. It was here the gentle Russian princesses were restored after seven years in Schamyl's cruel hands.

In all this weary round—in the marches in cold and mist, in the midnight darkness, at the dawn—a kindly pair of woman's eyes, "weary yet tender," beam on the young prince.

He hears in the sigh of the winds the one loving refrain, "Ahmed, my son!"

It is his fairy mother who speaks to him.

The slender wand of memory is broken. Yet around the cradle of his infancy that gracious presence lingers to hallow and to bless.

If "life is but a progress from the breast of one fond woman to that of another," Ahmed Schamyl claims a divided duty. Yet his mother's memory is only a gracious shade—a fleeting charm, like colors of the dying day.

On past the castellated gorges of the mountain ranges, out of the land where the religious exaltation of "Ben Mohammed Schamyl" still appals the simple warriors—far from Dargo's stately palaces (now in ruins, or tenanted by the meaner herd), Ahmed journeys. His horses' heads are turned toward the battle lines.

Shy girls in white mantles and silver-embroidered gowns, their dark tresses bound with silver lace, gaze kindly on the youthful leader. The heavy fruit trees fill the mountain roads with fragrant blossoms. It is the time of the singing bird. The painted pheasants mate in the forest shade.

In little villages deputations headed by the aged welcome the Czar's chosen officer.

On still, past Tarku, where the Russian legions died, over the nameless graves of thousands of forgotten soldiers, Schamyl speeds to the dark tryst of the Arpa-Tchai.

At "Amir-Hadje Yar" he views the old hall where a single Tcherkess killed three Russian generals before he was hacked to pieces by the guard. The mountain lion dies hard.

Camping at night, Ahmed wanders alone among the mysterious children of the Tcherkess—the land of free and merry girls, who proudly ride on their lovers' cruppers; the land where a woman's face shines openly on all until her marriage; the land where the bridal veil covers the wife forever; where the husband steals as a lover in the shades of night to his consort.

By day the man is busied with hospitality, with wise discourse, with war, or the songs of war. It is only the evening star which brings him homeward. A land of the sword and spear, of the chase and mighty woodcraft—Circassia!

Jealousy guards with a keen sword these mountain thresholds. Revenge, the vendetta, and kismet are the awful trinity of Circassian honor.

Blood is here atoned by blood alone, or a solemn tribal settlement. The sense of personal honor is fiercely fantastic. Here the young humbly respect and fear the old; here the wife crouches under the awful frown of her liege lord.

Purchased brides meet their lords, with open hearts. The forlorn widow is given away to some member of the clan who will shelter her. Alas for the widows!

Here, in Circassia, where the groom rips the bridal corsage with a sharp dagger, where the play of war heightens the festivity of the wedding day, among these olive-faced, dark-eyed, Grecian beauties, Schamyl dreams always of the starry-eyed one who pines for him behind the black walls of Kars!

The pretty Tcherkess lasses, in scarlet bonnets and floating braids, with gay jackets laced with silver, natty skirts and broad girdles, smile on him in vain.

Dainty hands with slender wrists wave unheeded their salutations to the lord of the Tcherkess. He heeds not the quaintly dyed finger-nails, the wonderful lace mittens of gossamer.

Schamyl rides the lanes unmoved. In vain the wild game spring up under his charger's feet. He goes to the chase of men. Village maid and blooming matron tempt not his eye. He is a faithful and pining lover.

He seems to see before him the presence of his great father—a white-haired chieftain, superbly mounted, in silk vestments and silver-steel chain mail. His gray eyes are shining under a golden helmet. At his side the priceless sabre of Omar swings. Pistols and the death-dealing rifle, his jewelled belt-dagger, and the shining white mantle, lend their aid to his martial presence. A god among men!

Beneath the princely rider, the fleetest steed of the Caucasus bears the blue velvet saddle, richly crested with its jewels and silver trappings. The black enamel of the Caucasus hides the glitter of the metals. The shade of Sultan Schamyl beckons his son to the red field of honor.

In all these visions, in the proud mystic stories of his race, Prince Ahmed (dreaming on his horse's neck) soon forgets his majestic warrior father, his princely brother who died as the son of a king, and thinks only of Maritza's tender dark eyes. Over his slumbers hovers the sweet womanly face, which, even here, beneath the singing pines—after long years have chilled her gentle heart—whispers, in the one unselfish love of life, "Ahmed, my son!"

Down, like an eagle in his fall, swings the impatient lover to the valley of the Arpa-Tchai. Past villages where stately men, in Persian caftans of bright hue, sit among their many fair wives; through the land where Persian, Russian, Arabic, Armenian, and Turkish voices mingle; past the tender-budded groves, where the returning birds sing in the cold, pale moonlight—Schamyl marches, his outpost duty done.

In another month this land will be a very paradise. But his sabre will flash in the sunlight of the Euphrates. Mountains of marble and alabaster, dim reaches of witching woodland, lovely meadows where the roses bud, stay him not. The veiled women sigh over his princely bearing. He gallops (hounded on by love, in its delicious torment) to the black plains of the Araxes, where the singing bugle calls thousands now to their death. Steadily threading the river, across which he can see the Kurdish camels playing around the conical skin tents of these men of blood, he rides in at the head of two thousand men, to hear Melikoff send the first shotted defiance of the Czar across the still waters.

BOOK III.

WINNING THE ROSE.

CHAPTER X.

THE CANNONS SPEAK.—HASSAN BEY'S MESSAGE.—MOUSSA'S BATTLE IN THE NIGHT.—FACE TO FACE.—TURNS OF THE TIDE.—THE MEDJIDIEH REDOUBT.

OUT of the gloomy forests, where from their high stockaded forts the Russians, goaded to madness, sallied on their wild foemen, the column swings past the Golgotha where Grabbe's thousands died under the dashing attacks of the Tcherkess horse. Away, far away from the rocky gorges, where the terrible war-cry of the children of Schamyl broke on the silent night, Ahmed leads his troopers to the black, stony plains of the Arpa-Tchai.

The cannon thundering loud as he nears Goomri bring his men to a gallop. The guns of the fortress are covering the crossing. His thirty poor captured conspirators, under guard, are left to the mercies of the Provost of Goomri. He draws his men into line. The great army is on the march.

The forces are crossing the Arpa-Tchai, for it is the 24th of April. War is declared!

As Schamyl leads his fierce riders up to the terreplein of the fortress, he meets Gronow in field attire. His own express rider preceded him by three hours.

"I am directed, General, to lead your men across and place you in the advance," Gronow cries.

There is a pontoon bridge over the Arpa-Tchai. Before Schamyl can collect his thoughts he is on the Turkish side. It is now a war, "à l'outrance," between the men who built the Ottoman Empire of the Dardanelles on the crumbling ruins of broken thrones, and the Czar's troops. Persian, Roman, Greek, Hun, the Slav, the Arabs under the great golden sceptre of Haroun al Raschid, give way to the dogged Moslems, who fight to-day the Russ of the North!

For two hundred years of the first thousand of the Christian era the Russians sought the city vainly, battling four times in siege for Constantinople.

The race of Alexis Comnenus, with their brief glory, gave way, after two hundred years of storm, to Michael Palæologus and his heirs.

In the fifteenth century the patter of the feet of Turkish horse sounded first outside the sacred walls. Amurath's weak assault was followed up by fiery Mahomet, who grasped the Golden City in 1453.

Unchallenged queen of the world in the fourteenth and fifteenth centuries, the Russians and English *together* assaulted it unsuccessfully in 1770. How fickle the faith of allied princes! In 1807

Admiral Duckworth led the English fleet to useless slaughter under the seraglio batteries *alone*. Now the Russian fights his old ally England in Asia *under cover*.

As Ahmed rides out, spreading his light cavaliers before the embattled hosts of the Czar on this bright April day, he grimly smiles to think that nothing will keep the children of the great Peter, the heirs of the mighty Catherine, out of the Golden Horn. A shadow falls on his mind!

His sabre drops loosely in its strap, for he remembers, with a thrill, the crash of the casements when he stood with wily Ignatief where the English boat swung, a gloomy black mass on the waters, that starlit night in the Golden Horn.

England fights for the Turk now!

"Defender of the Faith!" Which faith? O wearer of the crown of the Empire of the Seas! Cross or Crescent? No! The faith of the English is the faith in the sanctity of—the *British pocket*.

Schamyl watches his swift skirmishers press to the front in the beautiful work of the Russian cavalry. He turns to Gronow.

"You have news for me?"

"Yes, General," his old friend says, with an evident respect. Schamyl's heart is with Maritza. He hears not the salutation "General." Beyond his front, in the advance, lie closed columns of solid white-capped regiments, squadrons of heavy dragoons, and parked siege batteries, with an unending black mass of baggage trains.

Light batteries whirl by, going into action with lightning speed.

Gronow hands him several letters and despatches. On the broad plain before them, for they have now covered the slower movement of the heavy troops, a dropping fire shows that the sons of the Sultan are "en presence."

Schamyl gathers his charger. "To the front!" Gronow rides across his path.

"Pardon me! Prince, you are a *general* now. You cannot charge with your own skirmish line, like a trooper."

Schamyl's eyes seek his in wonder. Gronow points to the letters.

Calling to a captain, who gallops to the front, Gronow resolutely detains the prince.

Ahmed opens the first document. It recites his appointment as brigadier-general of cavalry. His tall form rises proudly in the saddle. A general, and a wearer of the white cross!

The cracking rifles of his troops salute the Grand Duke's youngest general.

The next letter he opens is from Abdallah. It is only a simple slip of paper, with a single withered red rose. The simple words are traced there:

"Ahmed, my lover!"

His eyes are dim. The soldier-lover's heart bounds with joy.

In a few moments the scrawling characters of Abdallah himself are deciphered. Schamyl knows now that his love waits for him behind the walls of Kars. She is there in the blue horizon to the southwest —and thither rolls the tide of war.

Thrusting the papers in his tunic, the young general hoarsely whispers:

"Forward! For Maritza's sake! On!"

He gives the fretting black the rein. He rides along his line under the cheers of the troops, who have caught the welcome news.

In an hour Gronow and Schamyl are seated under a plane tree. The light troops have swept far off, clearing a zone to the front. Schamyl's eyes are proudly fixed on the flashing sabres of his brigade. It is a knightly command.

Ten more sotnias give him the full present of his imperial master—a peerless command of his own wild liegemen.

Now he knows that the right column of the army has thrown itself toward Ardaban; that the dashing Tergukassoff from Erivan is marching with tiger tread on Bayazid. Along the Danube, two hundred thousand Russians press over the swamps toward the yet undefiled trenches of Plevna.

For Ignatief and Orloff, Gortschakoff and Schowaloff, have laid down the pen. The sword alone rules now. From Kirscheneff the veteran Czar Alexander, with Ignatief and Dolgourouki, hastens toward the Danube with a glittering personal train of four hundred cavaliers of the household.

The protocol was uselessly agreed to by the powers.

The Turk has resolutely refused the pressure of the powers, and will not sign. War to the knife! It is now Russia against the Turk.

The first rifle shot, with its puff of feathery smoke, blew away the relics of "protocol" and "conference," of "negotiation" and "wise discussion."

For the grass is waving now, the roads are firm,

the skies are balmy, and the harvest of blood is ready for the sabre sickle.

But one brief week ago Count Ignatief joined his imperial master at Kircheneff. The English falter and stand mute, while the Russian legions pour into the open gateways of the East.

Poor Burnaby threw himself desperately, in later years, on the Abyssinian spears. He died in vain for England's might; his warning voice was unheard.

Schamyl knows that if the cabinet of St. Petersburg sees the Russian eagles on Batoum and Kars, on Ardaban and Bayazid, there it will stay, blood hallowed in victory forever.

For Constantinople the Czar can wait. The future has its mysteries.

But the swinging car of Destiny rolls thither apace.

Schamyl, seated with Gronow, inspects the cowering prisoners brought in by his line.

He learns from them that the cavalry of Moussa and Ghazee Schamyl are in his front.

Leaving Gronow to his merry chat with the victorious officers, Prince Schamyl walks aside in the shadows of the night. The army has safely crossed.

Maritza's eyes shine on his shadowed heart.

The Czar's hosts battle for a new kingdom, on the old roads where Xenophon marched his unflinching Greeks back to the blue and beloved sea. From these storied waters the white-limbed Venus rose to hold all men in thrall. Schamyl fights for honor, his only prize, and the hand of the defenceless girl who is praying for him now behind those rocky parapets under the frowning Kara Dagh.

The empress of his soul! The dark-eyed beauty, whose withered rose rests upon his throbbing heart. It is a summons and a talisman.

He joins the dashing staff officer Gronow, who hailed him first as "General." By his side a horseman is dismounting. In the flickering light of the camp-fire, he recognizes gallant Tarnaieff.

The "dragoman" has given way now to the hardy "soldier," who exclaims joyfully:

"Prince! We will ride into Kars together!"

The wailing bugle sends the forward lines to the silence of rest. Only the watchful pickets and silent videttes strain their nerves to catch the mysterious voices of the night. Before Schamyl's limbs are relaxed from the ride of this eventful day, the reveillé is sounding.

A messenger is at his side on the line of the bivouac. He has grasped a treasure richer than gold and gems.

It is a letter from Maritza, who hears now from her convent refuge the dull boom of the cannon at the ford.

Hassan, the servitor, greets his lord, and waits to show him a *secret* way to scale the beetling heights of the Kara Dagh. For his argus eyes are everywhere.

No foot of the thirty miles toward Kars but trebles itself under the princely lover's impatience. Shall he ever see her beloved face again?

His renegade brother in his front! Schamyl's brow grows stern. Alas! Even with the goddess of victory smiling, it will be long months before Kars can be reduced. Mighty Paskiewitch spent a year in 1828 and 1829 to carry the double eagle in victory over the road now open to his horse.

And Mukhtar Pacha is a lion in the path, with fifty thousand armed men. Kars bristles with heavy guns.

Ahmed Schamyl's heart is filled with one holy purpose. Ghazee is in his front. To search the field and scatter his renegades, to save the innocent girl he dragged from her home—this is the heritage of the last bitter two months of agony.

When Sultan Schamyl blazed in glory at Dargo, holding royal state, three wives reigned over the palaces, before whose crested slopes twenty thousand Russian corpses lay in the three years' siege. By the dark mystery of his birth, Ghazee seems to have been his foe from the moment of his father's death. They never were brothers of the heart.

An undying bitterness, a hatred born of fanaticism, the scorn of a Moslem for the accursed Giaour, has been Ghazee's only brotherhood. Is it the succession to the shadowy coronet of the warrior prince which galls him?

Riding out to a knoll where a headquarters ensign marks the commander-in-chief's marquee, Schamyl receives his orders from General Dutrovskoi. He is the chief of staff of the princely commander Loris Melikoff.

The Grand Duke Nicholas, at Tiflis, holds the nominal command, surrounded by every enjoyment. But the iron truncheon of battle is wielded by Loris Melikoff, his keen eye fixed on his own rising star.

"Prince Schamyl, your brigade will be held for special service, as the reserve of the main advance.

Your task will be, especially, to watch and counteract the movements of Moussa's Kurds and renegade Circassians. They all know the ground. We rely on you, General, to cut them up.

"I am instructed by his Highness the Grand Duke Nicholas to say that your new rank is a reward for your splendid fight on the Arpa, and your successful guarding of our left flank and rear in your long scout. By the way, General, I suggest that the uniform of your grade will become you."

Escaping from a storm of congratulations, Schamyl gallops off to his own troops.

Gronow's thoughtfulness has provided him with his campaign baggage.

Surrounded by the officers of his hastily chosen staff, Prince Ahmed sadly misses the ubiquitous old Hassan, for that veteran servitor is a master of the arts of making camp comfortable.

The days fly by. All along the valley of the Arpa, hurrying hosts gather for the shock of battle. Telegrams tell of the movement on the Danube. The Kurds and Tcherkess are called out. From Poti, Sughum Kale, and Ardaban the news of sharp battle rolls along.

Seventeen thousand men, crossing at Ungheri, wait for General Melikoff's wild dash on Ardaban. Tiflis is in panic. The Turkish host is magnified into vast proportions.

Ahmed Schamyl, drilling and exercising his splendid riders, is in the saddle from dawn to dark. He inflames the haughty pride of his officers.

They are to meet in single combat the chosen irregulars of the Turks. Soon a swift courier takes to all-knowing Abdallah, Schamyl's entreaties for secret information of Moussa's and Ghazee's every movement.

It is their merciless horse he wishes to meet in the open field. By day, with his glass, he can see the cone-shaped Kibìtka tents of the Turkish camps. "His dearest foe" is on guard. His traitor brother.

Osman Bey glides through the army, in his serpent path, as chief of spies. He keeps up the line of Prince Schamyl's secret intelligence.

The days are stirring with fray and skirmish. At night, by the camp-fire, Ahmed reads the brief words of his beloved. Still dragging suspense! She is the loved and lost!

Her faded rose rests upon his heart. The mystic red rose beloved of the Turk! Born of a drop of Mohammed's precious blood, it is the lovely theme of their daintiest legends. The vulgar may not touch its sacred petals. Only on solemn feasts it may be plucked.

The precious attar distilled from its bosom consecrates the house of prayer, and sanctifies the body of the believer as a chrism of the holy Prophet's blood.

Dear as the red rose is to the pious Moslem, who prays before it, in penance, when wounded conscience stings the heart, the rose which Maritza's loving hand sends him as a token is holier yet to the ardent Circassian lover.

Her gentle hand lends it a charm more potent than the richest drops of great Mohammed's veins.

By this token he consecrates himself to the quest of the lovely prisoner, the sweet counterfeit nun of Kars. He will win the living Rose or die in seeking her.

Chafing at inaction, Schamyl's blood bounds when the cheers of the army welcome the glorious news of the day of May 17.

Melikoff, with Komaroff's column, has stormed Ardaban, and the river runs red with the enemy's blood. Now, to the front!

The bugles rouse the forces. The right and centre columns now close in.

Stealing into Schamyl's camp, a messenger from Abdallah brings to the general, news which makes his heart bound in mad delight.

Moussa and Ghazee are encamped half way between Kars and the front, and creep nearer for a night attack on the Russian cavalry.

A half-hour conference with General Melikoff gives Schamyl full power to throw himself on the enemy at his will. "Smash them!" says Loris.

Dearer than the tidings cheering his soldier's heart, of the rapid advance on the Danube and the splendid capture of Bayazid, is the latest letter from Maritza, which tells in burning words what the mute rose cannot say. For its fragrant petals are silent.

Hassan, the camel-driver, haunts the camp of the Turkish cavalry. His practised eye tells him of the movements day by day. A deserter crawls over the lines and gives the Russian pickets the tidings of the impending attack.

Day by day Schamyl's orderlies ride along the front. No message comes yet from Hassan.

Schamyl's brigade is ready. Gallant Tarnaieff, who knows every inch of the ground, volunteers to go as guide with the general, who has not yet fleshed his sword in open battle with the Turks.

The approaches of Kars are now beleaguered.

With his glass Schamyl sweeps the distant hills of the Kara Dagh.

There in that half moon of crowded houses below the high mountains, with the towering citadel in air, a blue cleft marking the path of the rushing river with its three old stone bridges, he can almost see the old convent where Maritza is safely hidden. Ghazee knows yet nothing of her.

From the Danube to Erzeroum, at Batoum, Kars, and along the whole theatre of war, the roar of fight rolls along.

Day by day Schamyl impatiently rides his outposts.

No movement yet of his enemy. He frets while the two generals watch each other twenty miles from the city.

Those ugly outlooks and the lofty walls crowded with heavy cannon make a sudden dash impossible.

To sit inactive while the town may be slowly bombarded, is madness. His heart is with the dear lonely girl who hides in the shadows of the cloister. Shot and shell may rain in on the devoted city. Her fate is joined with that of the other Christians now cooped up. For the Russian lines spread far around. A general battle impends.

Cautious Mukhtar stands at bay. Melikoff watches for an opening.

Schamyl leaps into the saddle when an order is delivered him by the gallant Gronow to head a column of cavalry toward the Russian outposts sixteen miles from Kars.

It is the hope that the Turks may attack this force which causes the advance.

Riding with the impatient Tarnaieff, Ahmed at nightfall bivouacs his men, without fires, around the little village of Beghli-Ahmed. He is among foes. A few sullen Moslem villagers glower from their huts at the invaders. He stations a guard to hold them.

A column of several heavy dragoon regiments follows a few miles in rear. They openly encamp, and leisurely occupy a favorable plain.

Schamyl's hidden pickets watch the woods and valleys.

Keeping his column in readiness, the prince waits for the shadows of the night to draw his men secretly away and leave the other camp apparently exposed.

Leaning on his sword, waiting the agreed signal to move his command into ambush, the young general at last springs to his feet. The guard drags along a straggler. He protests that he is a deserter.

Fiery Tarnaieff sternly says, "Shoot him in the morning. He is a spy!"

A sergeant approaches the commander. He whispers a message.

Schamyl, in briefest words, gains the wanderer's information.

He hands Ahmed a little twisted billet. Hassan Bey speaks at last. Russia's red gold was well spent.

"Moussa and Ghazee, with four thousand men, are bearing down to attack the exposed camp."

Old Sergeant Hassan also sends his slyly gleaned knowledge of their march. The straggler is *reliable*.

Dismissing his messenger to the care of the guard for the night, the Circassian draws his men off quietly to prevent any *chance* encounter. He sends Tarnaieff on a gallop to give the other commander the news. Four thousand crouch in readiness.

In ten minutes the dark squadrons of Ahmed's riders are swallowed up in the forest gloom. A few men are scattered across a high defile, a half mile away, to noiselessly announce the passage of any heavy force.

Two squadrons, led by the old captain of his escort, steal silently, holding their scabbards, to a dell, whence they can hold the pass and cut off the retreat of Moussa and Ghazee.

In solid line, Schamyl's brigade awaits one signal shot from a light rifle gun.

Behind their camp-fires, where a few men linger as a decoy, the heavy dragoons wait in the darkness until the enemy pour out on the plain.

Half the Russian force is posted, sabre in hand, to receive the charge. The other half, mounted, is drawn off the roads ready to charge in flank at their commander's signal.

Every squadron commander has his orders. Tarnaieff sits, stern and watchful, on his horse.

Schamyl has told him, in this silent waiting-hour, the story of his love. Ahmed's last words were:

"Stay with me in this fight. If I fall, lead the men out and avenge me. General Melikoff will rescue the princess. You can tell him all—only if I go down."

Tarnaieff mutely presses his hand. When midnight darkness wraps the broad valley, closed at its farther end by the narrow defile, there is a faint sound like the rustling of a breeze through a heavy forest. The enemy are coming!

Every man in the command knows the renegades and Kurdish thieves are pouring down the valley. They hope to surprise the camp.

The shadows deepen on the road four hundred yards away. There is a soft trampling of feet. Crawling back, a dozen scouts come running in. The head of the column is past.

When the last Turks are out of the defile, Schamyl waits for the signal volley of his skirmishers.

Ten minutes pass. Every rider is bending forward, sword in hand. A rattling fire in the gap tells of the passing of the Moslem rear.

Swinging his sabre, Ahmed calls out "Fire!" to his signal gunner, whose light piece is ready.

The ring of the three-pounder wakes the echoes of the night.

By its flash, a confused mass is seen surging over the plains. The Tcherkess dash on with wild cheers. The sword is at work.

Racing with Tarnaieff, Schamyl rides at the front, crying, "No quarter for renegades!"

His left squadrons wheel off to the pass, where they join the squadron cutting off the retreat.

Swinging his line, as previously ordered, Schamyl throws his brigade on the yelling and bewildered foe. It is a surprise, indeed! A *double* one!

Far to the front, the bitter rattle of the dragoons' rifles tell that the camp-lines have been reached.

A wild "Hurrah!" sweeps down the wind. The mounted dragoons are hewing away at the Turks. In the mad panic of flight, Moussa's force wheels to meet the awful shock of Schamyl's solid squadrons. By the dim starlight, the white caps of the

Russian troopers alone tell friend from foe. The Circassians have left their black turbans in camp.

Yells and savage cries rend the midnight silence. The crash of the volleyed firing at the front sounds high above the shrieks for quarter.

Schamyl has a knot of a dozen faithful troopers, who, even in the tangle of the slaughter, close around their young leader.

Tarnaieff clings at his general's side. The plain is already strewn with heaps of dead.

Forming up in knots, the Russians hew at the frightened mass, now pouring backward toward the pass.

Ahmed's arm is weary. He shouts in vain direction of this mad battle in the darkness. He watches by the flash of pistols for the horse-tail standard of a pacha.

In twenty minutes, the four regiments of Ghazee and Moussa are a bleeding mass of frantic fugitives. By common impulse, they pour backward toward the pass. The Circassian chaskas drink Moslem blood.

Schamyl has directed the squadron commanders to let the foe break backward and choke the pass.

There, they will be met by the rifles and sabres of his *fresh* force secretly posted. Tarnaieff rallies a hundred men beside the general. The retreating Turks fall on all sides. Schamyl's men hang on their right and left flanks, cutting them down.

The dragoons, now all in the saddle, bear down in line, driving the yelling fugitives to the gap.

Breathing for a few moments, Schamyl waits to form his body-guard once more, and hurl them on the flank.

A clump of a dozen lances twinkling round a pacha's horse-tail standard struggles toward the watchful knot of troopers around Schamyl.

Other Russians have dimly seen it. A crush of the white-capped pursuers presses toward it.

Is it the traitor Ghazee's ensign, or Moussa's?

With a wild cheer Tarnaieff yells, "Come on!"

Ahmed fights his way into the press. It is a prize to win Melikoff's general order.

Down go man and horse under the impact of that solid charge.

There is a struggle around the waving symbol. With the voice of a lion, there Ghazee fights at bay. Ahmed fights for the lost Rose of Tiflis. He forces his way to the standard-bearer. Encumbered with the staff, the Turk tries to turn. The wild black horse rears as Ahmed swings his keen sabre. He tears the staff from the falling man, for Tarnaieff's blade has pierced him through.

A dozen troopers dash at the burly Ghazee, who has cleared a ring. He is a devil!

Schamyl cheers on his men. He hears a growl of rage. Ghazee's splendid horse wheels and bears him out of the melée, a defeated fugitive!

In an hour the last broken remnants of the Turkish hosts have passed through the defile, under the merciless rifle fire of the ambush.

The forests and woods are filled with the panic-stricken fugitives.

Out in the valley the wild Russian bugles are sounding the recall. For Turkish hosts may come up to aid the irregulars.

Schamyl, rallying his scattered men upon the

main road, sends a squadron down to stop any rash pursuit over the ridge. A heavy force may follow Ghazee.

The white caps fall in as they may.

Two hours later the growing dawn shows a fearful field of carnage. There has been " no quarter."

By the earliest light the Turkish fugitives put miles between them and their pursuers.

Halting for a rest and a hasty meal, while the plunder and captured horses are secured, the two Russian commanders exchange felicitations.

Fourteen hundred of the enemy lie scattered over five miles of the road. It is a crushing blow.

At nightfall Schamyl dismisses his battle-wearied men on their lines in front of the main Russian army. The standard of Ghazee waves in triumph before Ahmed's tent. Moussa Pacha's wild irregulars spread panic to the walls of Kars in their retreat.

Prince Ahmed sends Tarnaieff to the commanding general with his trophy—traitor Ghazee's standard.

The day after, Melikoff sweeps by at evening parade, with his headquarter staff. He sends the men his verdict: "Brave fellows!" Schamyl is cheered to the echo.

Twelve days later, at Taghir, the whole main column breaks up on Mohammed Pacha's advanced half of Mukhtar's forces. Melikoff sees an opening at last. After a bitter battle the flying Turks leave three thousand dead on the field, besides their unfortunate General Mohammed.

Schamyl and Tarnaieff swept up the hill together

in that splendid charge of the Russian horse. The blue and white cross is in the ascendant.

Mukhtar with half his army stands at bay at Zewin. He hastens Ismail the Kurd's forces to join him from Erzeroum. It is salvation to him.

In these days of fierce battle creeping ever nearer to Kars, Prince Ahmed with an aching heart faces the Moslem foe. Maritza, queen of hearts, still a captive! All other rewards are nothing.

No news from Kars. The secret lines even are paralyzed. Abdallah is silent now.

Glorious news from Tergukassoff brings ringing cheers from the Russian line. Mukhtar himself has been routed at Eshek Khaliass.

The centre column is wild with joy. Will the great stronghold of Erzeroum surrender before Kars?

Two weeks of inactivity brings gloomy news. The tide turns! Victory veils her face!

Though Bayazid is in the Russian hands, Tergukassoff is beaten on the bloody hills of Zewin before Erzeroum. Mukhtar's sword is wreathed with laurel. For the Turk can fight!

Still the column is near Kars, and the Grand Duke, in person, now superintends the beginning of a bitter siege. The batteries are thundering away at the forts of the city.

Straining his eyes, Schamyl can see the shells burst over the town.

Fortune frowns her gloomiest now. Rumors of disaster on the Danube appall the battling soldiers of the Czar. A paralysis unnerves the Russian leaders everywhere. The long days wear away in grim siege and dull bombardment.

Bayazid is retaken by the Turks. Only the citadel holds out. The garrison is massacred.

The July and August days are days of defeat, sadness, and gloom. Horror follows on horror.

Great lines are furrowed in Schamyl's face. He hears not one word from the city which is the hidden refuge of his beloved. From Circassia the news of a rebel outbreak drifts down. The plains of Armenia are alive with Kurdish cut-throats.

Wearied, harassed, and baffled, Schamyl's spirits break when the besiegers suddenly fall back *from Kars*. In retreat, covering a dispirited army, Prince Ahmed crosses the burning plains, now one vast graveyard. Sickness, stifling heat, privation, and ruin reign over the Russian camps.

As the defeated troops file back over the hard-won ground, the awful news of the terrible butchery at Plevna dispirits even the boldest hearts.

Melikoff's brow is furrowed. His hawk eyes are haggard.

The cross pales before the crescent.

Two more terrible battles of indecisive butchery wear out the month of August. Will it ever turn —this tide of disaster? And Maritza! God!—not a word!

Schamyl *cannot* quit his post. Detaching Tarnaieff, he sends him to Goomri to gain from Abdallah any news of the imprisoned Princess Maritza.

In four days he is back. Victorious Mukhtar has almost driven the Russians into the Arpa-Tchai. Even Tiflis is no longer safe.

Abdallah at last sends a brief message. Maritza is yet in shelter. This he learns only from Hassan

Bey, for the whole land now swarms with bandit plunderers. Even the Russian graves are opened by the wild Kurds!

Still from the Danube comes the news of useless slaughter. Turkey and Russia force fresh thousands to the front.

On October 11 to 15 the fires of hell light up again the Aladja Dagh. Thousands of doomed men dye the hills with their blood. The Grand Duke and Melikoff throw their whole maddened army on Mukhtar Pacha. Ghazi no longer! He reels back at the head of a broken host.

Pushed to the very gates of Kars, the dispirited Pacha leaves ten thousand prisoners in the hands of the Russians, now desperate in their hour of victory. On they leap! The ringing siege guns roar once more! Fifteen thousand defeated Turks are cooped up in high-walled Kars, which is now surrounded on all sides. The Russian batteries rain a fearful fire upon the doomed city. It is the beginning of the end!

Along the road to Erzeroum, rallying his defeated stragglers, the great-hearted Pacha retreats to join Ismail, the wild Kurd, and stout old Faizi Kohlman Pacha. All is not yet lost. The Turk at bay is a hero.

Schamyl, ordered in hot pursuit, hangs for days upon the flanks of the retreating Moslems.

Tarnaieff with him urges the fiery Tcherkess mercilessly upon their foes. Even to the gates of Erzeroum, the Circassian sword reeks with blood.

Ah! Horrid wavering of the awful balances of war! Before Plevna, mounds of severed heads attest the fearful slaughter of the peerless Russian grand army. The sound of wailing goes up alike in the land of the crescent and of the cross. Darkness descends on thousands of Russian households. Is the road to Asia worth all this?

Sick of carnage, weary at heart, Schamyl led the terrific assault on November 4, which sent Mukhtar behind the walls of Erzeroum with a loss of ten thousand. The Moslem at bay appeals to his prophet. The dervishes wail in the mosques.

The crescent droops under these fearful blows at Kars and Erzeroum. Kurd and bandit flee from the plains of Anatolia.

On the night after the great defeat of the Turks at Erzeroum, Schamyl and Tarnaieff sit by their camp-fire. A courier rides up and hands Prince Ahmed a letter. It is the first tidings in three weary months from Princess Maritza.

Her lines are few:

"I am here unhurt in the awful bombardment. Every one says the city soon will fall. By the love you bear me, Ahmed, come as soon as you can to my rescue. Old Hassan will guide you. My Ahmed! come to me! I am yours to death! MARITZA."

There are streaks of gray in Schamyl's raven locks. For three months he has been under arms, day and night. Fifty skirmishes and combats and a dozen battles have made him callous to carnage. His blood has flowed more than once.

Will Erzeroum fall? He can then lead his triumphant horse back to Kars. Maritza waits him there.

Even if his own troops cannot be spared, *he* will ask to join in the Kars assault. Batoum, Ardaban, Bayazid, are all now in Russian hands. On the

Danube, starving Plevna totters to its fall. The end cometh. The camp is dreaming in silence.

Tarnaieff's noble face shines out by the camp-fire in deep thought. He has thrown himself on a roll of blankets. A gloomy master-thought possesses him.

All afternoon he has been in close converse with the higher generals. Sturdy old General Heiman knows that Tarnaieff can, in the dark, find every corner in Erzeroum. It may be taken by assault.

The stars are twinkling on the walls of the silent town where Mukhtar stands at bay.

Schamyl's face shines with the happiness of the news so long coveted. Tarnaieff lifts his head as an aide dashes up. "Orders for Colonel Tarnaieff." He dashes away. In an hour the returning hoofs of a horse ring out, and Tarnaieff swings to the ground.

His face is very grave.

"Prince," he quietly says, "I am going to lead ten battalions in a forlorn hope attack upon the Medjidieh fort. Sixteen more will assault the southern works. The troops move at midnight."

Schamyl is startled. His iron heart shakes.

"It is a desperate venture. The town is crowded with an army. The Azizi forts' heavy guns sweep every inch of your route," he says. "The citizens are all armed."

"True, Prince Ahmed. But *I alone* know the ground. The honor of leading is assigned me; we shall creep as near as possible, and attack precisely at the earliest flashes of day."

By the firelight Schamyl can see that his face is very pale, but firm as a classic Roman marble.

"Do you know who commands the Azizi fort?" Tarnaieff says.

"I do not," Schamyl wearily replies. He is sick of blood. More thousands for the ravens!

"It is our old friend Suleiman, now called Mehemed Pacha. He is the ablest and most gallant man in the Armenian army to-day, the equal of Mukhtar or Faizi Pacha in all but experience.

"I dislike to attack him; we were always close friends." Tarnaieff is musing. He feels the chill of an open grave. But—the Czar calls him!

"Prince Schamyl," he resumes, "I must leave you now. Do you remember the night we destroyed Moussa's cavalry? We watched the stars of victory together. I shall never see the stars rise again over Ararat."

He hands Schamyl a letter. "If I fall, please send that safely. That is all. I am a friendless man."

It is true. Lonely Tarnaieff has nothing but his stainless sword in the world.

Moved by some strange impulse, Schamyl says: "Tarnaieff, my dear old comrade, I will go with you." He cannot abandon the man who shared his first victory.

Without a word Tarnaieff clasps his friend's hand. There is a tear sparkling in his eye. Soldier brothers!

Just before dawn, the divided column of Tarnaieff, which has crawled forward at midnight, rushes into the Medjidieh lunette from its front and the open gorge. A roar to the south proves the other attack is in progress.

Schamyl leads the body over the redoubt; Tarnaieff, the party at the gorge. In five minutes the garrison are prisoners—five or six hundred sleepy wretches.

Ah! the clamor of the awakened city arises! Yells of rage fill the air. Fireballs from the minarets prove the crazy mollahs are on the watch. A wild mass of Turkish regulars dashes into the work, where the victorious Russians are forming up. At their head, Suleiman cheers on his men. In one body the Russians are fairly hurled out of the work or driven in knots from its gorge. Fighting hand to hand in the growing daylight, thousands of ferocious citizens stream out to pour a hell fire on the bewildered Russian columns. They all have arms. The huge guns of the Azizi work now open, with crashing shell, upon the Russian reserve battalions. The tired men go down in windrows.

Borne away by the retreating mass, Schamyl is breathless, bruised, and trodden down.

With a cheer of desperation, the Russians pour over the walls of the lunette once more, for gallant Tarnaieff's ringing voice leads them on.

Sword in hand, Schamyl throws himself over the parapet, followed by his eager men. The roar of cannon deepens into a steady crash. The guns of the Azizi are playing on the Russian masses, in rear, over the heads of the human fiends in the work.

Schamyl rushes toward Tarnaieff. With yells the Turks sweep forward. Tarnaieff dashes, with raised blade, upon Suleiman, who is in the van.

A flash from Suleiman's revolver! Tarnaieff falls heavily forward and never moves. Friend has met friend. Lonely Tarnaieff is a *dead* hero.

Schamyl springs toward his friend, and, in the very face of Suleiman, falls senseless from a blow of a cannon rammer.

In an hour, Schamyl opens his eyes. He is in a low, dark vault. Beside him sits an old Moslem sergeant. He feebly motions for water. The Turk hands him a gourd. Blest gift of God! water to the wounded! Roar of cannon and musketry resound. He is a prisoner, and yet the actions of the man are friendly.

In Turkish he whispers: "Silence, Effendi; when the stars rise, you are free."

Bleeding, bruised, and wounded, Schamyl sleeps even in the din of battle. He is in an underground magazine of the lunette. The old man is the guardian. Some friendly hand! The silence of death! Night falls. Silence reigns once more. In the darkness he can only hear the slow, wheezy breathing of the aged sergeant.

A man creeps into the magazine. Handing him a Persian conical cap and a long caftan, he says: "Come, now!" He offers a flask of brandy.

It is Suleiman, the victor of the most fearful day the ramparts of Erzeroum have ever known.

"I am going the picket rounds, and will take you out of our lines in safety. I have a horse on the sunk road, in rear. Don't speak. Come on, now!"

Crawling out of the magazine pit, Schamyl stumbles out of its opening. His wounds are sore.

By the glimmering stars, he can see double ranks of Turks sleeping on their arms around the parapet.

A few sentinels stalk along silently.

The interior of the lunette is piled with dead.

They are all stripped. In falling once or twice, he sees that they are headless.

A nameless horror seizes him. He would speak! Suleiman grasps his arm. Two horses wait at the road behind the fort; a squad of a half-dozen Kurdish lancers are in the saddle.

Mounting in silence, they ride over the field to where the picket fires of the Turks blaze in full view of the Russian position. The frightened steeds start at the piles of mangled dead. These are the work of the huge Azizi guns.

Ghastly forms, men and women, sneak silently over the field; the fanatics of Erzeroum are stripping and mutilating the dead. Schamyl is almost insane with the awful mental strain. Swiftly down the road the frightened horses gallop through the Golgotha. The Turkish lines are reached at last.

Bidding his escort wait, Suleiman rides out to the crest of a deep ravine sweeping toward the Russian outposts. Passing out beyond the sentinels' beat, Suleiman speaks. His voice is broken. "Go, now, my friend! May Allah guide! Ride straight down the ravine. You are safe. Beware how you come on your own pickets!"

"And Tarnaieff?" he whispers, as he clasps Suleiman's hand.

"Lies dead in my quarters, my friend. All that these fiends have left of the bravest of the brave. He fell like a star!

"Now go! Go quickly, my dear Schamyl! No thanks! Remember Suleiman, always your friend."

As the lithe steed springs down the sloping dell, Schamyl turns his head. Suleiman is seated on his horse, his soldierly figure sharp cut against the sky, watching over his flying friend with his face turned toward the enemies of his unhappy country.

In a half-hour Ahmed Schamyl rides into his own camp. Hailing a picket boldly, he is conducted to his lines by a squad wild with delight. He was already on the fatal black list. Victory has been torn from them. The assault has failed.

Throwing himself on the pile of blankets he shared with poor Tarnaieff, Schamyl, after calling his senior colonel to take command, closes his eyes in utter exhaustion.

Three thousand dead of each army lie piled around the Azizi fort. Tarnaieff, the gallant and gentle friend of his youth, lies silent and disfigured in the Turkish redoubt, where his heart's blood wet the sod.

Ahmed Schamyl's eyes are filled with bitter tears as he looks at the vacant couch of the daring young leader. Dead on the field of honor!

CHAPTER XI.

THE STORMING OF KARS.—AT THE ARMENIAN CONVENT!—OLD HASSAN'S FAITH.—GHAZEE'S FLIGHT.—SAFE AT LAST!

BEFORE the frowning walls of Kars, under the cover of its huge outworks, Ghazee Schamyl, the renegade, rides through his troops in bitter silence.

Now the glories of Zewin are faded. The telegraph brings from the Danube the news of a crushing defeat at Shipka Pass, and of the impending fall of Plevna.

It is the middle of dreary November. Day by day the Russian batteries pound away at Kars.

Ghazee spurs his horse in rage, till the blood streams. His eyes show him no golden crown hovering over the silver lines of the Caucasus.

Wearied Mukhtar is shut up in Erzeroum. The town of Kars, held by Hami Pacha, must finally yield, for the Russians press on its very outposts. An assault may come at any moment. And the princess still lost to him!

Every turn of fortune's wheel drives the traitor nearer madness.

The insurrection in Daghestan is crushed under the armed heel of the Russian. Circassia too is lost to the Turk forever.

In useless rage he has listened to the salvos of the Russian cannon in honor of their last victories.

Even the road to Erzeroum is in the enemy's hands.

Should the assault occur, he will be shot like a mad dog, if captured.

Even a soldier's fame is denied him, brave as he is. His troops are the veriest cowards and only braggart robbers of the dead.

Even Mustapha Bey, at Constantinople, has betrayed him. For Mehemet Pacha has been made a lieutenant-general.

Poor little Suleiman Bey, as Mehemet Pacha, is now commander, with old Faizi Pacha, of the last Turkish field army in Armenia. His laurels are fresh on his brow.

Suleiman, his Giaour brother's friend, wears the coveted rank of Ferik!

His prey, Maritza, has vanished—he knows not where.

Ah, God! He would grind her to the earth if he could find her! Revenge is his only hope!

Even the impotent commander of Kars, Hami, sneers at his comrade in command, Moussa, and himself.

The famous irregular troops are a miserable wreck. Carefully inspecting them, he selects and furnishes, as best as he may, a few chosen squadrons for his escort in flight. He must cut his own way out.

Defeated! Disgraced! A fugitive and a deserter! Is this whirling to Tiflis?

If he should meet his brother Ahmed at the head of that brigade, whose achievements ring through both armies! Then, death for one!

A baleful light glitters in his eyes. Money, property, jewels of untold value are his, taken safely out of Russian clutches before his treason.

He will not stay to die the death of a cur. He will escape in the confusion. He knows every secret path. Moussa can join him later. He, *too*, is a renegade. To gain Syria or Egypt. To work a deadly revenge on Ahmed. This is his only future. He swears it by the prophet's beard!

The blood boils in his brain as he bitterly dreams of Prince Ahmed Schamyl riding in review before the Russian Grand Duke, when the hated blue and white cross floats over Kars and Bayazid, Ardaban and Batoum, in triumph. His old colors! Prince of the Caucasus—perhaps an aide of the Emperor—and—and—Maritza's husband!

Never! by the fires of hell itself!

For he swears upon his soul that the *dagger* or the *bowl* shall work the revenge he dreams of—his only prize now; his last hope. He will reach the lovers, *even in Russia*. And then, after—after all!

While the stern-hearted fanatic rides back to Kars his heart softens for a moment.

There, in the beleaguered city, waits and watches for him the fearless woman, to whom the world is fair only when he is at her side.

It is so. Nadya Vronsky's love has been the anchor of his tossing bark.

She alone clings to him in his impending ruin. Love's crown of thorns!

Ha! she may be even dearer to him than in her hopeless love. If she will help him to a subtle revenge!

He will take her with him. Her wit may bring method to his madness.

While he rides up into Kars, to the retreat where the White Countess, under the thunder of the heated guns, waits for his return, he knows not that Ahmed with a few squadrons is sweeping like the wind to join in the grand assault which must be risked to prevent a winter siege.

Throwing himself moodily on a divan, Ghazee tells Nadya Vronsky that the town must fall.

Her pale cheek grows paler.

"We are so weak in cavalry we can only hope to save a few of the leading officers.

"*You* can be ready at a moment's notice. I will have a couple of wagons, with a few devoted men, over at Moussa's palace.

"No matter what happens, I will save you, for

the assault will give its own warning. We will go far into Syria, for when Kars falls the game is lost. We are beaten!" he growls.

"I shall seek you at once, for my mounted troops will not be in the walls. We go together. Moussa will convey us over the border. He has his *own* neck to save."

The frightened woman, clinging to the moody renegade, swears once more her faith to him, while the deep boom of the guns keeps time in wild music, as the siege crawls on.

Riding his lines, eagle-eyed Ghazee Schamyl cannot understand the ominous quiet reigning in the Russian lines.

Even aided by spies and worming sly dervish and mollah, nothing is known in Kars, save that the Russians have been heavily reënforced.

Since Mukhtar Pacha's departure for Erzeroum, Hassan Bey, the chief of the citadel, has been the genius of the defence of Kars. And well he plays his double part.

Ghazee avoids the general headquarters. The open contempt shown him by the leading officers is due to the cowardly inefficiency of his disheartened cavalry.

Since that fatal night when Ahmed smote them, they have been scattered a dozen times in battle.

The Russian horse have ridden through them, and spread them, yelling, to the four winds.

Yet the thirty thousand inhabitants and twenty thousand troops in Kars are provisioned for a winter siege. Mountains of military stores are yet on hand.

Hundreds of the defenders dream of a long winter siege. Several brave Russian assaults have been repulsed. Only Paskiewitch in 1828 ever stormed Kars.

Now three hundred Krupp guns frown upon its stony walls. Kars stubbornly clings to the crescent.

The fanatic riflemen are ready on bastion and redoubt. The Turks will fight a gun to the last.

Though Loris Melikoff is now prince governor-general of Armenia, a failure here may cost him that marshal's baton promised in return for the fourth jewel of Anatolia.

While Ghazee's eye moodily roves over every nook of Kars, he searches for Princess Maritza in vain. Is she yet here?

Never a trace of her! She may have been smuggled out of the city. Has she bribed her way out?

But he has never heard from deserter or refugee of her safety in the Russian lines.

Is she dead? Has the grave robbed him of a sweet revenge? He has sworn to reach her, even in the farthermost palaces of Russia.

Years are only days to a Circassian vendetta. While the November days fall clear and cold, Prince Ghazee, at the outposts, sees a flag of truce depart to the Russian lines.

It is *Hassan Bey*, the Russian spy, who is sent by the simple-minded General Hami Pacha to spy out the Russian lines!

Alas for the stolid general of Kars! He knows not that Osman Bey and Hassan are now plotting the last stroke of final treachery.

Ghazee Schamyl watches the party ride back

across the lines. His tiger blood would boil could he have seen Hassan, his brother's servitor, riding with that secret traitor Hassan Bey, as a horse holder.

The old Circassian has grown into his character of citizen of Kars. His disguise is perfect.

When Judas Hassan Bey and the Russian negotiator Osman together plan the sortie which is to leave the Hafiz Pacha Tabia fort in Muscovite hands long enough to spike the great guns, the old Circassian finds time to tell Osman Bey of the goat paths *he* alone has found. From thence the great citadel on the Kara Dagh can be reached with no serious loss.

Osman laughs for joy.

"Hassan, the Grand Duke shall make you rich for this," he cries.

The old spy in brief words bids Prince Ahmed Schamyl urge his way at once to the Armenian convent, for there his Maritza awaits the fearful day of the assault.

A letter in her own beloved hand gives Ahmed the history of her dreary life under the shadowy garb of an Armenian nun. Hopes deferred! When shall he clasp her to his heart?

Riding back to Kars, Hassan Bey, the citadel commander, grimly smiles. Treason's mines are laid.

The long siege is nearly done. For the Russians wait only to silence the huge guns of the Hafiz fort. Their massy columns are ready, led by the proudest of a victorious army, to throw thirty thousand desperate men on the city's defences.

In a few days the treachery is accomplished!

Dashing like wolves at the fort, under cover of a prearranged useless sortie, the Muscovites dismantle the great cannon, taking off the breech screws. Bravo! Judas Hassan! . . . Now the road is open. The Grand Duke, Loris Melikoff, Lazareff, and the other generals hasten every preparation.

Raining down a mock bombardment of days—while a snow-storm quiets the weary defenders,—the Russians prepare five huge columns to sweep into Kars. The cavalry on the Erzeroum road will be ready to cut down the escaping fugitives.

Two of these columns will open a false attack, while the others strike the three great forts Louvan, Kanly, and Hafiz Pacha, the key of the citadel.

Prince Ahmed Schamyl listens, with a beating heart, to the last conferences of the great council of war. November 17, 1877, dawns clear and cold. A full moon beamed over the silent batteries the night before. Thousands slept on their arms who saw the shining glory of the heavens for the last time. The field is ripe for the sickle.

As the rising moon silvers the splintered crags of the Kara Dagh, an unearthly silence settles down over mountain and plain. The batteries of friend and foe are silent. A ghastly mockery of peace!

Prince Schamyl creeps with the impetuous Gronow to the head of the forlorn hope of Count Grabbe's column. Gronow knows his secret. Schamyl's cavalry brigade is under the Prince of Abkhasia, for the Grand Duke has given the impetuous lover the right to enter the town with the *foot attack*. Two squadrons of his brigade await the earliest chance to dash up to the old convent. They are his special guard. They will cut their way to that point.

Following the two officers are twenty picked men from Schamyl's personal escort. Each man knows the quest now. They seek the Rose of Tiflis!

In the awful silence of the beautiful night, the three great columns of Lazareff, Grabbe, and Roop move out in the shadows; they silently steal toward the forts of Kars. Not a sound, not a light, not a standard; each stormer holds his breath and stills the noise of his arms.

The false attacks are all ready.

From his post, the Grand Duke, with anxious heart, receives quiet reports: "They are all off."

He draws a long breath.. At last!

The nipping air is below zero. The Turkish walls are silent. Not a dropping shot, not a gun.

In half an hour a few rattling musket shots tell that the farther columns are engaged.

The Grand Duke twists his mustache and stamps his armed heels. Suspense! Agony!

Ha! the false attack begins! A terrific Russian cannonade, on a distant point, to mask the real attacks.

Yells and clamor arise. The lines of Kars flash out in light. The roar of hell swells on the wintry wind. Each huge rampart blazes and rocks under the discharge of the enormous guns.

The Turk at bay fights like a devil incarnate.

Along twelve miles of line, fifty thousand men are struggling like demons.

The moon sails high above this fiendish clamor.

Still no cessation. Shock on shock—the great guns rend the night with horrid voice.

A wild wail, cheers, and mad yells sweep down from the key points. Victory hovers indecisive.

Ahmed Schamyl and Gronow, sword in hand, are swallowed up in a struggling mass of friends and foes. Gallant Count Grabbe falls dead from his horse within Fort Kanly. In an hour and a half the Turks are driven into a huge barrack. The new commander, heroic Belinsky, is shot dead at its doors.

From Fort Louvan, Schamyl can hear at last the victorious yells of the Russians. Melikoff has carried his great point. That work is won.

By the flashes of the advancing guns, Ahmed sees the solid Russian columns throwing the Turks in the river from the stone bridge they have bought with their blood.

Far away the frantic roar of victory swells from the Hafiz Pacha redoubt. Russian cheers tell that Lazareff has bought the second prize at fearful cost. Yes, it is true, for lines of flashing light tell now where his maddened troops sweep up the great heights, along old Hassan's secret path. A yell of wild triumph from the clouds proves that the great citadel has fallen. Hassan Bey's work is done. His treachery has saved thousands of Russian lives!

Schamyl rages vainly with Gronow at his side. His knot of devoted men cling to him. The roar and tumult from the town tells of the panic in its walls. The Turks cling to the gorge of the Kanly fort.

Far away a dropping fire on the road to Erzeroum

proves the Russian cavalry are grimly receiving the fugitives from the town.

Yet the quarter where Maritza hides, in the old nunnery, is still unreachable. "Daoud Pacha," fanatic and hero, fights at bay in the stone citadel. The Moslems swarm in to aid the defenders.

But the fierce Abkhasian cavalry under princely Wittgenstein sweep in and sabre the Turks, who are striving to cut out and rescue the Pacha. Hour wears along into hour. Still fighting! It is a deadlock! Schamyl is hemmed in. The fires of death sweep the gorge. The moon sinks to the west, yet the carnage reigns. It is a hideous night! The town is not yet won.

All the main works are in Russian hands. Only two stubborn forts on the heights and the Kanly barrack hold out. It is four o'clock before its doors are blown in. Grim old "Daoud Pacha" surrenders at last his five hundred heroes. *Now* the golden daylight streaks the east. The Russian victors can freely open the captured guns on the city. The twelve thousand Turks cooped up on the left bank are their prey.

The Grand Duke knows by report and the wounded victors, that a few hours will complete the victory. Melikoff's baton is won at last.

Roop's cavalry sweeps up. He surrounds the main body of the defenders. They capitulate. Hurrahs rend the air! Fighting, urging his way out of the Kanly fort, Prince Schamyl with Gronow, sword in hand, reaches the sheltered slope where his two superb squadrons wait him. On to Maritza, the day-star!

Now the way is clear! With the yell of a madman, Ahmed leads his troopers over the stone bridge. For the Russians are in the city at last!

The streets are filled with fighting fiends. Onward, by sheer weight, he forces his two squadrons which are now up. Friend and foe are intermixed.

The grim forts on the heights are still firing. Houses are shattered; gateways blocked with the débris of the awful bombardment. These guns are turned in on the town. Fire and flame are added to the night's horrors. In square and street, knots of ferocious horsemen cut down the fleeing Turks.

Away out on the Erzeroum road, the carbines are ringing. The cavalry are at their work.

At last the convent looms up. With a wild charge Prince Schamyl forces his men to within pistol shot. It is but a shattered ruin. Smoke pours from its windows, and its courtyard is deserted save by the heaps of dead. Schamyl drops his dripping sword. It dangles idly from his wrist by its knot.

Maritza! missing, dead, dying! The convent in flames. . . . His brain reels.

A yell rises. A man at his side raises a sabre to cut down a squalid figure.

It is old Hassan. Ahmed's heart leaps for joy!

"Master, master, quick, a horse! Follow me!" In an instant a trooper is out of the saddle.

"This way, down the bank!" Hassan has seized a dead man's sabre and leads in the wild race.

He shouts as he dashes along at the side of Ahmed. The two squadrons stretch out in a race for a life,—that darling Rose!

"The Prince Ghazee, with two wagons and a

squadron of his Kurds, carried off the day-star. We were driven out of the convent by the fire. He is escaping by the Olti road. On for her life!"

Twenty bounds carry the pursuers under the overhanging bank, out of the range of the guns still firing.

The desperate lover leads at a wild gallop! Down to the plain! On, on for life and love!

Yes, the Olti road. Away like a whirlwind, leaving the yelling fugitives unscathed! For on the plain a half mile ahead are wagons creeping slowly along.

The gallant black stretches his noble neck. It is a ride for life, for love, for Maritza!

Old Hassan's eyes are aflame. He points with his sabre.

In twenty minutes a dozen of the pursuers dash upon two wagons, urged along by their frantic drivers.

"Yes! yes!" yells Hassan, waving his blade.

As a score of the flying horsemen dash away in all directions, Ghazee's burly form is seen, with a dozen followers, circling around the wagons. The grim wild boar is at bay. The Russian squadrons are only a hundred yards in rear. The winners in the race fight at odds. Help comes!

It is a wild mêlée. Screams are sounding from the covered carts. Sword and pistol begin their work. Women wailing! Men dying! Ahmed dashes to the nearest wagon! He tears aside a leather curtain! Ghazee, at point blank, fires his pistol full at his brother! A sweep of old Hassan's sword! Ghazee's arm falls. With a yell of pain he wheels his horse into the bushes. He is gone! Ahmed is unscathed. What means that groan of suffering? The last men sweep up. Not too early! Gronow is standing over old Hassan, who has dropped heavily from his horse. A mortal sword-thrust has pierced his back. The wagons are halted across the road. Schamyl gazes wildly around as the devoted troopers gather.

There, in the wagon, white and pale, in the dark garb of an Armenian novice, lies his lost love Maritza! Is it death? No. Yet death is circling near. A dozen troopers are bending over old Hassan! He lies by the roadside. It is his last hour.

Gronow opens the curtain of the other wagon. Schamyl springs to his side. The White Countess!— bleeding and dying! Nadya Vronsky's heart's blood is welling out under the Persian shawl of her disguise. Ghazee's pistol shot was their divorce on earth. Her eyes are already set. A white hand grasps the shawl's folds over her bosom. Love's fatal gift!—death at her lover's hand!

A light from other days—from happier years— seems to gather on the devoted woman's face.

To spring to Maritza's side, to rouse her—dashing a canteen of water on her inanimate face—is an instant work for the princely lover. The plain is covered yet with fighting fugitives. Already the Russian troopers are scouring the field. The scattered escort is all rallied now. They form quickly around the wagons. Two of them spring to the reins, for the drivers lie under their teams. Gronow never loses his head. He is not *yet* a lover!

Gronow begs Ahmed to listen a moment. "He is calling for you—old Hassan, the man who has just saved your life!" It is even so.

Lying on a horseman's cloak, his grizzled head propped up, the old Circassian has but a few minutes to live. His life pays for his devotion to Ahmed's safety.

Ghazee's shot, aimed at his brother, has killed the only being in the world who loved him.

Some unknown hand brought Hassan low, while defending Ahmed.

Hassan mutters feebly, "Master." He beckons with a skinny hand. He gasps. The old soldier's day is done.

Schamyl is on his knees beside him. The aged servitor gasps feebly, for his life is welling away quickly.

"Master! my oath. I swore it to the dying. I am now free. Remember! Your mother was the lady! the Russian lady! the Princess Orbelian!

"Your father took you away; he would have you a Moslem. *You!* I kept faith with him and served you honestly. The dying are free at last. May you be happy with—the day-star—your princess. The other—the other—you can find—the little girl!"

His head drops back. The wild old rider has reached the last goal of life's race. His dead hand is closed over his master's fingers.

Ahmed hastily orders the body to be placed in the same wagon where all that is left of the White Countess stiffens slowly into marble. Shots and sounds of skirmish grow nearer.

Gronow and Schamyl, sword in hand, watch the suffering girl for whose rescue they dared the horrors of Fort Kanly. Princess Maritza revives slowly. Her lovely bosom heaves.

Her opening eyes meet the burning gaze of her

lover. There is a faint smile on her lips. She whispers:

"Ahmed, my lover, my own." The prince clasps her madly in his arms.

He covers her lips with burning kisses. He whispers loving words to calm her fears. Her breathing flutters faint and low, but she is unharmed.

Gronow speaks:

"Prince, we must instantly draw away. The Kurds and fugitives might bear down on us. I will command the detachment. Rouse yourself."

In five minutes, between two lines of the troopers, with a strong platoon at front and rear, the wagons move across the plain direct toward the Russian lines. *There* is peace and succor.

Schamyl's brain is soon quieted. The cannon slowly cease to roar at Kars. The whole city is now under the guns of the Russian victors. Victory folds its pinions.

Far up in the Kara Dagh citadel, a little flag is floating now. Schamyl knows it *is* at last the blue and white cross. Scattered musketry rings out yet, the roads are still black with prisoners herded by guards. The plains of Kars are a shambles, for the Circassian chaska is at its work.

His lovely charge lies silent and exhausted. Her beloved eyes meet his in the confident gaze of a child. She has no fear now, for her heroic lover's glance pledges her safety.

Safe at last! Thank God! She drops into the slumber of exhaustion. Arrived at the Russian lines, Schamyl directs his march to the field hospital. Maritza soon sleeps in a comfortable marquée, with a

Turkish waiting-woman wondering at the beauty of her worn and wasted face. An old army surgeon watches till she wakes in reassured peace. The death-watchers, in a tent near by, strive to divine what wayward fortune brought lovely Nadya Vronsky to die on an Armenian battle-field. For the White Countess lies pale and still! The proud, passionate heart knows no pang of anguish now!

Gronow is off to report to General Melikoff the rescue of Princess Maritza. Prince Ahmed soon learns of the complete possession of the city. Ringing cheers fill the air. The soldiers are wild with joy. Even now the staff are arranging for the triumphal entry of the victorious Grand Duke. Order is restored at the point of the sword. Schamyl knows full well that the Armenian campaign is over at last. Erzeroum will yield to a quiet siege. If the Danube army gains Plevna, it is the beginning of the end. And the fruits of victory!

Ahmed, while watching over his darling's safety, stands, after she is in quiet sleep, by the cold form of Nadya Vronsky. Dead! By a chance shot of her murderous lover! And Ghazee, now a hunted fugitive, wounded by old Hassan's sword as he struck down the murderous pistol—he has met the shipwreck of his last hope! Revenge is his only future. His life will be only that of the hunted wolf. Only Kurdistan opens its robber shelter to him.

All over the camp mad rejoicing begins. Yet, though fifteen thousand Turks are prisoners; though three hundred guns, and millions in stores and munitions, with the generals, the colors, and the great city are a gigantic trophy, there are grievous losses!

Five out of *six* column leaders lie dead or wounded! Five thousand slain or dying Turks have half as many Russian companions in the grave. Friend and foe lie in the grim windrows of the mitrâille,—fruits of military glory!

When the pale moon smiles once more on a quiet night, the Grand Duke enters Kars in triumph. The great dignitaries, Christian and Moslem, receive the imperial conqueror, who graciously gives Melikoff the marshal's baton he has earned! Golden honors crimsoned with the best blood of his peerless army.

Maritza de Deshkalin finds a fitting temporary residence. Clasped in the arms of gallant old Lazareff, her guardian, she feels again the dawn of a bright future. The telegraphs of victory to Tiflis bear news which brings happy tears to those she was torn away from. Madame Lazareff is at the summit of happiness! Her husband, the hero of Kars! Her lovely ward, safe!

Schamyl remains in Kars, though his brigade, with the advance, is driving the flying fugitives far out of the valley of the Euphrates and Tigris. Save at Erzeroum and Batoum, the Russian standard floats over the whole of Armenia.

Loris Melikoff, elated with victory, pushes his corps, with fifty guns, on to aid General Heimann at Erzeroum. The bayonets of the sturdy Turks still glitter behind their hard-held ramparts.

Fiery Komaroff throws himself upon Batoum to strengthen the Russian commander. That sea-port, as well as Poti, must be secured. They are Black Sea gateways of the railroad, over whose future route plotting Ignatief and wily Melikoff have dreamed for years, waiting the declaration of war.

Osman Bey, the secret agent, struts on the ramparts of Kars with pride. Hassan Bey, the Turkish Judas, wears his golden sabre proudly in the Russian lines. Under an escort of honor, he leaves for Goomri. He can safely bask in the harem of old Abdallah. There are coffers piled with Russian gold waiting for the man who sold both his fort and flag.

Ahmed is busied in sacred duties for several days. Though officially attached as aide to the Grand Duke, he is given a little time for personal affairs. His services at Kars claim every distinction. General Lazareff tells with gratitude how old Hassan's goat path led the stormers safely up to the Kara Dagh.

Bulmering, the grim old engineer colonel who blew in the doors of the Fort Kanly barrack, with joy embraces the princely young leader.

Schamyl clung to the assault with him in that awful two hours' struggle before "Daoud Pacha" gave up his heroic fight.

There is sadness on the brow of the young general when he stands by the open grave of old Hassan.

In the mosque burying ground a double squadron of his Circassian comrades fire the last volleys over the body of the quaint servitor. A stone with the graven turban surmounts the last resting-place of the wild feudal vassal. Faithful unto death!

The past, present, and future crowd in visions and dreams upon Schamyl, when the cortége of a few of his friends gathers in the Armenian church,

They hear mass, with bell, book, and candle, over what was once dazzling Nadya Vronsky.

Leaning on the arm of General Lazareff, Princess Maritza, with streaming eyes, strives to think that all of good was not worn away from Nadya's nature by her stormy, wandering career. As her own beautiful dark eyes meet Ahmed's, he can read in their splendid depths the thought, " She gave *me* back to you, Ahmed, my lover !."

The blood-stained ramparts of Kars are silent and peaceful.

New faces walk on the parapets, strange uniforms throng the headquarters. On bastion and outwork the flag of Russia floats. High in air over the palace the black and yellow insignia of the imperial family soars in pride.

The Grand Duke Michael holds the coveted quadrilateral for his imperial brother.

In abject defeat the waning crescent disappears forever from the old stronghold.

Three days after the entry of the Grand Duke, Schamyl receives an order to depart for the Danube with the personal despatches of the duke to his imperial brother who waits now for the downfall of Plevna.

Osman Ghazee Pacha is nearing the sunset of his glory. The tide of Russian victory sweeps along.

General Lazareff wishes to send Princess Maritza at once to Tiflis. Kars is no place for a gentle girl.

The congratulations of the Grand Duke, the honors of his personal reception are welcome to the loyal prince, yet they are worthless and empty to the priceless boon of escorting his Maritza to the safety and comfort of Tiflis.

Lazareff was a lover himself once. He smiles behind his gray mustache as he deftly tells Schamyl to prepare Princess Maritza for an immediate departure. Ahmed's heart throbs in exquisite happiness.

Seated in his private sanctum, the chief remarks, eying Schamyl closely:

"I suppose you will not be incommoded by the duty, Prince! There are several Christian ladies of rank here who wish to leave these scenes of horror. A travelling carriage of the Grand Duke will be placed at the disposal of the princess. She has reliable women attendants already.

"As I wish my wife and family to go on to St. Petersburg, I judge it safe for Princess Maritza to go with them. We will reunite when our gracious Emperor returns.

"If it will annoy or delay you, I will send *some one else*," the old fighter slyly remarks.

"Oh, by no means, General!" The prince's eyes are absently fixed on his wineglass. There is a red spot on his swarthy cheeks.

Even a *Circassian lover* can blush!

Strange to say, Schamyl is inattentive to the discursive remarks of Lazareff as to certain letters and little instructions with regard to his family in Tiflis.

"I think I had better prepare the princess for her voyage," Schamyl suggests.

"Most certainly, most certainly, my dear Prince," replies Lazareff, with a twinkling eye.

Prince Ahmed escapes with a celerity which amuses the old military governor.

The happy lover arrays himself in a style of military coquetry hardly suited to the grim hero of Fort Kanly.

As he clatters up the street on his bounding "Kara" his spirits are clouded by one haunting regret.

The half-told secret! His Mother, Princess Orbelian! Oh! that Hassan had lived another half-hour!

Alas! No more will old Hassan ride behind him —an unrivalled squire.

Past the dismantled walls of the old convent Schamyl rides. There are scores of workmen repairing it already. The scattered nuns are safely housed. The priests of the monastery are at home again. Love leads him to the Rose.

Schamyl enters the salon where Maritza waits him.

A tender delicacy has kept him from urging her to speak of her sufferings. The wise old Russian physician, who daily rides up to see his fairest patient, has ordained quiet and rest.

The story of her last days at the convent is yet unknown to him.

As he greets the woman he loves, Ahmed sees that the roses are coming back to her lovely face. She is the Rose of Tiflis once more.

Care and anxiety, long weary months of hiding in the dark convent walls, have strangely subdued her. Something of the nun clings to her!

But to-day, fleeting blushes mantle her cheeks; her eyes are downcast and dreamy.

She sees the great ruby flashing on his finger, and faintly smiles.

"I have news of importance for you, Princess," he says gently, seating himself at her side.

He tells her of the impending departure.

Home, friends, safety—Tiflis once more! To go far away beyond all reach of danger. The sudden prospect is too much for the rescued hostage of love!

Her eyes fill with sudden tears of joy. Burying her glowing face in her hands, she sobs like a child.

Schamyl's diplomacy yields to the burning ardor of a love which to him has been as *yet* only a torment.

His arms are around her. Silence reigns, till he softly says:

"Now, darling, sorrow and danger have folded their wings. In a few days you will be at Tiflis."

Maritza whispers softly: "Take me away, Ahmed—far away,—from this fearful place."

Schamyl presses his burning lips upon hers in answer.

"You shall go, my own poor darling—far away, in peace and safety. Go to St. Petersburg with Madame Lazareff, and give me the right to protect you forever, when the war is done. I must report to the Emperor in person. When the troops come home we meet again. Will you then be mine, my own, mine only?"

The beautiful dark eyes fill his very heart of hearts, as Maritza whispers:

"I will, my Ahmed! Yours while life lasts!"

Here, within the broken ramparts of the old

town, two happiest lovers bless the shining stars of Fate, which join their paths once more.

"But you must tell me of your last night in the convent," Ahmed asks.

Maritza shudders. "I can never remember all. It was horrible. I knew by the unnatural stillness some desperate measure was impending. Old Father Anastasius warned us to be ready to follow him, if we should be driven from our refuge. Your faithful Hassan told me of the assault. He promised to linger at the gateway and lead you to my refuge.

"Alas! It was all we could do to wait helplessly. I was ready for flight! I prepared to follow him to you.

"The streets were filled with excited people when the roar of the cannons told us your columns were attacking.

"Our servants and even the priests barricaded the doors, all but one portal. The Moslems were running from house to house sacking the Christians' homes.

"Louder than the yells and sound of the cannon, your crashing musketry fire crept nearer and nearer. It rivalled noonday, the flashing lights of battle.

"I was terrified. How I spent that awful night, I know not.

"When the morning began to dawn, the Kara Dagh battery fired into the town. We knew then the Russians had gained the citadel.

"Joy filled my heart! Alas! the bursting shells set fire to the monastery! I was dragged out of the side portal, more dead than alive.

"Hassan, watching and waiting at the door, had some nook of safety devised for me. The falling shells scattered our terrified priests and nuns.

"I ran blindly; in my fright, my veil was swept away. I darted toward a side street. I heard a wild yell. In a few moments I was thrust by your mad brother into a wagon. Menacing me with a pistol, he shouted to his followers. We plunged rapidly down the river road. Out upon the wooded plain the band dashed at wild speed.

"I never heard a sound from the other wagon, except once a woman's scream, as we passed through the line of fire at the outer gates.

"It was poor Nadya, who risked life to save me, and braved her lover's anger."

Maritza paused, covering her face with her thinned hands, to shut out the sights of that desperate ride.

"Enough," Ahmed cries. "You are safe now, beloved! The priests and nuns were all sheltered here and there. There are none missing.

"Did Ghazee speak to you on this flight?" Schamyl's mind calls back the fugitive.

"Only to scream, as he urged his men on: 'You are mine now, by all the fiends of hell! Where is your Giaour lover?' And then you came, darling, with your noble fellows."

Schamyl folds his love once more in his arms. "By all the angels of heaven, you are mine—alone, now and forevermore."

"I remember nothing of the pursuit and fight, save the firing and the yells around, until I saw your dear face bending over me."

The sweet girl blushes rosy red now, for Prince

Schamyl's *tenderness* is as demonstrative as his military valor is *dashing*. Always a Circassian!

Surrounded by a glittering circle, in adieu, conducted to her carriage by the overjoyed old General Lazareff, Princess Maritza drives out from the south gate of Kars, the next day, with the other ladies fleeing from its detested battle memories.

The Grand Duke himself deigns to ride to the outer forts with the Rose of Tiflis.

Old Father Anastasius in blessing lays his wrinkled hands upon her fair young head. He looks askance at the handsome face of the stately Ahmed, ever by her side. The good priest's reward for his devotion is the eagerness of the Russian officials to restore and refit his sanctuary and home of the religious. Maritza goes with his benediction.

In this wise, Kars loses the *sweetest nun* who ever peeped through a veil. Sister Agatha's name lingers as a gracious memory. Before the great altar, kneeling in thanks, she gave a splendid alms to be expended in masses for the repose of the soul of brilliant and wayward Nadya. She, poor lost one, lies sleeping quietly "after life's fitful fever." in the lonely "God's acre" of the old Armenian cathedral church.

In safety, in ease, under the too-anxious guard of her happiest of lovers, Maritza passes the gates of great Goomri and rests a day or two.

Here, across the Araxes, are bevies of ladies who flock to welcome the lovely Rose, now on the soil of Georgia once more.

Abdallah gravely bows his salutations. He, too,

must greet the Rose, whose singular and rapid recovery is a crowning professional triumph of the good old Russian army doctor.

In his adieu, the keen-eyed surgeon, pointing to Prince Schamyl, says gently, "Highness, I leave your case *now* to my *successor*."

Abdallah the jeweller has found a wonderful turquoise ring, of the peerless blue of Samarcand, which he offers as a gage of future happiness to the sweet captive of Kars. He wonders not at Schamyl's devotion.

"By Allah! A jewel!" he murmurs.

In easy and rapid movement, with relays, a few days' travel brings the escort to Tiflis. These hours are a dream of happiness.

Schamyl, with delicate consideration, sends two of his swiftest riders flying in advance to notify Madame Lazareff.

Bright tears of happiness sparkle in the eyes of the rescued Princess of Georgia when she is led through the portals of the Lazareff mansion.

There are four delighted enthusiasts madly embracing each other. Tiflis regains its day-star.

Madame Lazareff, the two sprightly demoiselles of the house, and the wanderer are a group of the happiest women in the Czar's broad domain.

Prince Schamyl has but a brief respite. On to Vladikaukas, to Kertsch and Odessa, down to the Danube, to press forward to the great imperial headquarters with the papers and despatches, he must speed. His two squadrons will escort him to the "Iron Gate of the Hills." Thence the railway leads to his destination on the Danube.

It is a happy circle at the dinner table.

Ahmed sees the household reassembled. Only its absent chief, who wears a warrior's crown of freshened laurels at Kars, is missing.

Madame Lazareff, the lovely Nina and her friend Tia, cast furtive glances at the unblushing Schamyl, whose love shines in every lineament.

These ladies realize that Princess Maritza has found her lord and master in the dashing hero of Fort Kanly. Madame Lazareff, reading her husband's letters, welcomes Ahmed as a member of the family circle. When the orderly reports his troops ready for the march, Prince Ahmed murmurs beseechingly to the lady of the mansion:

"I bring her back to you, madame. Before the snow melts on the Neva I shall come and claim her. Pray guard her for me."

Madame Lazareff smiles upon the young lover. His confident manner argues a very comprehensive agreement upon all future movements with the gentle fugitive of Kars.

Black Kara nods and tosses his proud head at the gateway. It needs a second message to rouse Prince Schamyl from his delicious day-dream.

The heaven of Maritza's happy eyes, the witching spell of her loving words, the chrism of her kiss—all these must give way to the stern fiat, "Forward! in the name of the Czar!"

Softly putting aside her clinging arms, he whispers: "Darling, wait for me in St. Petersburg. The war ends even now. It is only a brief separation."

And, as his lips press hers, the bright star of

love rises far in the eastern skies beyond the crested Caucasus.

When Maritza's eyes are lifted, the knightly train is sweeping down the causeway.

Her heart goes out into the silent night with her adored. She stands a radiant, blushing Rose!

CHAPTER XII.

BEYOND THE DANUBE.—VICTORY.—CONSTANTINOPLE.—GRONOW'S WARNING.—THE ENGLISH FLEET.—ON THE VERGE.—PEACE AT LAST.—SCHAMYL'S VISION.

UNDER the tranquil starlight Prince Ahmed gallops with his escort. Maritza's farewell kisses are yet burning on his lips. It is only when the gorges of the mountain road hide Tiflis from his eyes he is again the watchful leader.

The regular dropping of the horse's hoofs on the flinty road lulls him to rest. In revery he plods on. He is now an "imperial despatch bearer." He must make a forced march to the end of the railway.

All is peace around. The sweeping Russian victories have chased away all fear of uprisings in Daghestan and Abkhasia.

The wide expanse of Armenia shows from the Caspian to the Black only two defeated Turkish armies pent up at bay in Erzeroum and Batoum.

The fall of these cities is a mere matter of professional siege exercise. Ghazi Mukhtar the Great is Ghazi no longer.

Whither will his fanatic brother drift? Into Central Asia, into Arabia, or with his secretly exported wealth into some Pachalik of Syria or Far Turkey in Asia? Sybarite, renegade, deserter, fugitive!

Schamyl prays that he has seen that maddened face for the last time. Ghazee Schamyl dare never again venture north of the Araxes. The ancestral coronet will never rest upon his traitor brows.

As his nodding squadrons wind around the gorges, Ahmed recalls the dying disclosure of his old henchman. When the war is done he will trace out the history of the gentle shade whose memory seems to bless him even in these wild hills. He is Russian by blood! He can now see the springs of the deadly hatred of his Moslem brother.

Ghazee Schamyl, dreaming of empire, feared the influence of the Russian government in Ahmed's favor.

The Princess Orbelian! Ahmed dreamily remembers an old Russian family of that name.

There are few left to bear it. When St. Petersburg crowns his love with the sound of wedding bells, he will solve this mystery.

Tired and happy, proud of his mission, glad to avoid this border war, Schamyl pushes sharply toward the Iron Gate.

Three days later, in splendid array, his two squadrons rend the air with their wild parting "houras," as the train rolls away for Kertsch.

Schamyl is joyous. The magic telegraph brings him loving words from the fairy princess who holds the empire of his heart.

Before he reaches Plevna, the circle of his friends

at Tiflis will be safe on the Neva, far away from war's alarms.

At Kertsch, waiting for the train, he obtains his telegrams and letters. The route to Rustchuk and Plevna lies open. The Grand Army of the Danube is wild with joy. The ramparts of Plevna are at last under Russian colors. The grim Grivitzka redoubt is in the hands of the victorious Muscovites. Osman Pacha wounded and a prisoner!

Ten days later, Prince Schamyl, before his august Emperor, a crowned Cæsar, in the midst of his victorious army, delivers his sacred trust.

Over the historic Danube, past the scarred battle-fields, through the ranks of a huge army in panoply of victory, past the world-famous lines of Plevna, Schamyl has safely borne the papers from one victorious Romanoff to his imperial victor brother and master. Right and left the Russian legions are pressing on the flying Turks. It is revenge everywhere.

Shipka Pass and Philippopolis add to the glories of the winter harvest of victories. Gourko is over the Balkans!

Greeted by old comrades, happy in the telegraphed arrival of the Lazareff family at St. Petersburg, Ahmed Schamyl's heart is now at rest.

Princess Maritza is safe on the Neva, and her lover, the hero of the Araxes, is attached to the glittering staff of the Emperor as aide-de-camp.

Burning with ardor to rejoin the queen of his heart, Schamyl yet cheerfully heads his steed for Constantinople. The Russian's wild desire!

On to St. Sophia!—the army presses. Winter

snows, desperate Turks at bay, suffering and hardship, fail to withstand the gray-coated legions in their holy crusade.

One shadow only rests upon Schamyl. Platoff, friend of his boyish days, is not a sharer of the triumphant march onward. Desperately wounded in the battle of Lovtscha, he is now at St. Petersburg, just able to crawl around. A Turkish bayonet-wound makes his pale cheeks interesting to the ladies, who adore the man who pushed his rifled guns into the flaming crater with Skobeleff, the Ney of the Russian service. Assuring himself of his friend's safety, Schamyl rides proudly in the Emperor's train on that long path of glory which leads to Adrianople. The last guns are fired. The rifle rings no longer along the Danube. There are no more yawning grave-trenches to fill. For the magnificent legions of the Czar are encamped at San Stefano.

Six miles from Constantinople, the hosts of Alexander greet their Emperor, and crown him with the laurels of his greatest campaign. There before them lies the great city of the Moslem at the mercy of the Russian conqueror. Only—England?

The last day of January in 1878 ceases the work of the sword. It is the pen which, in a few brief flourishes, now consecrates the armistice. The veteran soldier sleeps upon his arms, victorious, yet warily expectant. The cup of victory is not drained to the dregs. St. Sophia yet bears the hated crescent above its desecrated shrines. Prince Schamyl, too, lays aside the sabre for the pen. The uncertain post, from the far north, brings him tidings of Maritza. Chafing like a caged panther, Schamyl waits for the word to return to the city which is now to him a jewel casket. *His* treasure is there! Paper missives keep alive Cupid's sharpshooting at long range.

In the splendid circle around the Emperor, great as Gourko shines in fame, high as soars the star of Skobeleff, no one is nearer the person of the master of the icy world than the indefatigable Ignatief.

Following in fire and flame his lord, he now coquets with Savfet Pacha over the veriest trifles of diplomacy. Harvest time in winter!

The cunning soldier-statesman has a list of demands which appalls even the Turk upon his knees. The road to Persia is safe. Armenia is Russian now. But there is no barrier between the autocrat of Russia and St. Sophia save his plighted word to the Queen of England, that he will not permanently occupy Constantinople.

The victorious army murmurs and demands its prey, now in sight. The long-wished-for goal of the Russian! Skobeleff rages and fumes at the sight of the golden domes from which he would tear down the Moslem's dishonoring crescent. Generals, princes, brothers of the blood, demand to be led in triumph into Constantinople.

Schamyl, tired of feasting and inactivity, weary of the hours idly wearing along, in waiting, learns by the telegraph that Batoum is in Russian hands.

The gallant Mehemed Pacha has led out his unconquered troops from Erzeroum. Peace reigns in Armenia. The road to India is clear for the Russian legions of the future.

Seated in his room, awaiting the assembly of the princely throng who gather at the Emperor's table,

Schamyl loses his occupation of counting the crawling minutes. A new quest awaits him.

A headquarters aide dashes up, saluting as he enters.

"Prince Schamyl will report instantly to General Count Ignatief for a special service."

He springs to his feet, gathering up his sword, cloak, and turban.

As he descends the stairway, his orderly hands him a telegram.

It is from Gronow, the faithful and gallant. As he hastens to General Ignatief's quarters, he tears it open. He reads with a wildly leaping heart:

"GOOMRI (by messenger from Erzeroum),
February 5, 1878.

"Treachery threatens Maritza. Ghazee plots mischief. I learn this here from Mehemed at Erzeroum by private message. Watch over her in St. Petersburg. Some deadly peril. Act instantly. He seeks revenge. He is with Ismail, the Kurd, in the hills. He has means of secretly communicating with Petersburg agents. Have notified Lazareff at Kars. Answer to Goomri.

"GRONOW."

Schamyl's heart-strings are thrilling when he gallops up to General Ignatief's quarters.

He knows now the bleeding crown of thorns which fate presses on Maritza's brow instead of a chaplet of roses. Still the implacable hatred of the deserter!

Maritza! Orphaned! Alone! Only guarded by gentle Madame Lazareff. What dark plot may be the supreme effort of this fanatic fiend? His murderous bullet pierced the one heart true to him in his reckless path. What is his fell design now?

Only a Circassian can know the Tcherkess heart, —the awful oath upon the amulets.

Nailed down by the iron hand of duty, he can only pray, only pour out his heart in invocation to the great Father of mercies for the safety of the lovely one who has already borne love's cross.

Seated at a table heaped with papers, a campaign map spread out before him, Nicolas Ignatief hardly sees the young general who waits the orders of the coming dictator.

The count's roving eyes follow the lines of the Bosporus and Sea of Marmora.

Lifting his head suddenly, a wintry smile plays on his worn face.

"My young chieftain once more! I have another task for you."

With intuition he sees the storm of internal mental conflict on the young man's mobile face.

Love against duty!

"Be seated, Prince. Are you ill?" he asks with a real concern.

"It is nothing, General. I am well enough, but I am in trouble," Schamyl wearily answers.

What to him are stars, medals, and honors if he cannot shield the one beloved head from the nameless death which hovers over it far away by the icy Neva?

"Let us talk of duty first, Prince. Then, if I can aid you, permit me to offer my assistance."

It is worthy of the world-worn champion of the Czar, for, strange to say, Ignatief *has* a heart.

He is not *quite* Machiavellian, *though* nearly so. With grave preoccupation Ignatief begins. Schamyl is the mute instrument of the Czar once more.

" Your perfect discretion, and the zeal with which you have fulfilled your duty in the war, place you *now* in a very important position.

" I know you are a good soldier."

Schamyl bows.

" I am going to make you a sailor, and also give you a glimpse of statesmanship.

" We stand on the verge of a fresh collision—perhaps a second bloody war. The armistice may be broken any moment.

" We have gained all in Europe we fought for. We have the royal road to Persia, India, and Asia assured.

" I am on the eve of signing the final peace with Savfet Pacha. But the Turks have lately assumed a defiant attitude. They are strengthening their defences. Every battalion released from Asia Minor is pouring in here. We fear a collision.

" The Emperor is urged on by the mad section of the army to enter Constantinople.

" He is holding back the turbulent chiefs, while I strain every nerve to sign this peace and save the solid fruits of this war.

" A new enemy menaces us. We may lose all. A single quarrel, diplomatic or military, would take the situation out of my hands."

"And the new enemy, General?" inquires Schamyl.

" Is England's fleet," replies the man of the hour. "I have borrowed a yacht from Prince Doria of Genoa. She is all ready. I wish you to run down to Tenedos and watch the English ironclads. I know they will come up as far as Besika Bay. The English minister Layard is coquetting with the other foreign ministers. The Porte fears *us*. It dare not give *them* permission to cover Constantinople. It dreads to refuse. We are using unstinted gold to gain secret service reports, from the attachés of the other embassies.

"I expect every moment an official threat from Layard that the fleet will come up, with or without permission. If they force their way to the city, it is an act of war. You will have a naval attaché to direct the yacht. It is the swiftest in the Orient. Here are your orders. You are to cling to the movements of the fleet. The yacht flies the Italian flag. I will line the shore with spies and signal men. Should the English ironclads steam to the city, you are to run ahead with all speed. When they actually move up to the walls of Istambôl, you are to hoist the imperial Russian standard at the mainmast, and run direct through the Bosporus. Your flag will be watched for from San Stefano. Hoist it when abreast of our lines."

Schamyl ponders. "And if fired at or chased?" he doubtfully mutters.

" Press your boat ahead, and keep the imperial flag flying as long as a plank holds together."

Prince Ahmed is very grave. His waiting bride may never see him!

Ignatief slowly closes. "I have selected you for your nerve, coolness, and judgment. The officer who goes with you will report every technical movement. He will have his own assistants. On you, Prince Ahmed, depends an awful responsibility."

The old Muscovite statesman-soldier speaks solemnly :

"If you come to the Bosporus with the imperial flag flying, the whole army will assault the Turkish lines. We will open our batteries on the fleet and city. It will mean war with England. It may decide the fate of India, or it may carry a new enemy to the gates of Moscow." He sighs wearily.

Schamyl accepts this as more desperate than a forlorn hope. He may *earn* the Emperor's sanction.

"I am ready," he says simply.

"For God, for Russia, and for the Czar, go, my young friend. England," says Ignatief, musing, "has one man at home who sees that the fate of India, the dominion of Asia, the railway from Batoum to Baku, the railway to the Chinese border, may be delayed twenty years by a fiasco here. It must not be. The pen must save now what the sword has gained. They have awakened too late to the enormous gains we have made in Asia Minor. We must not be embroiled here." Ignatief resumes:

"As soon as the treaty is definitely signed, you will be recalled. I will send down the legation launch. Till then, for life and death, for your honor, cruise carefully around the advance of the fleet. The Prince's Islands are a convenient cover. I will know what they *say* to me. You must show me what they will *do*."

"I depart at once, your Excellency."

"Instantly, as soon as you can get in mufti, I will send an aide to conduct you to the yacht. You have carte blanche.

"But you are in some trouble," Ignatief kindly says. "Let me help *you*, while you bear some of *mine*. What is it?"

Schamyl hands Ignatief the despatch of Gronow. He briefly explains its import.

The general's brow grows stern.

"Ah! that devil Ghazee! We must act at once." He rings his bell.

In an instant, a sheaf of telegraph blanks is brought in.

"Write any despatches you wish, to Petersburg, Kars, Tiflis, Goomri, Erzeroum. I will send them in the imperial cipher.

"The chief of the Third Section is here in attendance on the Emperor. He will have a special guard of the secret police watch the Lazareff mansion. I myself will telegraph Melikoff and Lazareff. You shall have the whole power of the Emperor to save that lovely girl."

Schamyl's pencil is flying. To Gronow, to despatch personally to Madame Lazareff, to—yes, to Paul Platoff. He is bright and resolute. To Maritza herself—ah, no! Only love and greetings to her.

Fast as they fly from his fingers the cipher clerks are transforming them. In an adjoining room the keys click.

Ahmed pauses. His work is done.

Is there any one who can counteract this devil's long-range villany? Any one else? He has, then, fellow conspirators in Petersburg!

He looks at the blood-red ruby on his finger. Yes, great heavens, Abdallah the jeweller! He is past master of the Moslem secrets of Armenia.

Schamyl explains to General Ignatief his faith in Abdallah.

"Say no more, Prince. I know him. I will have him sent by special train to St. Petersburg and attached to Madame Lazareff's household, as guest. He shall stay till you return.

"When this treaty is signed, when your duty is completed, I will give you that yacht to take you to Odessa, and you can receive us in Petersburg. I see you would be happier watching over her *yourself*." He smiles even in his friendly anxiety.

"It is so, General. She is my promised wife," Schamyl proudly answers.

"I myself will gain you the Emperor's permission for this marriage," the diplomat answers.

"Go now. Remember, your hand will throw the *whole army* on the works, if you hoist that flag. I will watch over your bride to be."

In a half hour the dark, snaky *Genova* is gliding, like a fleeting vision, down the blue waters of the Sea of Marmora.

Three days after, as Prince Ahmed walks the deck, gazing on the first evening stars rising over the bluest waters of old ocean—his great secret of state locked in his breast—he sweeps for the last time the southern waste of blue waters.

His colleague touches his arm. "There they are."

Four black specks in the distance—mere dots upon the water.

"What is it?" Schamyl questions.

"*It is the English fleet heading for Besika Bay!*"

Schamyl's heart gives one sudden bound. Will it be his fate to bring on the long-delayed war to the death between the lion and bear?

Southward the dainty yacht speeds, her delicate lines quivering under the throb of the superb engines.

In an hour he clearly sees the mighty floating fortresses forging sullenly along.

Monsters of the deep. Yes, the keen-eyed professional spies on board, make them out.

Alexandria, Devastation, Sultan, Achilles—the huge engines of refined human deviltry. Hornby's flag flies on the *Devastation*.

When their enormous anchors rattle down at the rendezvous, far down the gulf are two more grim sea monsters slowly following up in the wake of the first leviathans. England's might!

. Not a half-hour's sleep visits Schamyl's eyelids in this long night. The uneasy dreams of the warrior are a torture. When daylight blushes over the eastern hills, the yacht, rounding and curving along the shores, runs near enough to see the blood-red flag of England flying over these floating steel castles—their huge fires banked down. They are clearing for action!

Ominous, ready, imposing, they swim in sluggish menace on the ocean waves, yet ruled by Britannia!

A long day passed; there is time to exhaust every pretence of pleasure sailing.

Torn with anxieties, questioning the great white stars above him in his lonely watches, Schamyl holds his post with a bosom torn with a thousand fears.

Vessels pass up and down the gulf; all is peace so far, for no rumor reaches the little villages where the yacht enters. The black giants lie still in ugly readiness. They give but little signs of life.

Prince Ahmed's heart stiffens into stone. No relief, no change, no daily duty save to bear alone the weight of his responsibility, the burden of Ignatief's prudence. And Maritza in deadly danger!

It is the thirteenth of February when a fishing felucca drives down the gulf, like a wild sea-bird seeking its foamy nest on the ocean surge.

The *Genova* is artfully moving on her now familiar patrol. Each vessel, each shallop is keenly watched, for his orders tell him some means might be found to warn or guide him.

As the felucca nears the yacht, bearing down the gulf, a tiny flag flutters at the peak and is dipped three times.

Schamyl bounds to his feet. His colleague directs the course of the vessel. A signal!

In ten minutes the felucca is alongside. With a few reverse throbs of the screw, the course of the yacht is stayed.

A gayly dressed Greek fisherman throws a line on board. Drifting side by side, as the vessels float on the blue tide, the Cypriote springs over the low quarter.

Before Schamyl can advance, the fisher is at his side. A little billet is in his hands. Ahmed recognizes the brief signal which accompanied its delivery,—the secret service!

Tearing it open, he glues his eyes upon the few lines. It is from Nicolas Ignatief himself.

Involuntarily casting his eyes toward the English monsters, there are black clouds pouring from their funnels. Has it come at last?

As the dark smoke breaks away in wreaths, Ahmed reads again and again his last orders.

"13th:

"Layard, English minister, notified the Porte yesterday, the fleet would come up, permission or no permission. I have sent Onon, my dragoman, in with the Emperor's ultimatum. If the fleet comes to the city, the armistice ends when they pass the first battery. All in readiness for the assault.

"Remember your duty. The movement depends on you alone. The foreign ministers protest. We will fight!

"Treaty ready to be signed to-morrow. Watch the fleet every instant. Be ready to move at highest speed. Make no mistake. If they come beyond Besika Bay, we shall begin to move the troops.

"IGNATIEF."

An hour passes on; the felucca is far away—a mere speck dancing on the waters. Another hour; smoke still pouring from the funnels. Two hours afterward, the bows of the monsters are swarming with men. It is war!

Slowly, like drifting black clouds moving on a midnight sky, the fleet under way steams toward the Sea of Marmora.

Three miles before it, cutting across their path, the *Genova* leaps through the water and runs toward the nearest headlands.

The great yellow banner with its double-headed eagle is reeved on the halyards ready for the hand of Schamyl. Will they pass in?

Onward, moving grandly, the vessels forge along, like a school of enormous whales.

Two hours now will decide the fate of Constantinople. The blood clicks in Ahmed's temples like the movement of machinery.

By his side, the naval attaché quietly directs the movement of the yacht.

Ha! Far away on the headland a little flag which talks! It flutters, and at the masthead of the leading ironclad there are busy signal pennants displayed.

It is a message of awful import.

The feeble waving of those bits of party-colored rag brings the great ocean monsters to a halt.

In slanting course, as ocean birds wing the upper air, they draw in toward the sheltering shores and drop the mighty anchors once more.

The funnel smoke drifts away. The might of England stays its onward course. A breathing spell.

Is it peace? Is it the heavy hand of imperial Germany? The harsh challenge of fiery France? Is it the voice of the bevy of ambassadors crying, "Hold off—in the name of Europe!" which says, "No thoroughfare."

Ahmed Schamyl cannot tell. His whole nature sinks under the reaction of these exciting hours. Pride fills his bosom! His soldierly spirit tells him it was the gauntlet thrown down by the Czar, the defiance of the northern colossus, which seals those feebly guarded sea gates.

Ready at a moment to move ahead, the *Genova* clings to the advance of the war vessels. The night passes. Before Schamyl rouses from the deep sleep of exhaustion, the Russian embassy's launch is swinging alongside the *Genova*.

An aide in full uniform leaps lightly to the deck.

Saluting Schamyl, he hands him a letter. Worn with night watching, torn by anxiety, Prince Ahmed's hand trembles like a leaf in the storm.

The words are few:

"Return in the launch with your associate. Send yacht leisurely back to Golden Horn. Treaty signed yesterday.

"IGNATIEF."

In a half-hour the legation launch speeds like an arrow along the sheltering shores. Home to Maritza! Love's shining beacon leads him—home!

As Schamyl seats himself in the cabin, his merry associates are pledging the health of the Emperor.

A burning fever rages in his veins; he throws himself on the cushions. His papers, his secret orders, his belongings all there. His duty is done!

Yes! And the baffled sea monsters are receding in the distance. Back to the permanent anchorage of Besika Bay!

It is all over. The lion and bear will not yet grapple to the death. Layard's signals to the fleet told them the story of the peace.

And Schamyl is so tired, so weary! His eyes have been strained by day and night. His nerves are worn and shaken. His own love in danger!

Draining a glass of champagne, he dimly sees, though the blue wreaths of the papyrus, his naval guide and the aide most loyally going down the gradations of all the regular toasts in bumpers.

His aching eyes close in sleep. The yacht is far behind under half speed, steadily moving for the Golden Horn.

It is all darkness in the little cabin when Ahmed awakes. Friendly hands are on him; he is struggling violently.

A gleam struggles through the binnacle. His friends are holding him.

"Are you well, Prince? What is the matter?" They are both anxiously clinging to him!

"I know not," Schamyl mutters, "that dream, that vision! I am better."

Lights are at hand.

He wonders at the faces of his excited friends.

The aide laughs: "You nearly had me throttled, General! I fear you are worn out with your cruise. You are a tiger!"

The naval associate hands Ahmed a glass of brandy —the sailor's panacea for all the ills that flesh is heir to.

"Drink this, Prince. You were seized with a nervous chill. We had our hands full to quiet you."

The Circassian drains the fiery glass. His head falls exhausted on the divan. The boat speeds on in the hushed glory of the early morning hours, under the trembling stars of night, to the lines where a hundred thousand men sleep in peace around the ruler of the mighty frozen North! For the treaty is signed at last!

Schamyl cannot close his eyes! In his troubled sleep an awful vision froze his blood.

It comes back—that dream!

Yes; Maritza the beloved—never more lovely, never more radiant—in white, with clinging lace and great pearls of Ormuz around her snowy neck!

She smiles and leans forward. Heavens! that glimpse of paradise gives way to another tableau. While his outstretched arms are reached to clasp her to his bosom, she is changed.

Lying white and pale, her hands dropping by her side in death's relaxed abandonment, her lovely head low lying, her eyes closed, and one is bending over—a man; his face is turned away. He tears something from her hand. Who is he? Ah! Ahmed's leap and effort to stay the spoiler of this fairest of maids awakened him.

It was this!—Only a dream!—Thank God! Only a dream! a mad whirling of distorted hopes, wishes, fears, and fancies across his mind!

Silently, listening to the pulses of the engines, Schamyl drops into an exhausted slumber, with his whole soul lifted up in invocation for the orphaned queen of his heart so far away.

"The war is over," he murmurs, as his eyes close, "and now, and now . . ."

Gravely his friends watch him till the sunbeams dance on the blue ripples off San Stefano. Schamyl is in his wonted calm again.

Half an hour after the boat glides along the quay, before the tented homes of the Czar's legions, Schamyl is in the presence of Nicolas Ignatief. The camp is "en fête." Even the grave soldier-diplomat is merry to-day.

Bands are playing; review preparations are everywhere. Gilded aides gallop up and down, marshalling the great columns, setting out knightly squadrons and grim batteries. To-day the pride of Russia will march before the Czar.

Ignatief seizes the young Circassian joyfully by both hands.

"À la bonne heure! Schamyl, you have done well. Return me your secret orders."

Prince Ahmed hands over his directions. A mountain is lifted from his heart. The Czar's trust!

As Count Ignatief rings for the ever-flowing

champagne, he carelessly tosses the packet of *now useless* orders in the fire. It is a glorious winter day.

"Our English friends may just as well not know how near this *grand review* came to being a *storming assault* by a whole army," the great count merrily says. "They have baffled us; but, by Saint Vladimir, the day of Russia's reckoning with England will yet shake its rotten throne!

"We have the substantial fruits of victory. Turkey in Europe and the principalities are definitely and advantageously arranged. Erzeroum is evacuated, and the great quadrilateral of Anatolia is in our hands. Our position in Asia Minor will be made impregnable.

"In five years you will see a railway from Poti and Batoum to Tiflis and Baku. Then, Armenia can never be wrenched from us. We are now the lords of the Black and Caspian. Catherine's will is our guide.

"In ten years our military railway will reach Merv, Samarcand, Tashkend, and wrap our English friends in a steel band in Asia.

"Onward to Khuldja! to Irkutsk! to the Pacific! The railroad will hold us Persia, menace India, and control China. The English are asleep to our great march overland. We will seek a French alliance.

"Let us drink confusion to England's plotting. They spoiled our *last* glass of wine at Constantinople. Prince, they cannot spoil *this*. We will meet yet in a war to the death." And fiery Ignatief clinks glasses with the Circassian lover.

"Count," queries Schamyl, "are there any future operations in Armenia?"

"Not another shot," gayly responds Ignatief.

"The hundred guns salvo fired here to-day will be echoed at every post in Anatolia. The Grand Duke Michael also reviews his gallant army to-day.

"We will leave heavy garrisons in Asia Minor, for our interests lead us toward the Persian Gulf. We will have sea frontage there. England can then keep her useless Suez Canal.

"The millions of barrels of oil wasted now yearly at Baku must be spread over Asia and Russia on our railways when built. The great war with England will give us Constantinople or India. Every resource must be guarded for our national life struggles.

"I am sorry, Schamyl, that Prince Tchavachavadze will lead your brigade before the Grand Duke Michael to-day. They will miss you. But—the Emperor has directed you to head all the Circassian cavalry here in the march past. You are now the chief of Circassia."

"And then, Count?" Schamyl asks with anxiety. The compliment escapes him. Love's blindness!

"I beg your pardon, Prince! I had forgotten your private affairs. I have some letters and telegrams for you."

He commands a secretary to bring them.

Schamyl eyes them hungrily.

"Read your telegrams, Prince!" the man of many wiles kindly adds.

"You can enjoy your letters on the boat, for as soon as the review is over, you are to leave for Odessa with the *first despatches* to the ministry of the foreign office. Several of the imperial household go on the same boat. You will have a special train from Odessa to Petersburg."

"And will I rejoin my command in Armenia?" Schamyl's eyes are downcast.

"Not unless we must fight John Bull at once."

Ignatief laughs heartily, raising his glass. "Your duties as *aide-de-camp to the Emperor*, General, will detain you in St. Petersburg until the imperial staff arrive, for you must be presented on your *promotion*."

Prince Ahmed is neglecting his wine. A harvest of honors!

"To the health of the future Princess Schamyl!" cries the old count, heartily. "We can give you a leave now, but when we fight England you must lead a Tcherkess division into Asia. The day will surely come."

Ahmed understands the friendly care which hurries him to the Rose who waits him by the Neva. Ignatief has been a lover! A man of many arts!

The telegrams are reassuring—Platoff, Madame Lazareff, and also Gronow.

Thrusting his letters in his bosom, he departs with Ignatief's order to report at sundown for his despatches.

"Poor fellow! Hard hit by a pair of laughing eyes!" Ignatief muses. "Remarkably fine ones, by the way," he mutters, as he sends his subordinates flying on matters of moment.

To the sound of thundering cannon, with waving banners, singing trumpets, and rattling drums, proud, beautiful martial music thrilling on the thin air—the victorious host of Russia defiles before its lord!

Forests of bayonets, thickets of lances, lines of grim artillery, with the tossing crests of the rarest cavalry in the world, flashing by, the great panorama unrolls before the eyes of the aged Emperor.

Princes, generals, grand dukes of the blood, the whole imperial cortége of heroes crowd around their master.

Heroes of the Danube and Plevna, the war-worn veterans of Shipka Pass, of Loftscha, the daring stormers of the Grivitza redoubt, the men of Gorni-Dubnik, the iron-hearted soldiery who crossed the snowy Balkans, file by. The silent half of this grand army lies under the frozen clay of the Danube valley.

Proudly sweeping past: sword, lance, pennon, and banner droop before the mighty Czar of all the Russias.

The victors of Philippopolis rend the air with huzzas! The sturdy regiments who broke the pride of Suleiman Pacha, the grim warriors who forced Osman Pacha the Great out of his blood-bought stronghold, cheer the old sovereign who battles for the blue and white cross.

It is a day of wild rejoicing. The ground shakes under the tread of the mighty host.

Prince and paladin sweep by! Frantic yells greet great Gourko with his silver hair. Long rolling cheers announce the knightly person of the White General, Skobeleff, the man of the charmed life.

The invincible champion dashes by his Emperor, bowing to his charger's mane. The men yell with delight. He is their idol!

A wild, touching pageant, this,—the passing of the patient, plodding, gray-coated Muscovites, whose battle song for the Czar, welcoming the red death of the field, is their last sigh for Holy Russia.

Ahmed Schamyl leads the desperate column of the peerless Tcherkess past his Emperor. Nodding plume, twinkling lance, and jingling sabre excite the restive chargers whose dancing feet spurn the ground.

Prince Schamyl, lowering his sword before his sovereign, knows that the white cross flashing on his own bosom, gained in battle's desperate whirl, is no whiter than his own loyal soul. He has no fear to meet now the kindly eye of the lord of Russia's huge domains. Honor's chaplet is on his brow.

And so, saluting the ruler, all that is left of the Grand Army of the Danube passes proudly.

Shoulder to shoulder they have fought their country's fight! Thousands of gallant men's hearts beat sadly to think their bayonets may never glisten again upon the blood-stained ramparts they have won. Istambôl lies humbled at their feet.

Alexander, the mighty Emperor, gazes with dimmed eyes to see the flower of the service pass with depleted ranks. Thousands in the swamps of the Danube, tens of thousands before the dull red mounds of Plevna, myriads in the wild defiles of the Shipka, and where the forest ravens linger over the graves of the forgotten brave on the Balkans,— all these are missing from the lines.

His peerless Household Guards, in skeleton ranks, remind him, as they sweep on, of the countless homes in Russia, where, from palace to hut, the shadow of death and sorrow now lingers.

The awful heritage of the heaviest crown on

earth weighs the Czar down. The hereditary policy of Peter, the sacred will of mighty Catherine, drives the march of his legions ever toward India, Persia, the Gulf, the Far East. The Emperor is biding the time when (threatened and powerless in India), with a Franco-Russian alliance menacing China, England will not dare to block the way to yon glittering dome of St. Sophia.

Fate! Destiny! Treason! A strange and awful doom is leading the mighty victor homeward—laurel crowned—to die the death of a helpless victim, under the obscure plots of frantic conspirators.

Vanitas vanitatem!

As the legions march away, as the gray clouds roll around and wrap the city of Istambôl from his sight, Alexander the Conqueror, balked at the gates of the Black Sea, prays that some day the gray Russian horde may sweep in wild triumph over the walls of Constantinople.

Striving, plotting, building fort, city, mart, and railway, forge and arsenal, fleet and frontier defence, the Russian lives but to see the day of Constantinople's fall. Shedding new oceans of blood, the children of the Czar will take and gain Constantinople, in the face of even England's mighty power.

Far on the tossing Euxine, before the bugles sound the last signals of the night, Schamyl presses northward to lay his laurels at the feet of the proud and splendid woman who waits his coming in the old mansion of the Lazareffs on the Neva.

As he stands on the deck, the miles of lights of the great camp twinkle afar off.

He wonders at the embattled might of Russia in

arms. Its bugles sing reveillé from the Baltic to the blue Pacific.

The merry circle in the cabin, with joyous festivity, celebrate the coming joys. Their past victories are lived over. They pledge the hallowed memory of the gallant dead. The returning officers are mad with triumph. Ahmed's letters give him a quiet hour.

Paul Platoff, with trembling hand, announces his convalescence. The story of his services and wounds, his hours of pain and suffering, touches the friend of his bosom.

But the letter falls from his hand in blank amazement as Schamyl reads the close.

"I will say but little, for you soon will be here. I look forward with joy to meeting you, for I shall soon be married to a charming girl—an orphan. You will love her for my sake and her own. It is the young Princess Vera Orbelian. *You alone* must be my witness and my groomsman."

Ahmed Schamyl's wondering eyes read again. He is stunned, and his lips for the first time in his life frame the loving words, "*My sister!*"

CHAPTER XIII.

BY THE NEVA.—GHAZEE'S REVENGE!—AT THE OPERA.—THE LOST HANDKERCHIEF.—DR. ABDALLAH.

IT has been a winter of dark sorrow in St. Petersburg. Except by the officials, the valetudinarians, and the toilers, the capital is deserted.

The flower of Russia's youth has trodden the

frozen plains of Armenia with Melikoff, or followed grim Gourko in his deadly race to Adrianople.

And yet the streets are thronged. But the invisible thread, the nerve-life which makes the metropolis, is absent. War? Yes! horrid war! is the only topic.

Profoundly glorious in the gazette, serious in bureau circles, talked of with bated breath by the merchant, abhorred by the toiler and artisan,—the war broods over all!

There is to-day a common bond which knits together all Russian womanhood in one black band of mourning—the gallant dead.

Prince and general are missed from mess, club, and palace. The dark angel's wing sweeps unpityingly, touching now the mansion, now the hut. While all agree that certain glorious national results are sure to follow the wholesale blood-letting, many a gallant high-souled patrician woman eyes the picture of the unreturning brave in heart-broken silence. In the log huts, Marianka howls for Ivan, whose sturdy breast stopped a Turkish bullet.

War is woman's foe, her plaything, her fascinating enemy, her scourge. It leaves her widowed, sorrowing, husbandless, childless, loverless! And yet woman *urges* man on to conflict. All is vanity!

By all the crystallized tears of broken woman hearts, the proud tyrant, the juggling diplomat, the greedy conqueror, should pause before they incarnadine the peaceful fields with the loyal blood of a generation of brave bread-winners.

And still there is a forced and feverish gayety abroad. A reckless, shifting, insincere merriment agitates St. Petersburg.

Women steal from ball and opera, from rout and dinner, to gaze, heart hushed, on the last death bulletins. They turn from folly with white lips to murmur, "Who next?"—to say "Thank God!" if the whirlwind blast of battle spares the beloved; or to fall, stricken and crouching before God's altar, if the particular Dimitri or Sacha's name makes the long black death-roll one unit greater.

Blessed isolation of orphanhood! It limits the range of family griefs in times like these. Princess Maritza gazes on the leaden winter skies from the granite casements of the Lazareff mansion, and fears no bolt but one.

In "bashful, maiden art" she guards her secret. It is to God alone she whispers the fervent prayer that one gallant darling head may be spared.

Her princely lover! Her royal born consort to be! With a blush she bows her head before the shrine. He is even now the lord of her pure and stainless heart. In the high empire of her bosom he reigns a czar of love.

Laughing Tia Argutin, merry Nina Lazareff rally the Princess of Georgia upon her pale cheeks, her preoccupation.

Tiflis with its crowds of wounded, the city filled with the débris of a campaign, is no pleasant place for a family. So they linger on the Neva.

Watchful General Lazareff knows the mysterious fevers, the dangerous epidemics due to the crowding of thousands of soldiers in narrow areas.

The journey to St. Petersburg, long and tedious, was welcome. Each day's travel bore the family farther away from the war-clouds hovering around the Black Sea and the Caspian.

The shadows faded imperceptibly, until at Petersburg the absence of the court and the great mass of the higher orders was the only sign of the conflict.

Comfortably installed by the Neva, the sound and clash of battle now die into silence.

Maritza remembers only with a shudder her fearful dragging captivity. Those months buried from the world in the dark convent cells grow a memory. The awful scenes of the storming of Kars are forgotten. The grass is green on Nadya Vronsky's grave.

Madame Lazareff with graceful tact leads Maritza away from all sights which agitate.

Maritza owns to the sweet face in her mirror, alone, the depth and fervor of her passion for the young hero who is now the chief of Circassia.

A rosy cherub guards her pillow at night. He whispers—finger on his smiling lip: "He loves you!"

Every day, walking in the deserted gardens of the Winter Palace, she watches for one green leaflet, the forerunner of happy spring.

Dashing along the Neva bank in her sleigh, she prays for the day when that icy flooring will break up and tumble out into the tossing Baltic.

The great fleets of fragrant birch-wood barges will sweep in from mighty Ladoga soon, borne in on the crystal rush of the melting spring floods.

When the snows shall vanish from the Champ de Mars, the embattled host of victors will there parade their shot-torn ranks before the mighty Czar. The splendid, touching pageant will fade away, until another bugle blast shall call the millions ruled by the house of Romanoff to battle for Asia and India. None are feared save their hereditary, red-coated foes, the dreaded English.

Schamyl's letters but faintly fill the needs of Maritza's passionate soul.

Glaring black words cannot paint the ardent feelings which shine in her eyes as she dreams of Ahmed riding beside her carriage at Tiflis.

Pen cannot translate or fix the ecstasy of joy which thrilled her heart when Schamyl's loving words called her back to life on the plain of Kars. It was a paradise after an inferno!

She will not own, even to herself, the raptures of the thrills of love and sorrow in the fair bosom she is queen of, when he led her in the proud safeguard of his veteran riders back to Tiflis, the hero of the hour.

When the birds return from the south, in the glittering circle of the White Czar he will come. The bravest of the brave, loyal, true, and tender! And *then*, and *then!* She burns for the day when the evening shadows will show no parting for the pilgrims of love; the day when she can say in truth: "Ahmed, my own! Mine only!"

It is merry enough in a restrained way. Every day brings news of the sweeping and final successes of the Russian arms. At least, all the spent blood and treasure have not been wasted in useless defeat. The blue and white cross marches on.

There are stars and medals, titles and dignities, rewards and honors, to be showered by the aged hand of a grateful Emperor upon the living relics of the men who faltered not in Plevna's darkest hours.

With chastened hearts the butterflies of fashion mourn those spirited women of the court who thronged to the poisonous Dobrudsha swamps to nurse the wounded. They died as nobly as the men in arms.

As if the grave were never satisfied in its hunger for prey, disease has killed as many heroes as the bullets of the rampart-sheltered Moslems.

Scores of bright-eyed ladies, tender and true, laid down their lives in their self-appointed work. If there is a woman on earth whose spirit, fortitude, and tenderness will bear up against the thousand ills of life, it is the Russian wife, mother, and maiden. From high to low in rank—faithful, ardent, vivacious, and self-sacrificing—the charm of their singular beauty and devotion lingers around the homes of the icy north. The myrtle grows there only in these tender hearts, whose fires of love are perpetual.

Fit mothers of heroes! Worthy consorts of warriors!—these daughters of Holy Russia!

Maritza finds a wistful tenderness in Madame Lazareff's watchful love. Every movement, each step of her life, is guarded. And the roses are red in her cheeks; her eye beams in splendor.

Maritza, the Rose of Tiflis, knows not of the overshadowing threat of the fugitive madman.

One oasis blooms in the desert of her days. To whom can she pour out her heart life? To no one save the absent lover! To one only—Paul Platoff!

Yes! Paul Platoff is welcome daily at the Lazareffs. His noble face, pale with his sufferings, lights up as he leads her mind to the absent Prince Schamyl.

It is not strange his sleigh brings him every afternoon—that he is welcomed by the chatelaine of the house.

His bravery, his love for Ahmed, and his distinction give him a warm welcome. Another reason binds them together. For Paul has his own heart secret!

The beautiful and lonely Princess Orbelian is *also* an orphan. She is a ward of the Emperor. Platoff relies upon the unpaid debt of Loftscha's awful laurels, to obtain the permission of the great Alexander to wed his noble ward.

Till the Emperor's return, Platoff may not announce himself as the future husband of the princess.

Too delicate to monopolize her society—for there everywhere is a Mrs. Grundy, even in Russia—Paul artfully begs Madame Lazareff to aid his innocent strategy. He meets the queen of his awakened heart in the society of Princess Maritza, at her own home.

It is a charming trinity—*two* who love each other, *one* who loves another.

Educated in seclusion, Princess Orbelian with eager eyes looks forward to the day when the silent halls of her old family shall once more ring with the merriment of Russian hospitality.

With laughing eyes she promises Maritza a visit at the ancestral home when the sorrows depart.

"*Your* home is far away at Tiflis. When you are married, use *mine* as your own! I will make Paul take me to see you,—to your lovely Caucasus —your land of roses."

Princess Orbelian longs as ardently as Maritza for the return of the Emperor. He brings Ahmed to the fair Georgian!

For the magic permission may then soon be obtained for her own wedding. Two lovely suppliants wait for the Czar.

The Lazareffs, Paul, herself, and all their powerful circle may not be gainsaid in asking the maiden hand of the last of the Orbelians.

The two girls in these hours of confidence run over their strange family histories.

"I never knew my mother. She died when I was very young," is the whole of Princess Orbelian's memories. "My father was killed in the Caucasus wars. My lonely life has been spent in the institute, or with the families of my official tutors.

"When I come into my estate my mother's relics will pass into my possession. Her picture tells me she was very beautiful. Those who knew her say her heart was noble and unselfish."

St. Petersburg holds no happier hearts than the two lovely fiancées when the grand news of peace throws every door open in rejoicing.

A hundred guns fired on every square, a general illumination, a grand gala performance at every theatre, scores of splendid fêtes make the city by the Neva a scene of mad rejoicing.

The Emperor is coming! The army is coming! The court is coming! All laurel crowned!

Silent, upturned faces on the battle shambles of Turkey appeal no more to an inscrutable God. Pale lips murmuring, "How long, O Lord, how long!" are forgotten in the joy of to-day.

Joy reigns in the palaces of the Winter King.

Madame Lazareff finds her bevy of birds of paradise wildly excited.

Vera Orbelian chatters, "The Emperor is coming." Maritza de Deshkalin hides a telegram whose every word burns in her heart. The two nymphs of honor are vaguely happy to see their friends caught in the mighty net of love, so joyous. Cupid in ambush may even now be training his feathered artillery on pretty Tia and sweet Nina. Gronow the gallant is watching for Nina's return.

"Love is a queer thing—it comes and it goes."
"Incessa patuit Dea."

Great Venus swoops down to-day, as of old pale Diana wooed Endymion from starry heights—a touch, a kiss—the fatal fire is in the veins!

Venus victrix rules the stony hearts of men, the wayward impulse of woman.

The opera of to-night will be the only gala performance since the declaration of war.

Madame Lazareff is surrounded by a happy circle. Why not Major Paul Platoff as escort? Why not, indeed? His handsome face will represent General Lazareff and the absent Ahmed.

Before the evening falls old Abdallah spends an hour with Madame la Générale. He is happy. The jeweller of Goomri has settled his accounts with the foreign office. Secret service vouchers are not asked for. Abdallah makes *no mistake in his reckoning*. He would now offer to Princess Maritza a token of the devotion of the absent.

Shawled and turbaned, the aged Moslem gravely eyes the dream of beauty which is the living picture, Princess Maritza. For she has drunk of the honey dew of paradise. Her lover is coming!

In their fleecy cotton-wool wrappings, Abdallah

extends to Maritza a necklace of strands of the silver pearls of Ormuz, which makes the young patrician clasp her white hands in womanish delight.

"I have telegrams from the Prince Schamyl. He asked me to present, in his name, these pearls to the Lady Maritza. May Allah bless you! I shall see the day-star in the great music house of the Franks to-night.

"The pearls are royal and fitly bestowed." With bending salaams, the jeweller disappears.

His august brow is graver than ever, for in secret he watches for the blow which Ghazee may deliver! The traitor is as deadly as the fell cobra!

"Praise be to Allah! Royal Schamyl will soon be here, and my long vigil will be at an end."

Abdallah seeks his coffee-house and betakes himself to mocha and a narghileh. He muses upon the store of golden imperials he hoards for himself and Hassan Bey—the Judas of Kars!

When the carriages sweep up to the grand entrance of the opera, Abdallah, in a modest coupé, follows hard upon the two stately "glass fronts" of the Lazareff party.

They are late, for four ladies, each late a quarter of an hour, retard the appearance of a party.

Women are unexplained devourers of time! *Socially* desirous of being late, *astronomically* they are even more so than the code of "Noblesse oblige" demands.

Abdallah has arrayed himself in flowing raiment of price. His swelling port is the admiration of the few loungers in the foyer. The opera is on.

The mimic woes of the soprano heroine are thrilling the hearts of a vast audience; yet in the circular rows of boxes many are absent.

Dreamy, weird music floats upon old Abdallah's ears as he follows the party to their two loges. Paul Platoff, in the dashing uniform of the horse artillery, is handsome enough to satisfy even the exacting Vera Orbelian. Madame Lazareff, a stately swan, glides along with her beauteous cygnets.

"Bismillah! But the Frankish women are fair!" Abdallah murmurs, as he gazes upon the lovely girls.

"Yet, beard of the Prophet, they are bold unbelievers!"

For Abdallah likes not the unveiled faces of these glowing graces. His private delectations of the harem give him *monopolistic* ideas as to pleasing one alone.

Sultana, favorite, or meek slave, in his good old-fashioned conservatism he holds that these tender eyes should shine alone on the master.

It is his fortune to draw the admiring comment of envious ladies who watch the sheen of his costly jewels in the great box where he sits alone.

But his mind is far away. He has closely followed every movement of Maritza since her arrival. A letter in Arabic, crumpled in his hand, recounts to him the mad vagaries of Ghazee. The wild Kurdish princess, her scoundrel father, and old Ismail, are holding high revel with Ghazee Schamyl in the distant castle where Ghazee has taken his Kurdish bride.

Gallant Mehemet Pacha, marching out of Erzeroum with his army, forgets not to telegraph to

Lazareff at Kars, to Ignatief on the Golden Horn, and to Abdallah at Petersburg, the single word, "Beware!"

For all the world knows now that the Russian court will at once return to the Neva.

Mehemet's brief letter tells him that Ghazee has sworn upon the blood of the Prophet (the incarnation of the lovely red rose of Gulistan), that Maritza shall never be Schamyl's bride.

"Mashallah! There are lands of the Franks far beyond the sea. Prince Ahmed might bear his bride there, till the wild boar be brought to bay at last.

"He comes soon. In a Moslem harem she were safe. These Frankish homes are open alike to friend and stranger. It is a foolish custom."

Abdallah muses, as the sweet notes of the opera float, in golden ripples, around the splendid hall.

There is rustling of plumage and fluttering of draperies in the splendid loges. There Abdallah's reprehensible beauties attract the eyes of the gilded Russian youth by those charms he fain would veil from a Christian world. The Lazareff loge is a treasury of loveliness.

There are several cavaliers of high renown already wending toward the boxes. Madame Lazareff is a watchful keeper of these jewels. The curtain is down.

Before this swarm of butterflies can settle around the young divinities, there is a tap at the box door.

The box-keeper, with truly Russian servility, bows, extends a fan and handkerchief. From the darkened corridor a silken voice politely explains:

"Mademoiselle has lost these little articles?"

Before the grateful Maritza can fully express her thanks the polite unknown disappears with a formal bow.

The entrance to the two loges is crowded with the élite of young Russia—friends, devotees of the houses and fortunes of the Lazareffs, the Orbelians. There are others drawn by the radiant splendor shining in Maritza's eyes.

The passionate music stealing into her heart of hearts has but one voice : " He is coming ! He comes ! "

Her pretty toy, that most dangerous bit of woman's artillery—the fan—with its attached lace kerchief, must have fallen in the corridor. Or did she leave it in the carriage? A sudden thought— Ahmed's pearls ! Yes, they are there ! Their priceless circles cling to her lovely neck. As she steals a glance at herself in the mirror of the loge, Paul Platoff leans toward her. An attendant who hands him an envelope stands in the door.

Laughingly he whispers:

" Princess, *your* despatch is at home. *Mine* has followed me here."

His eyes challenge her merrily, as he hands her the little paper strip.

"Coming.   Arrive to-morrow night.
"Schamyl."

With one half-uttered joyous exclamation, the lovely waiting one leans back in her fauteuil. She presses her kerchief to her truant lips, whose half-spoken utterance of joy causes Madame Lazareff to gaze in wonder.

An instant later she is lying prone and lifeless on

the floor of the loge, her hand still clasping her handkerchief! There is a panic!

Platoff is on his knees beside her. The eyes of Madame Lazareff are frozen in fixed terror.

For the shimmering pearls upon Maritza's neck are not as white as the pale cheeks.

Her eyelids tremble; there is a light foam at her lips.

"The heart," some one whispers in a hushed voice.

"Is it death—the sudden blow of joy?" Platoff's brain boils with the surging blood.

Her hands are turning blue. She breathes not. Her heart is still.

Before the gentlemen can bear the prostrate girl into the corridor, Abdallah the Moslem is by the side of the dying, or the dead.

His keen eye notes the handkerchief clinched in the blue-shaded hand.

While several volunteers aid the distracted ladies, Abdallah grasps Platoff by the arm.

His skinny fingers almost meet in Platoff's muscles.

"Bear her in an inner room at once, quick! Her life is of a few moments. It is" (he tears off half of the pretty lace from the clinched and stiffened hands)—"it is the deadly 'Tchina.'"

Platoff almost screams, "Poison!"

The curse of Ghazee Schamyl has fallen at last upon the defenceless head of the lovely Rose of Georgia.

Maritza lies extended on a couch in an inner room of the foyer. The blue shade settles deeper on her face, the foam thickens on her lips. *Vera*

Orbelian alone is by her side, with Platoff and Abdallah.

The frantic girls are wailing with Madame Lazareff in a corner.

"A Frankish leech! Quick for your life!" Abdallah sharply calls.

As a leading court physician presses his way into the room, Abdallah solemnly says:

"Now, with Allah's blessing, bleed her at once and strongly." In a moment the satin dress sleeve is ripped up—the corsage cut. The polished argent of her stainless, lifeless bosom is bare.

No life, not a flutter. The blood will not flow.

Solemnly Abdallah draws forth a vial of cut and twisted Turkish glass.

"I appeal to the Holy Prophet. I know the Tchina poison. If the blood flows her life is saved. *Now*, force gently open her mouth!

"There!"

A half of the vial's contents in a crystal tumbler of water, in equal share, is poured down the girl's throat.

In the corner the sobs of the wailing ladies alone are heard. Silence surrounds the lovely victim. The blood drops slowly—a little drop at first, then larger drops, at last a little stream from the bandaged marble arm.

The Russian physician stares at the old man: "By what right do you take this risk?"

Abdallah simply says:

"I was a leech in the Sultan's harem once. I know the Kurdish 'Tchina.' No Frankish skill will aid—only this." He shows the half-emptied bottle.

Platoff is kneeling by the girl and chafing her hands. The shade is lighter on her face.

The Russian doctor's hand is on the silent heart.

The trickling blood flows more easily. The blue shade leaves the hands perceptibly.

"Hakim," says Abdallah, solemnly, "if her heart beats a few moments, the *second* half of this vial will save her life. Wait!"

The throng are silent now. All eyes are fixed on the veteran Russian surgeon.

Before his lips can utter the word, his smile tells the story.

The woman's fluttering heart beats faintly.

"Thank God!" cries the doctor.

Abdallah, the good angel, gravely notes the flow of blood. The trembling eyelid begins to waver more strongly. In five minutes there is a movement of the breast—the current of life, faint but regular. She breathes once more!

"Now bind the arm, Hakim," gravely directs Abdallah. It is quickly done.

"Aid me to give her the rest of this liquid without violence. Let all be silent."

The girl begins to moan when the second portion is taken.

A dozen trusty agents of police are flying over St. Petersburg in search of the stranger whose devil work lies before them. The opera drones along.

Carried to a carriage, the suffering girl is swiftly conveyed to the darkened home of the Lazareffs. Quiet reigns around the opera, where the police are swarming! A hundred secret agents search in vain for the poisoner.

Surgeons and physicians, in levee, examine the mysterious poison's work. Among them, lifted eyebrows and quiet sneers tell the story of doubting Thomas.

Abdallah gravely cuts a fragment of the kerchief he has carefully secured, and thrusts it in a candle flame. It lies limp and white, unburned.

"The deadliest curse of Kurdistan—the *Tchina!* When touched by moisture it acts at once!"

"Abdallah, whence comes it?" Platoff queries.

"From the deepest devil-broth of dark Eblis!" Abdallah says to all. "Leave now the maiden. She must rest. She must be quiet." Platoff selects the two or three physicians whom Abdallah indicates.

"Let there be a double guard around this house," he orders of Platoff.

"I have none of the saving potion left. Only in Constantinople can it be gotten. Its weight in ten times purest diamonds would not buy it.

"I shall stay here. I must watch the maiden for several days."

Madame Lazareff and Vera Orbelian carry out the wishes of Abdallah. His whispered conferences with Dr. Ostrokoff make the latter cry, "Wonderful! wonderful!"

Platoff obeys Abdallah's directions to quiet the house. A pile of cushions is thrown down in the corridor in front of Maritza's door.

"Here I will watch," he simply says. "Have some assistants watch the night there," pointing to the lower end of the hall. "See that they sleep not. The curse of Ghazee Schamyl never sleeps!"

"I shall be here," Platoff indicates. A room facing

the only entrance to Maritza's door awaits him. In her apartment two Sisters of Charity, noblest of God's daughters, are on duty.

The lonely house is silent. The hour wears late. Abdallah stands by Maritza's bedside. Platoff's eager eyes are watching her ashen face. She moans. Her arms pain her sorely. Deeply the surgeon's knife has sought the well-springs of her pure blood.

Her eyes are half open. An awful idea strikes Platoff. The women are strange to her. But *Abdallah and himself* are not! There is no flicker of recognition. Her eyes have *the stare of a child*. Great God! she is following the flashing of the foolish tinsel on his uniform!

He grasps Abdallah. He menaces him! She makes no sign.

"Tell me, tell me all!" Platoff hoarsely whispers. "Is there anything wrong?"

"May the angel of Allah spread his wings over the day-star! And the Holy Prophet make smooth the path of the lion of the Caucasus!

"He comes to-morrow night?"

Platoff's tears are blinding him as he bows his head in speechless woe.

"She may never speak or see him any more," sadly murmurs Abdallah. He leads Platoff from the room. "*Her mind is vacant.* Be it yours to meet this noble youth, and make this burden known to him. The future is with Allah."

The old Turk's uplifted finger implores the mercy of God. He sadly turns away, for Platoff throws himself on his couch in an agony. Madness: **Maritza** demented! An awful blow!

And, happy-hearted, the lovelight burning in the fiery eyes which faced the mad midnight battle in the Kanly fort to save her, Ahmed Schamyl is racing along toward the Neva.

"I shall see her to-morrow. I shall hear her say, 'Ahmed, my own! mine only!'" he whispers to himself.

God's infinite mercy lifts not the veil too soon which brings forth the manifold sorrows of the fate-stricken children of Eve.

CHAPTER XIV.

HOME AGAIN.—IN THE ORBELIAN PALACE.—FINDING A SISTER.—THE OPENING OF THE NEVA.

PAUL PLATOFF'S dreams in the Lazareff house are haunted by a suffering lily face. A sweet girl's vacant eyes roving over his person in childlike curiosity!

As he awakes to the saddest day of his life, his first thought is Dr. Abdallah's injunction, "You alone must tell Schamyl."

He rubs his eyes. It is, alas! not a dream.

The attendants in the halls come at his signal. Abdallah is in the sick-room. In a half-hour he noiselessly emerges.

Platoff's eyes ask the question.

"Better, my son! Stronger, but the spirit is still absent!"

Led by Abdallah, he enters the princely maiden's room.

There, pale and worn, yet breathing regularly, the Rose of Tiflis lies. No hopeful sign! The fearful blow of the poison upon the nerve centres has paralyzed her mind.

In the morning-room Madame Lazareff and the anxious girls wait for the report.

Abdallah forbids any one to enter, save the physician, the nurses, and herself. Only time, and gathering native nerve force, can obliterate the fearful shock to the mind.

A double-fanged serpent! If it kills not, the golden cord of the mind may snap forever. Only the old Aztec secrets of the Loco poison, guarded by fanatics from the Rio Grande to the dark wilds of Honduras, have a formula of such a dreaded poison as the Asiatic "Tchina." Poor widowed Empress Carlotta, after twenty years, bears the awful cross of a ruined intellect. Her deadly foe, Juarez (poisoned in his bath), and other wrecked minds and lives, are ghastly reminders of the work of the Aztec "Loco" poisons. Where the children of the Incas *sometimes* fail, the conspirators of the harem *always* succeed. To close the lips, to shatter the mind, to poison with a rose in one fragrant death-stroke, to reduce to mania or idiocy—is their work. They delight to bring on the fatal end under sudden excitement or after years of lingering pain. They can snuff out the mental candle like lightning. These are the gloomy secrets of the seraglio poisoners.

The Orient, mother of arts, languages, and kingdoms, has the fatal mist of conspiracy and concealed crime floating ever through its fairest bowers

Platoff mournfully orders his sleigh. To find the

news of the day; to learn if the miscreant has been caught; to locate the imperial train, and to meet Schamyl—this is his sad duty!

Abdallah calms the heart-broken women mourners. The extremest quiet must be the price of recovery, even if long delayed.

Platoff, in a boudoir, takes leave of the Princess Orbelian. Her noble soul goes out to the suffering sister of her heart.

"Paul," she says, with a rare smile lighting up her tears, "my palace, my country home, is the place! We will surround Maritza with *tenderest* love and care. I will offer it to General Lazareff when he comes. You know I enter *now* into my womanhood."

With a fervent kiss, Platoff dashes away to the heart of the city. He learns no news.

The police have been baffled. The whole opera thought the lady had only fainted. There is no social excitement. Tragedies are frequent in Petersburg.

The grim colonel in charge of the city police station is mystified. "Major Platoff," he says, "this devil must have slipped into the bazaars! In Oriental garb it would take years to find him. I fear he will escape us!" He grinds his teeth in rage.

It is too true! There are sixty thousand scattered Orientals in St. Petersburg.

Sorrowing, yet not surprised, Paul drives through the streets. Everywhere decorations and preparations for the imperial train. The Emperor may go to Gatschina. But the gala train of the imperial staff, the generals, princes, and great court officers, will arrive in the evening.

After conference with the Minister of Interior, Paul is given a special engine to meet the train.

The roads of Russia are closed to travel when the great Czar is en route.

With an hour spent in preparation, Platoff is in readiness.

Driving back to report to the circle at the Lazareffs, Paul learns the state of Maritza is the same. Away on the rail he speeds to prepare Prince Ahmed for this sad home-coming. It is too cruel!

No vigilance of the police is spared. The Lazareff house is searched in every nook. A cordon of the Third Section watches its every approach.

Dr. Abdallah, calmly smoking on his divan cushions at the end of the corridor, performs his daily ablutions. Facing the east, he prays in his solemn fashion for the lovely Frankish idol of his friend's heart. Nothing now surprises the old Moslem. His life has been spent in scenes of deadly conspiracy, of black intrigue and frenzied revenge.

Two hours' travel places Platoff's train on a siding awaiting the imperial party. The official wire has flashed a message to Schamyl.

"Waiting you here—special train. Important news for you."

Far away, with shrieking whistles, the gala train approaches. Petersburg, wild with delight, awaits its absent notables.

No heart bounds more gayly than Schamyl's; yet, when the despatch is handed him, he has once more a vision of a lovely woman, lifeless, the glistening pearls shining on her fair neck, and bending over her always *that man*. He cannot *even now* see the face.

With a roar and a shriek the great train draws up. One division proceeds to Gatschina. The other will go through to allow the citizens a sight of heroes laurelled in victory.

Platoff, standing on the platform, gazes at the train. In an instant, Schamyl, his eyes blazing like fire, clasps him in his arms.

"Maritza!" he hoarsely says.

"Is in St. Petersburg," Platoff answers, with averted face.

"She is ill—she is dead!" Ahmed's voice rises almost to a shriek.

"She is very ill, Schamyl," Paul answers. "Come into my train. I must talk to you, alone."

While the imperial convoy dashes away to Gatschina, the official division moves steadily on toward Petersburg. Ahmed sits in the car with Platoff, his head in his hands.

Strong man as he is, his frame is shaken with the fury of his rage. His ardent soul is torn with his frantic sorrow. He knows the story now!

To such a home-coming! To see the exquisite mind overthrown, to find her lovely face only a waxen blank, struck in her innocence by the coward fiend Ghazee! To be powerless to avert, to guard, to save, that one darling head! This is the crown of thorns—a life's misery!

He raises desperate eyes to his friend. Paul implores him to be master of himself. It is a blotting out of all the tender past—a shattering of the golden future!

All the scenes of war fade away. There is but one picture in their minds. That suffering woman's frozen smile may never change till another life shall be given her!

"Vengeance!" Ahmed hisses. "To the end of the world!"

Paul lays a hand on his arm. "Leave that to God alone, Schamyl," he solemnly says.

Moodily gazing from the windows, with eager glance Ahmed eyes the spires of Petersburg.

Descending in the station, where thousands frantically welcome the heroes of the hour, the two friends thread the joyous crowd.

"Take me to her at once!" Schamyl cries.

On through the illuminated streets the sleigh dashes.

Platoff precedes Schamyl into the Lazareff mansion.

While Ahmed paces the salon like a tiger, Platoff returns with Abdallah.

The ladies have not the courage to gaze yet on the princely lover in his despair.

"Come," says Abdallah, simply. At the threshold of the sick chamber the old man places his withered finger on his lip.

Schamyl bows.

Platoff, on tiptoe, sees the now familiar sight. That lovely pallid face, the wandering hands, the earnest, sad-eyed Sisters of Charity with tender woman hearts alive to human sorrows! On his knees beside the woman he has sought through fire and flame, the victor Prince of the Caucasus!

There is silence. Her eyes slowly meet his. They rove over his face, unchanged. She makes no sign. Ah, yes! a pleased expression, as of a spoiled infant. One lovely arm is extended toward him. He leans toward her. She *picks at the great white cross upon his breast.*

"Speak to her, Prince," Abdallah softly whispers.

"Maritza, my darling! My own beloved!" His voice trembles. Its accent is as sad as the wind sweeping over the tomb of the best beloved.

Steadily her splendid eyes are fixed upon the white cross of valor. She will have it—that bauble for which his life has been risked a hundred times.

Detaching it, he places it in her hand.

With a satisfied smile she sinks back on her pillow.

But she cannot hear the call of love from his heart of hearts.

He is on his knees and sobbing madly. "Come!" Abdallah touches him on the shoulder.

Pressing loyal lips on her brow, the princely Circassian lover staggers from the room.

In the next half-hour he knows how this sorrow has stricken the gentle hearts around her.

Abdallah—while Schamyl, lowly speaking, talks with Princess Orbelian, his eyes filled with a vague wonder—draws Platoff from the room.

"Watch him! Every moment, my son! Leave him not. There is a madness which kills not others, but the madman alone. Force him away. Make him talk of other things—the war, his own life. But this—this will kill him if he yields to his mood."

The night of general rejoicing sees Schamyl a guest at Platoff's rooms, and watched in his slumbers by faithful friends.

On the morrow Platoff resolutely occupies Schamyl's attention. To drive to the Ministry of War and obtain a leave; to notify General Lazareff, who cannot return for a month; to inform Count Ignatief by telegraph; to conduct the court physician to the bed of the invalid for a conference—all this is useful and distracting work.

With infinite patience Abdallah directs the treatment of the invalid. The Russian physicians marvel at the old Hakim. Before the evening the verdict of a council is announced—rest, quiet, and change of scene.

Madame Lazareff accepts the offer of the Princess Orbelian. In a few days Maritza is in the long silent home of the old family.

Schamyl, with a faithful detachment of soldiers, as well as police, finds his employment in insuring the safety of the gentle invalid.

The Emperor's aide-de-camp, sent to examine and report, bears to Prince Schamyl the imperial mandate to present himself at court, in due season, for special honors and rewards.

Ahmed's mind has recovered its balance. But a settled gloom and sadness weighs upon his soul.

The one bright flash of love and life in the splendid home of the Orbelians, near Tsarskoe-Zeloe, is the young heiress of the house.

Platoff has received the imperial permission to marry. It will not be as *Major*, but as *Colonel* Platoff, whose officers of his new regiment only wait for happier days, to give a rousing wedding feast to the hero of Loftscha.

The city on the Neva is in wild triumph.

The trees which Maritza watched begin to put

forth their little green shoots. Alas, her light foot wanders no more in the "lover's tryst" of the Winter Palace gardens! Attended by a faithful nun, or leaning on the arm of one of her three graces, the Dame Blanche silently walks the splendid corridors of the old Orbelian home. She speaks not. She notices the objects around her mechanically.

Ahmed's guiding arm assists her. In the frank abandonment of childhood, she follows. She *greets* not his coming. She *heeds* not his going. There is no smile to answer his loving gaze.

Seated by Vera Orbelian's side, she plays with the objects of Vera's daily examination. The guardians and tutors have delivered to Princess Vera her mother's jewels, personal mementos and papers.

Maritza grows stronger, but Abdallah's brow is carved with deepest wrinkles. He sees what *others cannot* see. Ahmed's heart is wearing out by inches. Hope not deferred, but gainsaid. No friendly ray on the gray horizon of these days!

Madame Lazareff, preparing for the general's return, is absent often.

Platoff tries to rouse Schamyl. Seated in the library, they discuss the war. Its solid fruits are now assured. Paul, with comrade-like delicacy, keeps his own happy love in the background. Yet he must see that Schamyl's eyes follow Vera Orbelian with a yearning tenderness. It is because of her gentle kindness to the stricken Princess Maritza, who sits and plays with the old letters Vera is reading for the first time.

The treaty of peace is published. Russia's enormous gains astonish the people—the whole control of Asia Minor; the great fortresses; Bessarabia regained; the loss of 1856 made good; the independence of Bosnia and Herzegovina; Bulgaria's autonomy; a huge war indemnity; Roumania, Servia, and Montenegro freed; the menacing Danube fortresses evacuated!

"Schamyl," Platoff cries, "we have gained all, save only the Dardanelles and St. Sophia.

" But *it will come!* " he cries, with sparkling eyes.

"I have done with glory and its dreams," Schamyl moodily cries. "I'd give the whole of Armenia, if I had it, to hear that angel speak *once more* to me."

He cannot be roused. He wanders away to lovely Vera, whose tender eyes are often dim with a child's tribute to a loved mother. She is reading her mother's heart—old letters. He hears a joyful cry. With sparkling eyes she hails Schamyl. Silent Maritza wonders at the royal jewels she fondly trifles with. The dark-robed Sister of Charity gazes on the lovely pair. For Maritza's glorious eyes mutely shine out in tender appeal: "Help me!"

Abdallah fears now the help is not in this world.

"Prince Ahmed!" Vera cries. "Come here! I am a Circassian, too!" She is holding a letter.

His brow lights up.

"Explain! I beg you!'

"I have just found this sealed letter, in which my dear loved mother tells me I was born in the Circassian mountains while the army was there."

Maritza's wistful eyes rove over the eager faces of Ahmed and Vera.

"And your exact age now?" Schamyl eagerly asks.

The wondering girl tells him. Abruptly, without a word, Schamyl leaves the room.

Returning with Platoff, whose face is blank with amazement, Schamyl leads the wondering girl up to her mother's picture. It is smiling down in the splendid boudoir, which her daughter now makes radiant with her own sweet presence.

"Vera," he softly says, "is that your mother?"

The lady looks up shyly. Is he wandering, too? Is his mind unthroned?

"My darling mother," she whispers, her hands clasped on her breast.

"Vera, she was *my mother* also," Schamyl softly says, with a tender smile; "and you, you dear child, are my own sister!"

Her head is buried in a brother's arms. Paul Platoff softly walks back to Maritza, seated, toying with the jewels.

Beside the mother's tomb in the old family chapel, brother and sister kneel together. The hallowed air seems full of rushing spirit wings.

When they unfold to Paul all the story, he knows that his bride and his friend are both children of the great Schamyl.

The seal of years is lifted from the strange history. Schamyl knows now the dying Hassan would have named in his last gasp the gentle sister whose smile is shed on his darkened soul like moonlight on the waters.

As he seeks his couch, Vera whispers with her good-night: "Ahmed, my brother, God's mercy may save you yet! Maritza's happiest days may come with the *roses budding now!*"

Platoff and Schamyl make a pilgrimage of two days to the city of Peter.

Closeted with General Ignatief, they learn the whole story of Princess Orbelian. The brothers in arms are soon to be united by a closer tie. The marriage wraps Princess Maritza with a nearer cordon of loving friends.

Ignatief accords the right of Colonel Platoff to know the birth of his wife. Master of the policy of the Russian government, he explains to the young men the long captivity of Princess Orbelian at Dargo, the *enforced* marriage of the lovely hostage with Sultan Schamyl, the Lion of Daghestan!

General Orbelian's death, his long absence on service, the seven years' disappearance of the princess, were matters incident to the romantic border service of Russia.

The policy of the great Czar in advancing Schamyl's *second* son, in surrounding Vera Orbelian's girlhood with tenderest attentions, was suggested by the importance of the succession to the princely suzerainty of Circassia.

For the first time in his life, Ahmed Schamyl grasps the secret of the Moslem cunning of his royal father.

Breaking the oath of his first capitulation, betraying his soldier's honor pledged to General Fesi, at Tileth in 1837, he was later bound by personal gratitude to the Czar for the return of Jamal-Eddin, his darling first-born.

When the death of Jamal-Eddin in the foreign Turkish service plunged him in frantic sorrow, his final surrender to Prince Baryatinsky left him, at last, helpless in the power of the Czar.

His people scattered, Circassia devastated by forty years of war—his own career was ended.

From the palaces of Dargo, he descended in royal state with two new bonds tying his faith to the Czar. His legitimate successor, Ghazee Schamyl, might die or be the victim of treachery!

"He was a grand old diplomatist," Ignatief enthusiastically cries to his young listeners.

"Desirous of wielding the sceptre of the Caucasus through his sons, he remained quiet at Kaluga in Russia for nine years—a stately captive!

"When he allowed Princess Orbelian and her infant daughter to return to Russia in exchange for his first-born, he withheld the *son* of their marriage.

"You know, Prince Ahmed, *your* education differed from Ghazee's. There were interviews, now covered with the mantle of eternal silence, between Sultan Schamyl and his lovely Russian wife during his years at Kaluga.

"The fiery Moslem must have deeply loved the gentle woman, who drooped into the grave soon after his downfall, for he educated you *as a Christian*.

"Some pledge of love, some last desire to do tardy justice to the beautiful woman whom he roughly wooed in her long captivity, must have softened the old rebel's heart.

"To Ghazee alone he poured out his political plans of the future—his Jesuitic schemes to replace a Schamyl on the warrior throne of Circassia!

"*You* he was content to see in the Russian service, knowing that from policy the government would advance you in your career. He felt that years would bring your sister and yourself together. He knew it was your right to be a Christian.

"The Orbelian inheritance provided for her. Your own wealth was set aside by your father, with our government's approval."

"Mysterious and wonderful man!" Ahmed murmurs. "Count, I cannot understand his last years."

Ignatief resumes.

"We did not ourselves until the events of the last war. After the death of Princess Orbelian his mystic moods returned. The dreamer longed for a death in the holy places—a voyage to Mecca and Medina. It was part *policy*, part *devotion*.

"He outwitted the Czar in his old age. He well knew as a *mere rebel* Ghazee could never succeed in regaining the Caucasus.

"He trained Ghazee in all his own dark wiles. Leaving him here to penetrate our policy, he retired to Arabia and died there.

"His master mind built up at Constantinople, with the higher Ulemas of the Moslem church, the plan of Ghazee's counter rebellion. He knew the inevitable Russo-Turkish war was near. Turkey was to aid in driving Russia back to the natural line of the Caucasus, and Ghazee was to reign alone.

"It was for this he sent him these solemn last messages. He bound your servitor Hassan to never reveal your birth while living. Ghazee hated you as the son of a gentle Russian who swayed your royal father's mind. It was mere state policy with us to forbid public acknowledgments of that union. But Ghazee failed in exciting the wild enthusiasm of your father among the mountaineers. Cold, selfish, and brutal, he was not loved. He only desired to wed Princess Maritza to strengthen his claims.

"Besides, my young friends, he failed to recognize the Russianizing of his native provinces in twenty years. The railway and modern arms made the renewal of a Circassian rebellion wild folly."

Prince Ahmed sees clearly at last.

"A great tribute to Schamyl's prophetic mind! He knew Turkey could not conquer us, but hoped that England would *actively* aid with her enormous fleet. He hoped they would hold the Black Sea, while the Turks, with the Circassian rebellion, swept away our power in Asia Minor."

"And Europe?" Ahmed asks.

"There again his genius shines. He dreamed that Austria would be strong enough to hold Russia off the Danube by mere jealousy. The rise of the Prussian power cleared away the strongest active enemy of Russia in the principalities. *Austria* is dead.

"These future schemes were dinned into Schamyl's ears by the diplomatic agents of France, England, and Austria. He was persuaded by his own Turkish friends. There were continued offers of aid to him, even to the last."

"These agents deceived him," Ahmed murmurs.

"Ah, my dear Prince!" Ignatief replies with a smile. "Diplomacy is only refined lying! When the game of war opens, the strongest takes all the prizes. It is a poor trade, modern diplomacy!

"Look at Russia! *We never go back!* Forced to be cunning, we win and hold by the strong title of the sword.

"Onward to Asia! On to the Pacific! On to Constantinople! On to the Persian Gulf! Such is our natural path."

The count pauses, his roving black eyes watch the eager listeners.

"And yet *England is in our path.*"

The great count smiles as he rises and directs the traditional wine to be served.

"Both you gentlemen may live to ride as generals of division in the death struggle for India which will be fought with England on the lines of the Asiatic border. We shall flatter and hold France as our ally. We will give them a part of the great East."

"Communications!" both the soldiers cry.

"Gentlemen, General Anenkoff is already ordered to build the railway from the Caspian shore to Merv, Tashkend, and Samarcand.

"Within a year the railway from Poti and Batoum to Kutars, Tiflis, and Baku will be in construction.

"We may not live to see it, but in less than a quarter of a century the Russian military roads will control in one unbroken line, without change of car, the Indian, Chinese, and Siberian boundaries. `We' will gain territory on every border.

"The locomotive will have a clear path to the blue Pacific at Vladivostock.

"*Where* will our English friends be then?"

He pauses in triumph. The dictatorship drifts toward him now. A dangerous honor!

With warm greetings the coming dictator dismisses the two soldiers.

"I expect to hear of your marriage at a very early day, Colonel Platoff. Pray believe me, it would be the wisest step. The late Princess Orbelian arranged her papers before her death, so that her daughter would know, only at the right time, the secret of her birth.

"Prince Schamyl, on behalf of the Emperor, I am authorized to say that should Colonel Platoff and his wife, or the Lazareffs, wish to take Princess Maritza abroad for travel or medical assistance, every official aid will be freely given. Your presentation to the Emperor only awaits your happier days."

Before the mid-April leaves are timidly unfolding their delicate green fronds to the warmer sunlight, there is a quiet wedding in the chapel of the Orbelians. Vera is given away by General Lazareff's honored hand to Paul Platoff in marriage.

Madame Lazareff, a few of the knights of the sword, and the two lovely belles of Tiflis are the witnesses.

As the white-robed priests raise the deep swelling tones of the Russian marriage service, while the boy choir alternates in music of the angels, Ahmed Schamyl's eyes grow misty. Supported by Abdallah, whose loving-kindness endears him, silent Maritza watches all. The good Sisters of Charity meekly tell their beads near by. Maritza, the Rose of Tiflis, wonders at the mystic ceremony. She makes no sign.

Clad in rich, clinging white robes, the beautiful girl's face is childlike. No words escape the sealed portals of her rosy lips, but she smiles and points in glee at the golden crowns held over the heads of bride and groom.

Ahmed's pearls are gleaming to-day on her neck. On her bosom she wears the white cross of Schamyl. With a strange childish fancy, she will not part with it, but plays with it for hours.

Quietly, royally, the wedding-breakfast ends the celebration. Maritza, gentle soul, follows meekly the happy bride. For pain and sorrow, joy and hope's high longings, touch not her idle mind.

It is two weeks after the bridal, when the advice of the wisest, Abdallah's utter lack of hope, and General Lazareff's wishes, decide the loving circle to go abroad with the stricken one. Perhaps change of scene, some skilful specialist, some providential chance, may break the silence of this affected daughter of princes.

General Lazareff, a lion of the triumphant court circles, aids with his widest experience in every plan. To Schamyl he brings news from Mehemet Pacha. Ghazee Schamyl and his Kurdish bride have disappeared. Tiflis is in general sorrow for the loved princess. The utmost skill of spy and agent, secret section and refugee, fail to connect Ghazee *directly* with the blow so foully struck.

Rejected by the Turks, Ghazee has fled to Egypt, to Arabia, perchance to Morocco.

Grim Lazareff recounts the positive threats of the Russian government to the Turkish authorities, that any appearance of Ghazee on the border would be followed by prompt and unpitying punishment. He is *useless* to the Turks now. Mustapha Bey seeks vengeance for Nadya Vronsky's death.

Old Ismail Pacha knows the fate of a Russian renegade, traitor, and deserter. The wily Kurd aided the disappearance of the would-be assassin!

Gathered in St. Petersburg, the little circle makes ready for its departure.

It is high time. The court is bidden to the gorgeous ceremony of the opening of the Neva.

From the huge polygon, the gloomy fortress of Petropaulosk, with barbaric opulence of display, the governor of the great fortress of the crown in state proceeds. He offers in a golden cup the waters of the Neva to the imperial lord of the frozen north.

When the blue waters race to the sea, once more clangor of bell and boom of cannon peal out. The lord of the waters receives the announcement of the return of the short summer.

General and Madame Lazareff attend this royal ceremony. Countless thousands line the banks to welcome the imperial victor.

The splendor of Asia wraps the peculiar ceremony of the Russian court with mediæval display. Priest and dignitary, fashion and the multitude, lend their aid.

Platoff and his happiest of brides are with the party. The departure is only delayed for Madame

Lazareff, who must take part in the great reunion of the court.

Seated at an open window in the family mansion, Prince Ahmed guards, alone, his suffering loved one. Not a single moment has she been unwatched since the fatal stroke of the demon enemy.

The breath of spring wanders through the casement. There are roses by the side of the gentle invalid. Save for her vacant silence no one could tell how sadly the Rose of Tiflis is weighed down by the paralysis of the mysterious poison.

In the corner, faithful and devoted, the Russian nun sits, praying for the afflicted.

Proud music swells in street and square. The legions of the Czar are marching to the great review of victory. For the Champ de Mars to-day will see the flower of Russia march past with the banners, battle consecrated, of Plevna and of Kars, of Shipka and of Loftscha. It is the great feast of victory. At high noon the boom of a single gun announces the departure of the official message.

"The Neva is open. Its waters are once more under guard of his Majesty's legions."

The golden tribute cup is offered in midstream to the Emperor.

Schamyl sadly gazes on the beautiful girl who heeds not the swelling martial music. Boom of bell or the joyous cries of the multitude in the streets stir her not.

He cannot ride to-day before the eyes of the great Emperor, and the dangerous beauties of the northern world.

In twenty minutes a terrific salvo of all the guns of the fortress shakes the ground. The casements rattle again with a second grand peal from a hundred steel throats.

Schamyl hears a voice. He turns like a flash.

Maritza is standing, her hands clasped. There is surely a strong effort of her will. Her lips are moving!

The nun springs toward the fair girl. When the last salvo shakes the room Maritza cries, "The Russians are coming! Ahmed, my own! He comes to save me!"

As she totters and sinks, the strong arms of her lover are round her.

Resting in a chair, the kneeling nun is gazing in rapture on her brightening face. As Schamyl's kisses warm her waxen hands, she slowly murmurs:

"They are coming to save me! Ahmed! Killed? Oh, my God!"

With a shriek she falls exhausted in the chair.

That sound brings Abdallah from his noon-day prayers, in a haste which proves his devotion.

"Quick now!" he cries. He knows the voice of the silent lady.

"A flask of brandy!"

A restoring draught is given the unconscious girl. Ahmed whispers the tidings.

Abdallah motions the nun to leave the room. The black robe glides to the door.

"Watch her, Prince, ALONE, when she wakes. It is our last chance!"

He shuffles behind a curtain.

A faint fluttering of the eyelids. Schamyl's heart beats as if it would burst its bonds. O God! have mercy!

The lids open slowly. He is kneeling before her. A flash of lovelight gleams on her sweet face. She softly says, clasping him in her clinging arms:

"I knew you would come. My Ahmed, my lover! Let us fly—away, away from the cannon!"

The seal is broken. She knows him now. When the carriage sweeps up, late in the afternoon, with Madame Lazareff and the ladies, old Abdallah in majesty receives them.

"Praise be to Allah! Go not up! The prophet of God has sent his blessing upon the angel of your house. She is saved!"

The excited ladies throw themselves upon the Moslem. Platoff's witching bride, the stately lady, and the nymphs cause him to think that the Frankish women are marvels. He gently leads them into the drawing-room.

It is his hour of supreme triumph. In a half-hour, with clattering escort, General Lazareff and Colonel Platoff ride into the courtyard.

Platoff is astounded! His sweet wife almost throws herself under the feet of the chargers.

"Paul! Paul! Come! She is saved!" she cries. He leaps to the ground.

With an agility which the young men envy, old General Lazareff throws himself also out of the saddle. Plumes, stars, and medals, jingling sabre, and all, he dashes into the house. Platoff is in his wife's arms. She is weeping and laughing.

"Softly, great chief," entreats Abdallah. "I will

go up and find if I may show you this child of Allah's grace."

Lumbering up the stairs, blessing the prophet's name, Abdallah returns.

He leads the procession and entreats silence.

Into the room, one after another, the delighted throng softly pass.

It is a dream of heavenly peace and joy! For there, under the mild smile of the jewelled picture of the Virgin Mother, lies the Rose of Tiflis. Schamyl, with the light of his new-found happiness transfiguring his face, holds one slender hand which peeps out of the coverlid. The great ruby ring gleams upon the snowy finger he is caressing. On his bosom shines once more his own white cross.

Her lovely face beams with the radiance of the old days. Her arms close around Vera Platoff in the first kiss of a new sisterhood.

One by one the circle greet with tenderest words the beauty of Tiflis returned from the dark land of shadows.

Abdallah leads them from the room. But by her side, in rapture, the prince of the Caucasus watches the lovely one whose eyes are now closing in the slumber of happy excitement.

The delightful days following the return of Princess Maritza's consciousness bring but one disagreement among the dwellers in the house of joy.

General Lazareff ascribes the cure to the sage and doubly venerated Abdallah.

The old Turk gravely relates how, at the hour of

his noon-day prayer, the mighty hand of the prophet was stretched forth in aid.

The Russian ladies, aided by the gentle Sisters, in grateful prayer bow before the holy picture of the jewelled shrine. It is a new miracle!

Practical Paul Platoff, with pardonable professional pride, insists that the terrific shock of the salvos of the fortress artillery recalled the awful cannonade of Kars. It broke, with overmastering power of fear, memory, and love, the seal of silence.

The gallant and stately Schamyl, whispering burning words of love's long silent story to the now blooming beauty, is too happy and thankful to *argue*. He thinks he can hear the silver chime of wedding-bells.

CHAPTER XV.

AN EMPEROR'S GIFT.—THE BRIDES OF DARGO.—TIDINGS OF GHAZEE.—A LAST SHOT.—UNDER THE WHITE TOWER. — TREASURE - TROVE. — KISMET.

BENEATH the fragrant spring blossoms, Ahmed and Maritza take up the golden threads of love's precious story. They walk the gardens of the Orbelian palace.

Her recovery is absolute. Calmly Abdallah eyes his completed work. All the physicians demand that she be spared every excitement.

Ignorant of the cause of her illness and the insidious attack on her life, Maritza de Deshkalin looks forward only to her coming marriage.

The departure of the Lazareffs is delayed for the

bridal. The wedding-bells ring out. Happy Maritza accedes to Prince Ahmed's wishes for an immediate union.

Before the altar where Paul and Vera joined their hands, Schamyl takes the Rose to his bosom for aye. It is a dream of quiet ecstasy, the solemn pageant!

After the ceremony, lovely Maritza learns of the strange tie doubly binding to her heart the budding matron Vera.

A wedding of surprises! An imperial aide presented himself as a witness for the Czar. A delegation of the officers of the Circassians of the royal guard appeared on behalf of the army.

Count Ignatief; in stately grandeur, gazed on the beautiful scene. Standing in the halls of the palace, gazing on his long unknown but ever-loved mother's face, Prince Schamyl, ready for the ceremony, receives as a personal gift from the Emperor the storied sword which his father bore in his kingly sway over the Caucasus. His rank as major-general with it!

A mandate to appear, in special audience, before the Czar, at Tsarskoe-Zeloe, accompanies this crowning honor of a sovereign's grace.

On behalf of the Empress, the courtly Ignatief presents to the bride a necklace of diamonds, which, glistening on her neck at a special presentation of the groom and bride, is a signal mark of the favor of the august Czarina.

Ahmed Schamyl, among the roses blooming in his mother's fairy bowers, finds no rose as fair as the blushing bride whose sorrows have melted away under the sun of the wedding-morn.

In the old hall, seated as master of the feast, Paul Platoff toasts the loveliest bride in Russia. His eyes fondly rest upon Vera, a matron of *brief* but *wondrous* experience, sitting in piquant beauty—the lady of the castle.

While the feast is at its height, Count Ignatief takes his leave. Yet he lingers for an hour of earnest conference with Colonel Platoff and Abdallah. A man of mysteries! The book of the past has yet its sealed pages.

Golden days run away, lightly linked in rosy bands. There is happiness in the home of the Orbelians. Maritza's face glows with the olden beauty and a newer light.

Abdallah with majestic mien takes an affecting farewell of his friends. He has a secret mission. The gloomy fastnesses of his Goomri abode will soon receive him. "Inshallah! The peace of the prophet be upon you all!" he utters, as he salaams. He is not loath to revisit his own harem.

The return of the brides to Tiflis, and a visit to Dargo, is the finale of the weddings. The brother and sister long to see the old castle of their birth. It will be graced by the presence of Abdallah. He is charged with secret missions from the foreign office. A special duty is laid on him also by Count Ignatief. He goes rejoicing on his way.

Platoff alone knows its import. The Prince and Princess Schamyl, in state, as due their rank, bow to the rulers of the great empire.

Schamyl's chosen command, the cavalry of the frontier, awaits him. To Circassia! Away!

It is his dearest wish to restore and reoccupy the

vacant halls of Dargo, where his father's white mantle once glittered in pride.

To show Paul the glories of the matchless Caucasus; to wander hand in hand with Vera where their gentle mother lingered in her cloud-capped palace; to see the star-like eyes of Maritza shining on him among her own roses at Tiflis, where the silver minarets of great Ararat rise far in the sapphire sky—is the prince's fondest desire.

Week after week of Petersburg's fêtes and splendors have exhausted the public capacity for frantic rejoicing. The court and its gilded circle begin to seek the bosky woods and the fragrant dells of the romantic country palaces. Old *boyar*, great noble, proud prince, and powerful courtier disperse to Finland, the Crimea, or family mansions far away from the shadows of the Winter Palace.

The Lazareffs make the "grand tour." It is a family party of four which, in merriest mood, leaves for the storied mountains of the Tcherkess. Russian prestige demands it.

Platoff and Ahmed recount their campaign scenes as the plains of the Kherson fly by. The happy brides are waiting to see the white peak of Elburz rise from the southern line of the steppes.

Day by day the long panorama unrolls. In the gorges of the royal peaks the song of the pines welcomes the wanderers.

Fragrant breezes fan the brows of the merry beauties.

At Vladikaukas, an escort of honor awaits the Prince of the Caucasus. Schamyl's heart bounds with pride when he recognizes in the wild "Hourra," the voices of the men who followed him when he first smote the Kurdish raiders.

It is his *own body-guard.*

General Prince Melikoff would honor the man who bears the magic sabre of great Sultan Schamyl.

The special favor of the Czar radiates around Ahmed's head in glory.

Once more in her girlhood's home, at Tiflis, Maritza wanders through the leafy shades. They are now blooming with rose and myrtle. The Caucasus is a paradise. The gardens by the Kara are a dream of witchery. By Ahmed's side, the Rose of Tiflis, a happy wife, with bated breath shows him where she was hurried to the river, a helpless captive. These are golden days!

There is no fear now! For looking far to where Kars frowns upon its beetling cliffs, beyond the swift Kara, it is all Russia!

Russian land evermore!

Tiflis en fête is a Paris en miniature.

Paul Platoff, envied by the men, adored by the ladies, is captured by Gronow and the gallant staff.

The review of Schamyl's brigade, in all its wild chivalry, on the square where he first told his love in spite of the gentle chaperon, brings happy tears to the eyes of Maritza.

A grand ball, at which the courtly Grand Duke honors each bride impartially, revives memories of the night when Schamyl broke his word.

For, as a penance, this evening he dances the mazurka with the beauty who missed that last grand ball.

While the music floats out into the delicious

night, and Princess Vera Platoff queens it with her sister rose—in an alcoved recess—Platoff gravely confers with Abdallah.

"May the smile of Allah lighten the pathway of the just and valiant! I have good news for you. I have discovered the truth!

"You may telegraph the wise count!" Abdallah is cheerful. He resumes.

"There are *great stores of gold and jewels* left by the lion of Daghestan in the old palace at Dargo.

"Count Ignatief is a diviner of the buried treasures. A mighty chief!"

"Explain!" cries Platoff. His eager looks betray his anxiety.

Abdallah strokes his beard.

"Patience, my son! When I returned I talked with the wily Melikoff. I urged on him that now, if any knew of the treasure, they would be lurking around the castle of Dargo."

"Go on, go on, Abdallah!" cries Platoff.

"Gently, my son! We sent a strong column of the Prince Ahmed's troops to surround the castle. They had secret orders to permit no one to depart. The refitting of the castle gave reason to retain them all. Yet there is much to do in examining the tower from the old description. It shows no sign of a hiding-place."

"But do you know the right tower?" Platoff interjects.

"Of a truth! We found one or two suspicious dwellers in the old halls. With a little help they told what they knew. The treasures are there.

Some day Lord Ghazee will come secretly to regain them. He alone knows the hiding-place."

"How do you know this?" cries Platoff.

"Of a verity, these were the *last words* the dogs urged to prevent their death!" Abdallah rejoins.

"Can they point them out?" Platoff is now wild with curiosity.

"Alas! great friend, they died, refusing any further disclosures. They protested only the tower was known to them. Ghazee *alone* knows the whole secret."

"They died!" Platoff repeats, stunned.

"It was the only way to prove their sincerity. They knew not. But we will discover the exact spot. We will remove the *whole tower*."

"And Ghazee?" Platoff anxiously asks.

"Far away, waiting for coming years to cover the memories of the past. These treasures are all that is left to him of his birthright." Abdallah slowly answers. "Ahmed is now the lord of Daghestan."

"True, Abdallah! but the spoil of the Russian armies is there," Platoff rejoins.

"Very good! Let the White Czar have his own. The rest goes to the dark lord of the eagle eye."

In a fortnight a splendid cavalcade leaves Tiflis for Dargo. By a strange desire for travel, Abdallah is at the old palaces before the double wedding party.

Seneschal and trusted friend, he meets them at the door.

Only Ignatief, Platoff, and Abdallah know the

story of the secret treasures left by great Schamyl before gallant Woronzoff drove him out.

In summer-time and hey-day of youth, life *before* them, love *around* them, the two comrades wander in the splendid halls of the romantic castle. They are under the witching eyes of the brides of Dargo. Watch and ward is kept by the faithful soldiers who followed the "White Cross" in the dark days of defeat and danger.

Bluest skies, brightest sunsets, moonlight dreaming on the peaceful river, and the wild song of the swaying pines mark these happiest days, never to be lost from love's golden calendar.

Schamyl and his lovely sister, hand in hand, clamber over the old ramparts and stray in the glens. Princess Maritza, queen of the flying hours, calls all her truants together.

For Platoff and Abdallah waste hours in exploring every nook and cranny of the great keep.

Under guard of their gallant horsemen, the old battle-fields are visited. Deep reaches of the romantic forest, smiling valleys where the ripening fruits now hang in clusters, are explored.

Shy Circassian girls wonder at the fairness of the two ladies who gayly gallop through the forest arches with their lords. An ideal life in a matchless land!

Days slip by unheeded. The foot of Time falls softly on the roses beneath the feet of the brides of Dargo.

Platoff and Ahmed chase the forest game far afield. The old halls gleam at night with banquet mirth.

Schamyl, gazing on his lovely wife, whose smile is sweeter for the sorrows once printed on her peerless brow, wonders if she will ever know of the dark vow of Ghazee dooming her innocent life. Would he were dead! Then the future would be secure. The renegade still lives! Though far away, still he lives!

A Circassian is always a Circassian. Ahmed gravely questions Abdallah. He knows naught of his haunts. Even Mehemet Pacha, who sends a royal gift of jewels, Persian shawls, and gossamer from rarest India's looms, writes that the deserter is gone forever, the wild Kurdish princess with him.

In a few months Ahmed will meet Mehemet at the border. Can he ever reward him for that old comradeship, which saved him from gallant Tarnaieff's awful doom?

To ride in grand battue the woods, to chase the boar and bear, to show Platoff a true Circassian field hunt, the mingled train of soldiers, attendants, and hill dwellers rides out at early morn.

They enclose, by a sharp secret night ride, twenty miles around the great mountain range overlooking Dargo. Dozens of mountaineers, in lines, drive down the game at morn with fires, with sound of horn, with chase of hounds.

It is the sparkling hour of early daybreak. The mists hang yet on the mountains, when Ahmed and Platoff merrily spring to the saddle. The two ladies, superbly mounted, are conducted, with a dozen retainers, by their lords to see the frightened game break from the covert and seek the glen toward the river, its only escape.

The violet's fragrance is fresh on the dew-diamonded grass. The birds whirr away before the horses' feet. Far on the hills, horn and hound sound Diana's greeting to the rising sun.

Platoff, a veteran sportsman, rides with the advance. Ahmed guides the ladies—rosier and lovelier than the blossoms of the perfumed forests. They wind down below the old castle toward the river. Down into the mouth of the glen the cavalcade moves. It is here the startled game will break cover.

Under the shadow of a beetling crag the advance halts. The lord of the chase stations his ladies with their attendants. As the party draws up, Schamyl bends over to say a whispered word to the woman whose sunny smile lights this new and happy life. A merry laugh is on her lips.

Sharp and clear from the crag a rifle shot rings out! The horse of Princess Maritza falls, rolling over her! There is a wild shout! She lies motionless! Her face pale as ashes! Before Schamyl can spring from his black Kara, a second answering volley echoes near him. There is a wild yell of defiance! A dozen men aid the prince! The loved one is only bruised and stunned. Her gallant steed lies dead, shot through the spine.

While Schamyl makes a couch of cloaks, and learns from her own words Maritza is unwounded, Paul Platoff, standing by his side, his smoking rifle in his hand, says: "I fear I missed him. The wretch!"

A baying of hounds! A chorus of yells arouses the prince'

Springing wildly along the face of the nearest crag, a man is running for his life! He is in flowing Persian garb. A rifle is in his hands! Half a dozen of the Tcherkess gallop around the crag to cut him off!

Darting in and out among the jutting rocks, he glides like a hunted animal.

In an instant twenty armed men are scaling the rocks to secure him! Some lurking spy unearthed by the beaters! He was stealing up from the river when sighted.

Schamyl gazes at the castle not three hundred yards away. Its old keep hangs over the bastioned wall commanding the glen.

"Platoff, direct this man's capture. I will take the ladies back and rejoin you," Ahmed calls.

With the aid of the attendants the frightened Maritza is hurried in safety to the castle! *Who was the assailant?*

Some hunted fugitive Moslem!

Keen-eyed Tcherkess are swarming over the crag. They return to report empty hands. The bird has flown.

"I saw him stealing through the bushes toward the castle," cries Platoff, as he aids in the removal of Princess Maritza to the quiet of her rooms.

Shaken and startled, bruised, but, thank God! safe!

Vera Platoff watches her friend! Abdallah is again Dr. Abdallah.

Schamyl dashes back to the guard gate, and orders a patrol to scour the country. Platoff returns with him to the hunt. The attendants slay the game now pouring down the glen. With grave brows, Schamyl and Platoff examine every inch of the path followed by the murderous refugee. Not a sign of his presence! The copse leading to the castle walls, the growth of twenty years, affords a hiding-place.

Schamyl sends in a platoon to search every yard of the shrubbery.

While Platoff and himself, seated on a rock, discuss this mystery, a shout of joy is heard. In five minutes one searcher hands Ahmed a heavy rifle, another lays at his feet a Persian skin water-bottle. It is full. There is a girdle to which the water-bottle was attached. It was torn off in the flight.

Ahmed examines the rifle carefully. It is the *Turkish* Martini-Henry. A shade settles on his brow. The girdle is heavy. With a stroke of his dagger he cuts it open. Cartridges, fresh and new, all of the American make! It is the *Turkish army* ammunition.

"Platoff, this is some Turkish assassin!" Schamyl slowly says.

"I will put a chain of concealed guards around the castle at night, and keep a cordon around the vicinity. This devil never got far away. He was too heavily loaded. My guards will be in blindings, and keep quiet. We will get him when he tries to sneak away. He is near here yet."

"Why so?" Platoff questions.

"The heavy, full water-bottle, its outside skin still wet, shows he *came up from the river*. He risked his life to sneak down there and fill it," Schamyl reflectively answers.

"And then?" Platoff grows pale.

"He has some place of hiding! Some object in lingering near here! Paul, it looks bad! I am going to take the ladies to Tiflis. *This old haunt is accursed!* I go not till I catch this rascal!"

Schamyl muses. His brow is dark. The hunt is still ringing in the vale. The keen warriors are making a royal bag. It is a scene of wild excitement.

"I have it! I will station a few men secretly. They can be changed after dark. I will let the hunt run out. We will return to the castle."

These orders given, Paul and Schamyl enter the gateway, where the old white tower hangs over its frowning bastion wall. An attendant bears the rifle, water-bottle, and the cartridges.

Platoff examines the belt. He swings it in his hands. It is of the finest Persian embroidery on leather—a money or jewel belt once, now a mere cartridge pouch. A paper flutters from its cut sides. Platoff picks it up.

Schamyl grasps it. It is a *sketch plan of the white tower*. The cold sweat stands on Paul's brow.

"Schamyl, not a word! Come in and see Abdallah. He can tell you a strange story. Hasten!"

In Schamyl's hunting-room the old jeweller, Platoff, and Ahmed bend over the plan. It is an *exact* sketch of the white tower.

Schamyl's eyes glow as the old Turk tells him of the fabled hidden treasure of Dargo.

He turns reproachful eyes on Paul.

"I kept this secret, Ahmed. *We did not wish to*

excite you till we verified some part of the old tale. It is now time to act."

"Yes!" Ahmed cries. "This mysterious enemy is lurking to reach that treasure. His arms and all signs show he came from over the Araxes."

A horrible thought flashes over Schámyl. The vendetta of the amulet! No, it cannot be!

As Abdallah tells of the executed spies, Platoff cries, "I have it! This man knows the secret of the entrance to the white tower! He *alone* has the whole knowledge!"

And yet the plan is perfectly plain. It shows no secret vault. Schamyl muses. "I'll catch him first, and then blow down the tower!"

Platoff is at the window, examining the mysterious paper. It is an old and worn parchment.

"Here!" shouts Platoff. "Here is the secret chamber!"

The two friends spring to his side. Triumphantly holding it up before the light, a faintly traced line *shines through.* It shows a vault under the foundations of the old tower.

It is true! And yet no egress or ingress! There is the royal secret!

Schamyl raises his head after pondering. "I will not delay a minute. Abdallah, you join the ladies and stay with them. Tell them we are going to fire some of the old cannon.

"Paul, come with me. We will blow out the wall."

The two officers, in half an hour, have satisfied themselves there is no manner of reaching the concealed crypt from the interior. With plan laid down, examining keenly the bastion wall, Platoff says: "This is the nearest point to the chamber. Blow out the side wall here. The tower will yet stand. We can then tunnel in behind the heavy face wall."

In two hours the preparations are complete. The huntsmen are returned. Concealed guards have their orders to shoot any fugitive.

Reassuring the lovely Maritza, and privately informing Vera of the intended explosion, Schamyl and Platoff send in a line of guards to clear the west angle of the old courtyard.

All is ready. A couple of heavy powder bags affixed to crowbars driven in the loose crevices of the old bastion wall, will bring down twenty feet of the wall on their explosion.

A half dozen resolute men are at hand.

With *his own hand* Schamyl fires the mine. A flash, a rumble, a crash! From their safety refuge the friends can see a yawning gap. The old wall is thrown out. The tower stands still, firm and strong.

Schamyl is the first man at the breach. Lanterns and lights are at hand. He is ready to enter.

"Beware!" cries Platoff. "The air may be foul. Let the mass settle also."

A lantern on a long pole is pushed in. A regular opening is seen—a tunnel leading in under the tower. It is no idle tale!

Cautiously advancing with lights, which burn clearly, Schamyl gropes his way into the narrow tunnel leading to the crypt.

Platoff is behind him. Ahmed picks his way toward the tower.

Platoff calls to the others to hold back till needed.

He gazes down the long hole burrowed under the bastion wall. It is blocked by a man's body!

With a half shriek he calls Schamyl back.

"Ahmed, for Heaven's sake! Here, there is a man buried!"

"Wait!" calls Schamyl. His voice sounds *strangely muffled.* "Let me go first."

The treasures of the chamber can be later examined. It may be only an empty cavern of bats. But crushed and pinned by the falling stones, twenty feet beyond the rent in the wall, is the body of a man, doubled up!

Platoff crawls down after Schamyl.

"This is the spy, caught by the explosion!" Ahmed excitedly says. They near him. It is the fugitive in the Persian robes. His breast is pinned by the blocks of the bastion wall sliding down. His head covered with fallen dust and sand. He is dead! Tons of stone rest on his silent breast.

Prince Ahmed scrapes away the sand and grime.

Platoff's heart stops beating, for his friend drops lantern and screams:

"Ghazee, my brother!"

It is indeed so! Crawling up, Platoff satisfies himself. The heavy, malignant face, its red beard, the staring eye, his well-known burly form—on his head the peaked caftan of the Persian!

Schamyl quickly cries:

"Go back! Let no one come! Leave me with the dead! I want no one to enter here!"

Platoff, crawling and stooping, works back to the crater's opening. He stations a guard and gropes back to the death-chamber.

Rejoining Ahmed, Platoff asks his wishes.

He is yet working and digging in the débris. His voice is a hissing whisper.

"Paul, there is some one else over there! I cannot see. I can only feel a foot. *It is a boy!* Dead also!"

With ten minutes' labor the two friends clear away enough to see. They dare not loosen more. The bastion wall might settle. Neither body can be removed.

Platoff forces Schamyl to desist.

"It cannot be reached, Ahmed! I will not have you risk your life! I will pull off the riding-boot. It is a small man or a boy." He throws the boot away.

Schamyl picks it up.

He crawls to the front. Catching Platoff in a vice-like grip, he shows him by the light the boot.

"This is a *Kurdish* boot, Paul! Look there, that is a woman's foot and ankle!"

Platoff shudders.

"It is!" he mutters.

"The *Kurdish princess!*" Schamyl replies hoarsely. "This shall be their tomb, Paul!"

It is indeed Ghazee and his wild bride. His girdle is gone. He has no arms but a dagger. Platoff picks it up. By his side a *small sack* is lying. It is heavy.

Crawling out with dagger and sack, Platoff joins Schamyl. At a sign, the artillerist assists Schamyl to block up the tunnel way with loose stones from the opening of the rift.

Five minutes later they are in the crypt under

the tower. It is a strongly vaulted room made by the recesses of the huge foundations of the tower.

At a glance the friends see that the vault has been lately occupied. It is filled with chests, bales, and bundles.

Swords and armor, old vessels, and a mass of Asiatic articles—the booty of old victories! The secret hiding-place of Sultan Schamyl the mystic!

Prince Ahmed examines the bag which Platoff carries. Cutting its cords with the dagger of the dead man, its contents are blazing jewels. There is a princely fortune in the sack.

Schamyl quickly makes his plan.

"We will send Abdallah here to take charge. I wish this secret to be kept. It is God's justice by His own hand on Ghazee's crimes.

"We will remove all, in charge of Abdallah. You and I will see the rift in the wall filled in solid with stone. The ivy and creeper will cover it in a month."

Before the evening shades have fallen, the vast treasures of the old sultan are removed to the castle—gold and jewels, cups and masses of the precious metals, jewelled weapons and horse-gear of untold value! The bastion wall is roughly closed up forever.

The delighted brides, aided by Abdallah, are classing the jewels and choosing the princeliest of the treasure-trove for themselves.

They know not the secret of the tunnel, with the fugitive lovers lying dead under the massy blocks of the old bastion.

Their excited happiness in the discovery of the hidden treasures chases away all other thoughts. Even the morning's adventure is forgotten.

Prince Schamyl and Platoff wander on the ramparts. They agree upon a course of action. It is easy for them to locate the near vicinity of the concealed tunnel mouth.

Looking down from the base of the old tower, his stern, martial face now in repose, Ahmed Schamyl traces the fugitive in his career.

"He alone knew how to enter the tunnel and thus reach the crypt. Perhaps the last death-message of my warrior father revealed it. The drawing may have been delivered to him, with the secret, by the Turkish authorities, after the declaration of war. That mystery is sealed in his cold breast.

"Disguising himself as a Persian, and taking the Kurdish dare-devil girl-wife, *dressed as a boy*, he secreted himself near here. It was clearly his idea to remove the choicest of the treasures. Abdallah's slyness caught his spies. Forced to live in the crypt, it was while bringing water he risked his life and was accidentally discovered. His last shot may have been for me. He may have tried only to delay pursuit till he could hide. At night he could have stolen away. It was with that purpose he packed up the sack of jewels. The glens were known to him. The first horses caught, with a noose-rope bridle, would have carried them to friends. They would then have left the Araxes valley forever."

"It is true!" cries Platoff. "Yet our guards might have caught them at night."

Schamyl says solemnly:

"It was flight or *death by thirst!* Ghazee met the vengeance of God! Let him rest forever there, under the old tower where he played as a boy. He was a Circassian to the death! The hand of the Almighty ends his vendetta. It releases us from the curse of the amulet!"

Down through the shrubbery the friends wander, through copse and thicket.

Sagacious Platoff, with his trained eye, discovers a cleft in the rock. There is a moss-grown stone which has been moved. A dozen men with crowbars pry it off. A tilting rock! Its rough hinges are clogged by the explosion. It was thus the *wily old warrior Schamyl* arranged his hiding-place.

Ordering it securely walled up, as a seal to the tomb of the two wild spirits, Prince Schamyl leaves the spot, which is *now* hateful to him. Twice in his life had the great foe of Russia thus escaped death, by using similar retreats prepared before. Sultan Schamyl's mysterious exits!

"There must have been an interior entrance, walled up after the treasures were deposited during the long siege. The defeated sultan knew further resistance was useless. Great Dargo was doomed. Perchance he thought he might return some day and reach the treasures himself."

Thus speaks Abdallah, his hands deep in jewels.

"True!" cries Paul Platoff. "But the Russian government never permitted his return after the surrender of Baryatinsky."

A guarded train draws out, a week later. Ahmed Schamyl, gazing on the bright and splendid face of the lovely Rose, whose one dark enemy is at rest, conducts her in triumph to Tiflis. To her own home with the radiant Vera! Sagacious Abdallah, with Platoff, under the secret orders of General Ignatief, delivers over to Governor-General Loris Melikoff the governmental share of the recovered booty.

Colonel Platoff, recalled to the court, takes away from Schamyl his sweet sister, whose new-found love is the crowning glory of Schamyl's happy marriage.

The old palace-home is vacant now. Dargo, its keep occupied only as a guard-post, is deserted as a residence. Ahmed Schamyl likes not its memories. The eagle, soaring high in the sapphire sky of the Caucasus, looks down on the lovely glens and witching woods, where the wild winds murmur the requiem of the bold refugee and his wayward Kurdish bride.

Where is the happiest home in Russia? For, even in Russia, are homes crowned with truest love.

Paul Platoff thinks it is the old Orbelian palace, where Princess Paul rules, under the sweet eyes of her mother, looking down from her picture on the circle, whose Russian hospitality embraces often the princely lovers from Tiflis.

Prince Ahmed, watching the splendid and loving woman who bore her sorrows so long, is persuaded that the happiest home under the Czar's rule is the one where blooms Maritza, the Rose of Georgia.

Gallant Mehemet Pacha, meeting his brother in arms, at the border, learns the fate of Ismail's daughter and wild Schamyl. He bows his head, looking at his beloved Ahmed, solemnly saying, "May your happiness ever abide!"

He waits the time when perhaps the cannon will roar once more over Asia Minor. With steadfast faith to do his soldier's duty, only wishing "Bonnes chances aux braves!"

Gallant Gronow, released at last from duty for urgent reasons, is said to be returning to Tiflis with the bright and laughing Nina Lazareff, who remembers a certain promise made to the dashing staff officer. Her sister nymph, Tia Argutin, contemplates a similar capture of one who is dearer to her than all the jewels of Russia's crown.

Abdallah, full of years and glory, enhanced in wealth, high in confidence, bows his head with fervent devotion at the noon hour, when he remembers how the prophet aided Dr. Abdallah.

The fatal Kismet hangs over the affairs of men and nations in the mighty Orient.

Alexander, the old Czar, is gone! Skobeleff and Melikoff sleep with the unforgotten brave!

Still toward the Dardanelles, onward to India, Asia, and China, the Russian flag crawls apace!

For under a new Emperor, with steadfast eyes fixed toward the future, great Ignatief, mighty Gourko, and far-seeing Anenkoff toil and labor at the secret roads of Empire.

In the name of the Czar!

The wild vines have covered the broken bastions of Dargo. There is eternal peace in the sweep of the wild winds and the rush of the river past the crumbling battlements. A palace once! A tomb now!

Over its ruined archway the words of Sadi might tell the mournful story of to-day.

"The spider has woven its web in the palace of the Cæsars.

"The owl shrieks its nightly song on the towers of Aphrasiab."

Welcomed by Press and Public.

THE LITTLE LADY OF LAGUNITAS.

By RICHARD HENRY SAVAGE,
Author of "My Official Wife," etc.

Published simultaneously in New York, Leipzig and London.
A STRIKING, POPULAR SUCCESS!

American Press Comment.

"A good story and well told. It is a book that will hold the reader's attention from the first chapter."
—NEW YORK RECORDER, June 5th, 1892.

"Lively, interesting, and will hold the reader's attention in every line."
—BOSTON GLOBE, June 13.

"An exceedingly interesting romance; a remarkably brilliant picture of a very remarkable episode in our national history."
—CHICAGO TIMES, June 18.

"The 'Little Lady' is a very winsome person."
—PHILADELPHIA BULLETIN, May 30.

"Entertaining—strong—instructive."
—SAN FRANCISCO CALL., June 5.

"The story is one of absorbing interest—thoroughly American in character and spirit."
—NEW YORK HOME JOURNAL, June 15.

"Holds the attention throughout."
—CLEVELAND PLAINDEALER, July 2.

"Exceedingly interesting."
—PHILADELPHIA CALL., June 6.

"Told in an engaging manner."
—CHICAGO MAIL, July 5.

THE LITTLE LADY OF LAGUNITAS—AMERICAN PRESS COMMENT.

"A stirring romance."
—New York Sun, July 16.

"A fine sense of the picturesque—a brilliant panorama."
—San Francisco Wave, June 11.

"Vividly portrays the wild, strange scenes attending the acquisition of California."
—Columbus, Ohio, State Journal, June 20.

"The reader's interest does not flag."
—Town Topics, May 19.

"A charming story."
—The Boston Traveller, June 3.

"Vivid character sketches."
—Cincinnati Commercial Gazette, June 25.

"A correct conception."
—San Francisco Report, June 18.

"A strong story. Will keep the reader wide-awake."
—Newark Advertiser, July 2.

"An historical romance of exceeding interest. Of the highest literary merit."
—Lincoln, Neb., State Journal, May 30th, 1892.

"The purchaser will have his money's worth."
—Springfield Republican, June 12th, 1892.

"Of great interest. The 'bonanza era,' with its reign of luxury and wantonness, is depicted in glowing colors . . . most dramatically rehearsed."
—Denver Republican, June 19.

"One of the most thrilling historical romances which the Spring has produced. A stirring story."
—Boston Times, June 26.

"An exciting story."
—Denver News, June 17.

(And many others.)

SIXTY THOUSAND COPIES SOLD IN THREE MONTHS IN AMERICA, GERMANY AND ENGLAND.

Sold by The American News Company.

THE LITTLE LADY OF LAGUNITAS.

Foreign Words of Approval.

"Offers much interest,—well worth perusal."
—MORNING POST, London, June 28th, 1892.

"Mr. Savage in a former novel gave evidence of an unusual capacity for the construction of an elaborate plot, but in this work he has excelled even that splendid performance, 'My Official Wife.'"
—GLASGOW HERALD, June 23d, 1892.

"The descriptions of the lawless life in California are exciting and vivid." —LONDON DAILY CHRONICLE, July 15.

"Distinctly interesting . . . the tale becomes intensely exciting." —SCOTTISH LEADER, Edinburgh, July 2.

"Plenty of excitement in this narrative."
—MANCHESTER EXAMINER, July 7.

"Much that is original and deserving of commendation. The dialogue is never at any time dull."
—NORTH BRITISH DAILY MAIL, Glasgow, June 20.

"The story is lively, beyond the common. The reader will hardly be able to stop."
—THE SCOTSMAN, Edinburgh, July 4.

"Stirring incidents, set amid a surrounding of picturesque uncivilized life."
—PUBLISHERS' CIRCULAR, London, June 25.

"Mr. Savage's descriptive powers are undeniable. He paints with a firm hand, and is picturesque."
—SATURDAY REVIEW, London, July 30.

"For those who want a really exciting book, we recommend 'The Little Lady.'" —MANCHESTER COURIER, July 30.

(Many other reviews.)

Continental English Edition by Tauchnitz of Leipzig.
British Edition by George Routledge and Sons of London.
French and German Translations in Press.

Richard Henry Savage's

ROMANTIC NOVELS:

✻

My Official Wife.

The Little Lady of Lagunitas.

Prince Schamyl's Wooing.

ORIGINAL! BRILLIANT! SUCCESSFUL!

MY OFFICIAL WIFE

BY

Colonel RICHARD HENRY SAVAGE,

Author of "The Little Lady of Lagunitas," etc.

Publishers in Europe.

George Routledge & Sons,	London	(English Edition)
Bernhard Tauchitz,	Leipzig	(Continental Edition)
J. Engelhorn,	Stuttgart	(German Translation)
Messrs. Hachette,	Paris	(French Translation)

Foreign Reviewers' Remarks.

Welcomed from Japan and India, to Berlin!

"There is not a dull page in this book."
—TIMES OF INDIA, Bombay, Feb. 20th, 1892.

"Can not fail to make a mark."
—NEWS OF THE WORLD, London, Jan. 24th, 1892.

"Very exciting."
—SCOTTISH LEADER, Edinburgh, July 9th, 1891.

"A wonderfully clever 'tour de force.'"
—LONDON TIMES, Aug. 10th, 1891.

"No recent story surpasses it."
—YORKSHIRE POST, July 8th, 1891.

"As bright as the best French comedy."
—BERLIN POST, Germany, Nov. 26th, 1891.

"The vivacity, movement, and style deserve warm praise."
—LONDON DAILY NEWS, Dec. 25th, 1891.

"A well conceived sensational story."
—LONDON SPECTATOR, Sept. 12th, 1891.

"This story would dramatize well."
—BRADFORD OBSERVER, Oct. 1st, 1891.

"One of the 'livest' and most entertaining novels we have read for many a day."
—LEEDS MERCURY, Sept. 9th, 1891.

"Told with delightful spirit."
—THE SCOTSMAN, Edinburgh, July 6th, 1891.

SOLD BY

THE HOME PUBLISHING CO., 3 East 14th St., New York City.

MY OFFICIAL WIFE

BY

RICHARD HENRY SAVAGE,

Author of "The Little Lady of Lagunitas," etc., etc.

For Sale Everywhere! Shortly to be Dramatized!

The American Success of the Season!

The Voice of the Press.

"A vivid and stirring story."
—New York Tribune, August 2, 1891.

"Abundance of Action. Very cleverly written."
—San Francisco Chronicle, June 21, 1891.

"Something thoroughly stirring."
—Omaha Bee, June 27th, 1891.

"The denouement is intensely dramatic."
—Boston Advertiser, July 3d, 1891.

"A striking story."
—Portland Oregonian, May 31st, 1891.

"Something extraordinary. Worth reading."
—Louisville Commercial, July 6th, 1891.

"Full of life and go and very entertaining."
—Chicago Times, June 20th, 1891.

"Events and situations increasing in excitement. The reader will dash through with wild eagerness."
—New York Herald, June 21st, 1891.

"A very exciting web of complications."
—New Orleans Picayune, July 12th, 1891.

"A story of absorbing interest."
—Cleveland Plaindealer, June 14th, 1891.

"Occupies the close attention of the reader."
—San Francisco Call, June 21st, 1891.

"Amusing and exciting."
—Town Topics, Nov. 12th, 1891.

"Overflowing with human interest and intensely dramatic."
—New York Home Journal, Dec. 16th, 1891.

"Decidedly original. The making of a very effective play. Ingenious and daring in conception."
—New York World, Aug. 2d, 1891.

"The story is racy and will be a favorite at the clubs."
—San Francisco Evening Post, June 27th, 1891.

"Abundance of action. Extremely interesting."
—San Francisco Newsdealer, August 1st, 1891.

"The novel is of unusual interest."
—New York Journal, June 28th, 1891.

"A story of great power and originality."
—Minneapolis Commercial Bulletin, Oct. 24th, 1891.

My Official Wife.

BY

Col. Richard Henry Savage.

The Little Lady of Lagunitas.

A Franco-Californian Romance.

BY

Richard Henry Savage.

Prince Schamyl's Wooing.

A Story of the Caucasus—Russo-Turkish War.

BY

Richard Henry Savage.

My Official Wife.

DRAMATIZED BY

Archibald Clavering Gunter

UNDER LICENSE FROM
THE AUTHOR.

UNIVERSITY OF CALIFORNIA LIBRARY

THIS BOOK IS DUE ON THE LAST DATE STAMPED BELOW

SEP 27 1916

DEC 15 1926

30m-1,'15

50163

www.ingramcontent.com/pod-product-compliance
Lightning Source LLC
Chambersburg PA
CBHW032046220426
43664CB00008B/887